Ethics and Research with Young Children

Also available from Bloomsbury

Children, Religion and the Ethics of Influence, John Tillson
Theorizing Feminist Ethics of Care in Early Childhood Practice,
edited by Rachel Langford

Ethics and Research with Young Children

New Perspectives

Edited by Christopher M. Schulte

BLOOMSBURY ACADEMIC
LONDON • NEW YORK • OXFORD • NEW DELHI • SYDNEY

BLOOMSBURY ACADEMIC
Bloomsbury Publishing Inc
50 Bedford Square, London, WC1B 3DP, UK
1385 Broadway, New York, NY 10018, USA
29 Earlsfort Terrace, Dublin 2, Ireland

BLOOMSBURY, BLOOMSBURY ACADEMIC and the Diana logo are trademarks
of Bloomsbury Publishing Plc

First published in Great Britain 2020
This paperback edition published in 2022

Cover design: Adriana Brioso
Cover image: ChristinLola/iStock

A catalogue record for this book is available from the British Library.

A catalog record for this book is available from the Library of Congress.

ISBN: HB: 978-1-3500-7643-3
          PB: 978-1-3502-1374-6
          ePDF: 978-1-3500-7645-7
          eBook: 978-1-3500-7647-1

Typeset by Integra Software Services Pvt. Ltd.

To find out more about our authors and books visit www.bloomsbury.com
and sign up for our newsletters.

Contents

Figures

Contributors

Bronwyn Davies is an independent scholar, a professorial fellow at the University of Melbourne, and an emeritus professor at Western Sydney University. She is a writer, scholar, and teacher and has been a visiting professor in the last few years in the United States, Sweden, Denmark, Belgium, Finland, and the UK. She is well known for her work using collective biography, her work on gender, literacy, and pedagogy, and for her critique of neoliberalism as it impacts on university work. Her most recent books are *Listening to Children: Being and Becoming* and her first work of fiction for children, a new version of Pixie O'Harris's classic story *The Fairy Who Wouldn't Fly*. She is currently writing a book called *Remember Me ... Tracing the Web of Family*, which looks at the early colonization of New South Wales. More details of her work can be found on her website at bronwyndavies.com.au

Candace R. Kuby is Associate Professor of Early Childhood Education at the University of Missouri. Her research interests are twofold: (1) the ethico-onto-epistemologies of literacy desiring(s) when young children work with materials to create multimodal, digital, and hybrid texts and (2) approaches to qualitative inquiry drawing upon poststructural and posthumanist theories and the teaching of qualitative inquiry. Candace is the coauthor of *Go Be a Writer!: Expanding the Curricular Boundaries of Literacy Learning* (2016, Teachers College Press); author of *Critical Literacy in the Early Childhood Classroom: Unpacking Histories, Unlearning Privilege* (2013, Teachers College Press); and coeditor of *Disrupting Qualitative Inquiry: Possibilities and Tensions in Educational Research* (2014, Peter Lang). Journals in which her scholarship appears include *Qualitative Inquiry, International Journal of Qualitative Studies in Education, Journal of Early Childhood Literacy,* and *Language Arts.*

Christine Marmé Thompson is Professor Emerita at Penn State University and has been a visiting professor in the Art Education Department at Virginia Commonwealth University for 2017–2018. Her research on early childhood art and children's culture has appeared in national and international journals, handbooks, and numerous edited volumes.

Christopher M. Schulte is Endowed Associate Professor of Art Education in the School of Art at the University of Arkansas. His research on children's art, specifically drawing in early childhood, has appeared in handbooks and other edited volumes as well as in national and international journals in art education, early childhood education, and qualitative studies. He is the coeditor (with Christine Marmé Thompson) of *Communities of Practice: Art, Play, and Aesthetics in Early Childhood* (2018, Springer) and editor of the *International Journal of Education & the Arts*.

Hayon Park is a Ph.D. candidate in Art Education at Penn State University with particular interests in studio art practices, childhood studies, and art education. Hayon received a B.F.A in painting from Ewha Womans University in South Korea and a M.S. in art education from Penn State University, with a Fulbright scholarship.

Heather Kaplan is Visiting Assistant Professor at the University of Texas El Paso. She is an artist, educator, and researcher. Heather's research interests are studio art making and early childhood art education, and she considers her research to inform and be informed by her teaching and artistic practices. Her research explores notions of play and materiality, community, contemporary art and making practices, and storytelling. Decidedly, her work engages with contemporary notions of how we come to know and be through relations with others and art.

Jaye Johnson Thiel is Visiting Research Scholar at the University of Georgia, where she serves as the Research and Activities Co-Director of a community place-based research center. As a qualitative methodologist, her research explores the co-constitutive entanglements of class, gender, race, literacies, and educational equity. Specifically, she considers how phenomena entangle to create unique opportunities for children and adults to find intellectual fullness during creative play and how these moments serve as counter narratives to deficit discourses surrounding women, children, families, and teachers.

Jayne Osgood is Professor of Education at the Centre for Education Research & Scholarship, Middlesex University. Her present methodologies and research practices are framed by feminist new materialism. Her work maintains a concern with issues of social/worldly justice, and she critically engages with early childhood policy, curricular frameworks, and pedagogical approaches. Through her work she seeks to extend understandings of the workforce, families, "the child" and "childhood" in early years contexts. She has published extensively and is currently coeditor of journals *Gender & Education* and *Reconceptualising Educational Research Methodology*, and also book series coeditor of *Feminist Thought in Childhood Research* (Bloomsbury).

Kylie Smith is Associate Professor in the Melbourne Graduate School of Education at the University of Melbourne. Her research brings theory and practice together to support children's participation in research, curriculum development, and the formation of public policy. Over the past twenty years, she has explored and developed ethical research protocols and practices that support children under the age of five years to engage with issues of informed consent, research design, and reporting. Informed by rights-based practices and sociological perspectives of childhood, Kylie advocates and develops research methodologies that support research *with* rather than *about* young children.

Laura Trafí-Prats is Senior Lecturer at the School of Childhood, Youth and Education Studies at Manchester Metropolitan University, former associate professor at the University of Wisconsin-Milwaukee, and Lecturer at Universitat Autònoma de Barcelona. She is a member of the Children and Childhood Research Group at MMU's Education and Social Research Institute. Her research connects the fields of visual arts, childhood studies, place-based pedagogies, and video. She is interested in poststructuralist, new materialist, posthumanist, and decolonizing philosophies and methodologies. Her work has been published in journals like *Studies in Art Education, Qualitative Inquiry, Journal of Curriculum and Pedagogy*, and *Cultural Studies ↔ Critical Methodologies*.

Leslie Rech Penn holds a M.F.A. in Studio Art and a Ph.D. in Early Childhood Education. She has engaged in a wide range of scholarly presentations, publications, and exhibits of her artwork. The majority of her work over the last five years addresses children's drawing as a site of material, embodied, and sociocultural exchanges. She is Assistant Professor in the Department of Educational Theory and Practice at the University of Georgia.

Marek Tesar is Associate Dean International (Strategic Engagement) and Associate Professor in Childhood Studies and Early Childhood Education at the University of Auckland. His research focuses on childhood, children's lives, policy, and methodology. Marek's scholarship and activism merge theoretical work with a practical impact on the mundane lives of children and their childhoods in Aotearoa New Zealand and overseas. He has published and disseminated his work in many books and journals, and also to the early childhood community. His work received numerous national and international awards and accolades, and recently he has been leading international and local teams of experts in Indonesia to establish a research center of excellence for early childhood education to serve the South-East Asia regions (SEAMEO).

Margaret M. Coady is Honorary Researcher at the Youth Research Centre, University of Melbourne. She has published on children's and families' rights and on professional ethics. She has held Research Fellowships at the Center for Human Values at Princeton University; the Rockefeller Center at Bellagio, Italy; the Kennedy Institute for Ethics at Georgetown University; and the Uehiro Centre for Practical Ethics at Oxford University. She has received three Australian Research Council grants. She has lectured on children's rights in universities in Singapore, China, the UK, and the United States. She was an ethics consultant to the Royal Australian and New Zealand College of Psychiatry, the Australian Association of Social Workers, and the Victorian College of Optometry. She was a member of the Psychosurgery Review Board, the Victorian Government Child Death Review Committee, the Victorian Assisted Reproductive Treatment Authority, and is still a member of the Victoria Police Human Research Ethics Committee and the Royal Women's Hospital Ethics Advisory Group.

Marissa McClure is interested in contemporary theories of child art, constructions of childhood and children and visual and media culture, community-based art education, feminist theory, and curriculum inquiry, theory, and design. Throughout her time in preschool and elementary classrooms, Marissa worked with young children as co-researchers. She has been especially interested in enriching understandings of culturally and linguistically diverse groups of children within the broader context of educational research, curriculum theory, and policy. She is currently an Art Education and Women's and Gender Studies faculty member at Indiana University of Pennsylvania and Coordinator of the Art Education Program.

Melissa Freeman is Professor of Qualitative Research and Evaluation Methodologies at the University of Georgia. Her research into different philosophically informed traditions examines the variety of interpretive strategies researchers use to make sense of the world. She is the author (along with Sandra Mathison) of *Researching Children's Experiences* (Guilford Press, 2009) and *Modes of Thinking for Qualitative Data Analysis* (Routledge, 2017). Dr. Freeman's work is cross-disciplinary and she is committed to addressing social and educational problems in ways that contribute meaningfully to new ways of conceptualizing the role of inquiry in everyday practice.

Shana Cinquemani is Assistant Professor at the Rhode Island School of Design. Her research interests include theories of early childhood art education, conceptualizations of children's art as a meaningful sociocultural practice, ethical research practices with children, connections between art and play, and relationships between children and adults in the art classroom space. She has published her research in multiple venues and has presented at various national and international conferences. Currently she is President of the Early Childhood Art Educators Issue Group for NAEA and serves on the editorial review board for *The Journal of Art Education.*

Sonja Arndt is Senior Lecturer at the Faculty of Education, University of Waikato. Her teaching and research interests intersect early childhood education, cultural studies and indigeneity in education, and philosophy of education, at undergraduate and postgraduate, and national and international levels. Sonja's research addresses the complexities of Otherness through philosophies of the subject and beyond the subject, and her interest in both the known and the unknown leads her work into the post- or more-than-human realm. Her research uses a philosophical approach and method, in an attempt to recognize and address the complexities of children's and teachers' lived, everyday realities.

Sylvia Kind is a faculty instructor in Early Childhood Education at Capilano University and an *atelierista* at the Capilano University Children's Centre. She has a particular affinity for the pedagogical values and approach of the schools in Reggio Emilia and their commitment to relational and artistic ways of knowing. Her work is motivated by an interest in young children's studio practices, their lively material improvisations, and collective experimentations and how the early childhood studio takes shape as an eventful place. She has coauthored the book *Encounters with Materials in Early Childhood Education.*

Tara Gutshall Rucker is in her eleventh year as an elementary teacher in Columbia Public Schools in Columbia, Missouri. Tara has taught first, second, and fifth grades. She received her M.A. in curriculum and instruction through the Teaching Fellows program and an Elementary Mathematics Specialists Certificate at the University of Missouri. Through the Fellows program Tara began her journey as a teacher research. Tara is the coauthor of *Go Be a Writer!: Expanding the Curricular Boundaries of Literacy Learning* (2016, Teachers College Press) as well as published articles in *Language Arts, Talking Points*, and the *Journal of Early Childhood Literacy*.

Acknowledgments

My sincere thanks and appreciation to Mark Richardson, whose encouragement made this project possible; to Maria Giovanna Brauzzi, whose ongoing support was instrumental in helping me to craft this volume; to the reviewers, who generously gave their time to read and provide feedback; to Shanmathi Priya Sampath at Bloomsbury: thank you for the attentiveness and care that you brought to the manuscript; to the incredible authors who contributed to this volume: I am not only indebted to each of you but also deeply inspired by your commitment to innovating the ways in which we think about ethics and research with young children; to Sarah Nachtman, who graciously helped to edit some of the photographs featured in this volume; to the School of Art at the University of Arkansas for supporting this project; and to my family (Jill, Sophia, and Liam): This project would not be possible without your love and support.

Thank you to all involved.

Introduction

Christopher M. Schulte
University of Arkansas, USA

Ethics, research, and young children: New perspectives

There is no shortage of literature on the subject of ethics and research with children. This is especially true in the social sciences, where, as Canella and Lincoln (2011) have suggested, the "social, intellectual, and even political positions from which the notion of research ethics can be defined" are subject to an increasingly broad array of "knowledges and ways of experiencing the world" (p. 81). For example, there are practical handbooks that aim to provide resources to students, researchers, and others whose intention is to inquire with and about children (e.g., Anderson and Morrow, 2011). There is also a growing list of edited volumes, each uniquely positioned and with a frame of reference that adds to the broader conversation about ethics and research with children. There are texts that focus on researching children in context (e.g., Bresler and Thompson, 2002; Graue and Walsh, 1998), those that center on the study of children's experience (e.g., Freeman and Mathison, 2009; Greene and Hogan, 2009; Mayall, 1994; Tobin, Wu and Davidson, 1991;), and others that address the complexities of including the perspectives and voices of children (Harcourt, Perry and Waller, 2011; Lewis and Lindsay, 2000; Soto and Swadener, 2005; Tobin 2000).

Adding to this conversation is an increasingly diverse list of single-authored and co-authored books (e.g., Bloch, Swadener and Canella, 2018; Dahlberg and Moss, 2004; Davies, 2014; Lenz Taguchi, 2009; Moss, 2018; Murris, 2016; Olsson, 2009; Pacnini-Ketchbaw, Kind and Kocher, 2016; Schulte and Thompson, 2018), as well as peer-reviewed journal articles (e.g., Barker and Weller, 2003; Blaise, Banerjee, Pacini-Ketchabaw and Taylor, 2013; Morrow and Richards, 1996; Punch, 2002; Soto and Swadener, 2002), each acknowledging in its own way the situated work of research with children and the complex ethical realities in which this work takes place.

Of course, this is not by any means a comprehensive account of the literature on ethics and research with young children. Rather, it offers a snapshot of some of the work that has been done to date. More importantly, though, I point to this literature in order to reference the broader conversation that this volume seeks to contribute to. Importantly, this conversation is far more extensive than how it has been represented here. For example, there are many texts that do not directly take up the problem of ethics but have nonetheless played a significant role in reorienting how researchers conceptualize the matter of ethics and the extent to which these conceptualizations take root, informing new or at least different forms of ethical practice with children (e.g., Crinall, 2019; Fraser, Lewis, Ding, Kellett and Robinson, 2004; Kuby, Spector and Thiel, 2018; Osgood and Robinson, 2019; Rautio and Stenvall, 2019; Thompson, 2009).

Ethics and Research with Young Children: New Perspectives seeks to further augment this dialogue. As researchers and theorists, teachers and teacher educators, parents and grandparents and advocates for children, the authors featured in this volume share a common inclination to work against traditional humanist frameworks (e.g., developmental and psychological frameworks), which have historically premised children as "human becomings" (Lee, 2001, p. 2), whose lives and experiences are viewed through a lens that not only perceives them to be "lacking independence, rationality, intelligence, autonomy and confidence" but also positions them as "objects of the researchers' gaze" (Smith, 2011, p. 14). This is especially problematic for children whose lives and experiences do not align with or aptly reflect the universalist, white middle-class heteronormative beliefs that these frameworks tend to value most (see, e.g., Blaise, Banerjee, Pacini-Ketchabaw and Taylor, 2013; Janmohamed, 2010; Osgood and Robinson, 2019). It is for this reason that *Ethics and Research with Young Children: New Perspectives* is situated within the interdisciplinary tradition of childhood studies (see, e.g., Corsaro, 1997; James and James, 2004; Qvortrup, Corsaro, Honig and Valentine, 2009).

The perspectives offered in this volume are foregrounded by the recognition that childhood is a sociocultural space (James and Prout, 2003) and that children are social actors (Prout, 2002), whose lives, experiences, and subjectivities are situated and intersectional. The researchers featured in this volume understand that this recognition is essential to the ethical work of questioning whose knowledge, experience, values, and context get to matter. As such, the authors in this volume build out from this recognition, activating a range of theoretical frameworks to engage the "difficult differences" (Osgood and Robinson, 2019, p. 29) that emerge when doing research with children (e.g., critical education studies, feminist poststructuralism, posthumanism, and feminist science and technology studies). Grounded in relationships between and among adults and children, the shifting social, cultural, and political contexts in which these relationships materialize, and the world of ideas and experiences that impel them to face and reorient each other, the authors in this volume take up the project of conceptualizing an ethics and research that is situated and contingent, relational, shift-inclined, and that values the ways in which ethics and research with children is always more-than-one and more-than-human.

While this volume has not been divided into separate sections or organized to center a particular set of interests, per se, it has been structured to scaffold for the reader a sense of momentum—conceptually speaking. Many of the chapters featured in this volume are inspired by the posthuman turn, specifically the movements of new materialism and feminist science and technology studies. That said, not all of the chapters in this volume are oriented to this perspective. Nonetheless, it is a perspective that tends to linger, continuously bubbling up, sometimes indirectly, even tacitly, with different questions and new demands. For this reason, this volume has been structured to slowly and strategically familiarize the reader with the complexities of what it might mean to think of ethics and research with young children as a more-than-human project. While this volume attends to and constructs this consideration over time, the process of becoming acclimated to this possibility is ultimately inclined toward a more decisive set of purposes. For example, to value the productive potential of the ordinary and unremarkable in one's research with children; to challenge, supplement, and extend the terms, values, contexts, and boundaries that have traditionally shaped how research with young children comes to matter; to orient researchers to both the possibilities and demands of an ethics that is situated, intersectional, and relational; and to further the recognition that the researcher is always involved and implicated in the production of what counts.

In Chapter 1, Kylie Smith and Margaret Coady address the complexities of informed consent in research with children under the age of three, questioning in particular the extent to which adults fail to recognize children's capacity to participate in consent processes, thus belying the interests and points of view that children bring to these situations. In Chapter 2, Melissa Freeman reexamines the drawings and transcripts that were left behind from playing the "squiggle game" with three- and four-year-olds in the 1980s. Through this reexamination, Freeman brings into visibility the ways play performs an ethics of response-ability, a sense of becoming-with that recognizes children as competent interpreters and creators of meaning. In Chapter 3, Hayon Park utilizes the work of Jacques

Ranciére to argue for a relational ethics of ignorance. In doing so, Park attends with greater care and criticality to her experience of drawing popular culture figures with children in a university-affiliated kindergarten classroom.

In Chapter 4, Sylvia Kind explores an ethics of attention and the obligation to listen to children and their multiple ways of knowing and being. Drawing on her work as an artist, educator, and researcher in an early childhood art studio, Kind situates research as an ethical process that is co-composed and co-constructed, as lived processes of inquiring with young children. In Chapter 5, Chris Schulte writes about his experience of playing school at home with his daughter. In doing so, Schulte tends to this occasion of parental play in order to grapple with and re-personalize the complexities of being a father, who doesn't always know the *right way* to love and support his daughter. In Chapter 6, Shana Cinquemani draws on her experience as an artist, educator, and researcher in a Saturday morning art program to explore the between spaces that exist in teaching and research relationships with children. Through this sense of the between, Cinquemani argues for a conceptualization of ethics, teaching, and research with children that is fluid and multiple, and that resists the tendency to position children in realities that are singular and that constitute children as knowable and predictable subjects.

In Chapter 7, Christine Marmé Thompson draws on the work of Miranda Fricker and Sheri Leafgren to articulate a conceptualization of epistemic modesty that, in the context of doing research with children, demands that we (researchers) work against the assumptions that we bring with us to our encounters with children in order to remain open to the possibilities and pleasures of being surprised by children. In Chapter 8, Marissa McClure shares narratives that she has written from arts-based participatory research projects with young children, highlighting the tensions that often exist between the more general assumptions about doing ethical research with children and her own post-qualitative collaborative approach. In Chapter 9, Jayne Osgood provides a speculative account of the ways in which her enactment of feminist new materialist philosophy makes thinking about her entanglements in early childhood contexts more expansive. Specifically, Osgood considers the ways in which Donna Haraway's figure of the "mutated modest witness" offers the means to exercise heightened ethical responsibility. In Chapter 10, Laura Trafi-Prats draws on various anecdotes (e.g., walking in the neighborhood, being alongside snails, making, looking at, and talking about pictures created with mobile phones and GoPro cameras) to activate a posthuman ethics of care in which parents and children learn to think partially, sensuously, and intensively about how to care with/for others, in ways that stretch beyond the normative frames of neoliberal governance.

In Chapter 11, Bronwyn Davies draws on her experience of witnessing the intra-actions among a boy, his mother, and a pond, in order to ponder how we might generate ethical encounters where both children and adults are open and alive to both human and more-than-human others, readied to affecting and being affected by the other, and open to engaging in a joint project of finding ways to live justly. In Chapter 12, Heather Kaplan writes about two art education–related research experiences (the first in an early childhood setting with emergent curriculum and research practices, the second in a local high school with a newly instituted project and outcome-based curriculum and fairly removed observational approach to research) in order to explore different notions of ethics after the material turn. In Chapter 13, Leslie Rech Penn utilizes a diffractive method of analysis to articulate a critical return to a drawing event that she has presented on and published about in the past. In doing so, Rech Penn generates an ethical intervention into the reflective tradition of representing children's experiences, especially as artists.

In Chapter 14, Sonja Arndt and Marek Tesar take up the concept of "mundane abjection" in order to unsettle their own pedagogies of researching with young children. Through this lens, which is informed by the work of Julia Kristeva, Arndt and Tesar explore how our encounters with children, which are neither fixed, stable, or normalized, not only provoke questions about otherness but also expose the need to continually rethink existing research imperatives. In Chapter 15, Jaye Johnson Thiel directs readers to attune themselves to world's smaller, more intimate happenings—to those "deep and simple" moments that instruct us about the ways children actively and perhaps unknowingly work against the tacit rules of a hyper-capitalist society and the manner in which their bodies get produced within it. In Chapter 16, Candace Kuby and Tara Gutshall Rucker write through poetry to share about how their practice of teaching literacies to/with children is critical to their own conceptualization of a relational ethics with children and to sustaining their long-standing teacher–researcher partnership.

The hope of this volume, and of those who contributed to it, is that as reader you will feel inclined to play with the ethical worlds that are presented; to both vary and experiment with the ways you enter and reenter thought—about research, about children, and about ethics; to attach to the contexts and sensibilities that the authors in this volume share your own thinking and experience as a researcher; and, most importantly, to remain willing and ready to think of research with children in ways that generate new possibilities and different forms of ethical practice.

References

Alderson, P., and Morrow, V. (2011). *The ethics of research with children and young people: A practical handbook*. New York: Sage.

Barker, J., and Weller, S. (2003). "Is it fun?" Developing children centered research methods. *International Journal of Sociology and Social Policy, 23*(1/2), 33–58.

Blaise, M., Banerjee, B., Pacini-Ketchabaw, V., and Taylor, A. (2013). Researching the naturecultures of postcolonial childhoods. *Global Studies in Childhood, 3*(4), 350–354.

Bloch, M. N., Swadener, B. B., and Cannella, G. S. (2018). *Reconceptualizing early childhood education and Care: A reader: Critical questions, new imaginaries and social activism*. New York: Peter Lang.

Bresler, L., and Thompson, C. M. (Eds.) (2002). *The arts in children's lives: Context, culture, and curriculum*. Dordrecht: Kluwer Academic Publishers.

Cannella, G. S., and Lincoln, Y. S. (2011). Ethics, research regulations, and critical social science. *The Sage handbook of qualitative research* (pp. 81–90). Los Angeles, CA: Routledge.

Corsaro, W. A. (1997). *The sociology of childhood*. Thousand Oaks, CA: Sage.

Crinall, S. (2019). *Sustaining childhood natures: The art of becoming with water*. Cham, Switzerland: Springer.

Dahlberg, G., and Moss, P. (2004). *Ethics and politics in early childhood education*. Routledge.

Davies, B. (2014). *Listening to children: Being and becoming*. New York: Routledge.

Fraser, S., Lewis, V., Ding, S., Kellett, M., and Robinson, C. (Eds.) (2004). *Doing research with children and young people*. New York: Sage.

Freeman, M., and Mathison, S. (2009). *Researching children's experiences*. New York: Guilford Press.

Graue, M. E., and Walsh, D. J. (1998). *Studying children in context: Theories, methods, and ethics*. Thousand Oaks, CA: Sage.

Greene, S., and Hogan, D. (Eds.) (2009). *Researching children's experience: Methods and approaches*. Los Angeles: Sage.

Harcort, D., Perry, B., and Waller, T. (Eds.) (2011). *Researching young children's perspectives: Debating the ethics and dilemmas of educational research with children*. New York: Routledge.

James, A., and James, A. L. (2004). *Constructing childhood: Theory, policy and social Practice*. Basingstoke: Palgrave Macmillan.

James, A., and Prout, A. (2003). *Constructing and reconstructing childhood: Contemporary issues in the sociological study of childhood*. New York: Routledge.

Janmohamed, Z. (2010). Queering early childhood studies: Challenging the discourse of developmentally appropriate practice. *Alberta Journal of Educational Research, 56*(3), 304–318.

Kuby, C. R., Spector, K., and Thiel, J. J. (Eds.) (2018). *Posthumanism and literacy education: Knowing/becoming/doing literacies*. New York: Routledge.

Lee, N. (2001). *Childhood and society: Growing up in an age of uncertainty*. London, UK: McGraw-Hill Education.

Lewis, A., and Lindsay, G. (Eds.) (2000). *Researching children's perspectives*. Philadelphia: Open University Press.

Mayall, B. (Ed.) (1994). *Children's childhoods: Observed and experienced*. New York: Psychology Press.

Morrow, V., and Richards, M. (1996). The ethics of social research with children: An overview. *Children & society*, *10*(2), 90–105.

Moss, P. (2018). *Alternative narratives in early childhood: An introduction for students and practitioners*. New York: Routledge.

Murris, K. (2016). *The posthuman child: Educational transformation through philosophy with picturebooks*. New York: Routledge.

Olsson, L. M. (2009). *Movement and experimentation in young children's learning: Deleuze and Guattari in early childhood education*. New York: Routledge.

Osgood, J., and Robinson, K. (2019). *Feminists researching gendered childhoods: Generative entanglements*. London: Bloomsbury.

Pacini-Ketchabaw, V., Kind, S., and Kocher, L. L. (2016). *Encounters with materials in early childhood education*. New York: Routledge.

Prout, A. (2002). Researching children as social actors: An introduction to the children. *Children & Society*, *16*(2), 67–76.

Punch, S. (2002). Research with children: The same or different from research with adults? *Childhood*, *9*(3), 321–341.

Qvortrup, J., Corsaro, W. A., Honig, M. S., and Valentine, G. (Eds.) (2009). *The Palgrave handbook of childhood studies*. Basingstoke: Palgrave Macmillan.

Rautio, P., and Stenvall, E. (Eds.) (2019). *Social, material and political constructs of arctic childhoods: An everyday life perspective*. Cham, Switzerland: Springer.

Schulte, C. M., and Thompson, C. M. (Eds.) (2018). *Communities of practice: Art, play, and aesthetics in early childhood*. Cham, Switzerland: Springer.

Smith, A. (2011). Respecting children's rights and agency: Theoretical insights into ethical research procedures. In D. Harcourt, B. Perry and T. Waller (Eds.), *Researching young children's perspectives: Debating the ethics and dilemmas of educational research with children* (pp. 111–125). New York: Routledge.

Soto, L. D., and Swadener, B. B. (2002). Toward liberatory early childhood theory, research and praxis: Decolonizing a field. *Contemporary Issues in Early Childhood*, *3*(1), 38–66.

Soto, L. D., and Swadener, B. B. (2005). *Power & voice in research with children*. New York: Peter Lang.

Taguchi, H. L. (2009). *Going beyond the theory/practice divide in early childhood education: Introducing an intra-active pedagogy*. New York: Routledge.

Thompson, C. M. (2009). Mira! Looking, listening, and lingering in research with children. *Visual Arts Research*, *35*(1), 24–34.

Tobin, J. (2000). *"Good guys don't wear hats": Children's talk about the media*. New York: Teachers College Press.

Tobin, J. J., Wu, D. Y., and Davidson, D. H. (1991). *Preschool in three cultures: Japan, China, and the United States*. New Haven, CT: Yale University Press.

1

Rethinking Informed Consent with Children under the Age of Three

Kylie Smith

University of Melbourne, Graduate School of Education

Margaret M. Coady

University of Melbourne, Graduate School of Education, Youth Research Centre

Introduction

Since the Nuremberg trials after the World War II, informed consent has been taken to be the primary ethical concern in research with human subjects. In much of research involving children, informed consent is obtained solely from adults (guardian). With the influence of the United Nations Rights of the Child (CRC) and shifting theoretical paradigms related to the changing conceptualization of children in disciplines such as sociology, history, and philosophy, there has been an interest in exploring how young children's consent might be obtained. The United Nations Convention of the Rights of the Child, Article 12, states that children have a right to be heard in all aspects of life including research.

This chapter explores how two researchers have grappled with and developed research pedagogies and protocols to gain informed consent from children under three years of age in research. The first author has worked as a researcher and educator in early childhood service and has challenged developmental paradigms that limited very young children's opportunities to engage with discussions of informed consent. The second author has been engaged in teaching and research in relation to early childhood issues for approximately forty years and seen the changes from the U.N. Declaration of the Rights of the Child, and the challenges to this by the child liberationists, particularly John Holt, who wanted children's rights to be identical to adult rights, through to the 1989 U.N. Convention on the Rights of the Child. She has also been a member of several government committees in which a primary consideration has been decisions on informed consent of children and of adults. Together we would describe our view of childhood as very much aligned with the views embodied in the CRC, and we hold that the CRC[1] resolved, particularly in Articles 12 through 16, many of the issues which liberationists identified in the earlier declaration. We have been involved in debates with members of research ethics committees, one of whom told us very firmly that young children do *not* have points of view. We see children, like adults, as agents in having interests and points of view (Coady, 2008). We take seriously Article 12 of the U.N. Convention on the Rights of the Child and see research as a matter that affects children, and therefore one on which they should have a say (MacNaughton and Smith, 2008; Palaiologou, 2014).

Douglas MacLean (2006) wrote: "Informed consent is a fundamental component of moral justification. It distinguishes love-making from rape, employment from servitude, and life-saving surgery from felonious assault with a deadly weapon, to mention just a few examples" (p. 668). Less dramatically, but more fundamentally, informed consent is a central notion in society, governing relations of power and agreement between human beings. Referring specifically to research, Guillemin and Gillam (2004) say "informed consent is at heart an interpersonal process between researcher and participant where the prospective participant comes to an understanding of what the research project is about and what participation would involve and makes his or her own decision about whether, and on what terms, to participate" (p. 272).

This chapter will explore the theoretical and practical implementation of research methods to support children under the age of three to participate in providing informed consent in research. We chose the age of three partly because we have worked with children of this age and partly because this age creates the greatest challenge to the idea of informed consent. In the adult-centered research environment, children can be assessed and constrained in their experiences of research (Punch, 2013), through narrow universal developmental categories that normalize and limit how young children's cognitive and linguistic capabilities are understood. The result is that adults question or fail to recognize children's capacity to participate in consent processes.

Since the ratification of the United Nations Convention on the Rights of the Child, there has been a major shift from seeing young children as passive recipients to viewing them as active participants in their own learning,

---

[1] For an overview of the articles in the United Nations Convention on the Rights of the Child, see https://www.ohchr.org/en/professionalinterest/pages/crc.aspx.

development, and engagement with the world. General Comment (No. 7), on "Implementing Child Rights in Early Childhood," has played a significant role in researchers beginning to explore participatory methodologies for and with young children.[2] General Comment (No. 7) states that the young child's right to express his or her views and feelings should be taken into account in the development of policies and services, including research. This comment stresses that these are the rights of all children, irrespective of their age.

The National Statement on Ethical Conduct in Human Research (NHMRC) sets out the national guidelines for ethical conduct in research, stating the need to specify how researchers will judge the child's vulnerability and capacity to consent to participation in research. The statement also describes the form of proposed discussions with children about the research and its effects; information given should be at their level of comprehension. However, this aspect of the statement remains somewhat open for interpretation and does not provide guidance on the types of protocols and practices to support young children's engagement. While protocols and practices should be contextual to the research project and particular groups of young children, forty years of our research work with the Graduate School of Education, added to qualifications in child development and learning, have led us to some specific methodologies and protocols that are useful when researching with children under three years. While there is a growing body of research and writing that uses participatory research methods with children under the age of five, there is a paucity of research that provides specific research protocols outlining practices and processes in gaining informed consent from young children. Some of the exceptions to this are Palaiologou (2014), Dockett, Perry and Kearney (2013), and Alderson (1992), though in most cases these authors are referring to children over three.

Tensions between informed consent and children's rights

There remain tensions between several of the elements of the CRC. In particular, there is a tension between the protective elements of the CRC and the claim that the child who is capable of forming his or her own views has "the right to express those views freely in all matters affecting the child, the views of the child being given due weight in accordance with the age and maturity of the child" (Article 12). The protective elements in the CRC could be seen as a continuation

---

[2]   General Comment 7 examines how to implement child rights in early childhood.

of earlier statements of children's rights, such as the U.N. Declaration of the Rights of the Child. This earlier document contrasts markedly with Articles 12 to 16 that flow from the more recent conception of children as agentic, as having points of view. Legal philosopher John Eekelaar (2017, 1994) addresses this tension, recognizing that many decisions must be made for children but that there are dangers in paternalism where adults may be deciding, whether consciously or unconsciously, in their own interests rather than in the child's. To resolve this tension Eekelaar (2017) proposes the idea of self-determinism, which interprets the concept of "best interests of the child" in a way that "allows scope for the child to interpret what those interests are" (p. 129). Solving this tension is particularly relevant to informed consent in research with very young children. This self-determinism when applied to the child under three requires great empathy on the part of the parent, guardian, teacher, or researcher. Self-determinism is captured by the Latin word *consentire*, to be of one mind and feeling, a word from which consent is probably derived and which best describes the state of mind required between the more powerful adult and the less powerful child. Self-determinism thus constitutes the child as still active in the decision-making but not necessarily in determining the result. Protection must always be there.

Our own practices in gaining consent

While our guiding ethical philosophy is clear, the practice of self-determinism as informed consent with very young children becomes complicated, continually evolving and very different from that with adults. Drawing from Edwards and Cutter-Mackenzie (2011), we would explain this process as ethical intentionality, where seeking consent starts at the recruitment phase and continues during all of the research encounters with the participants. Ethical intentionality ensures that self-determinism and consent are an ongoing process throughout the research rather than an administrative task to tick off at the beginning and file away as a compliance activity. One of the first methods to gain children's consent was the use of images as props to explain who the researchers are, the activities in which we are asking children to participate, how we will record or document what they say and do, what we will do with their ideas (for example, write = image of a pen and paper or computer, or talk with other people = image of a group of people talking), and that they can say yes or no to participate (consent = image of a head nodding yes or no or a hand with a thumbs up or down or a smiley face or frown). This can take the form of a paper document with the images on one page or it could be a series of individual photos or pictures.

One caution is that focusing on elaborate designs can mean both researcher and participant lose sight of the ethical purpose of the material, which is to inform or explain what the research is that children are being asked to participate in, what they would actually do, and that they have rights to agree or say no to being part of the research. These rights continue throughout the research so that even after initial agreement they can change their minds and say no to participation at any stage of the research. This method of obtaining informed consent reminds us to continually return to the key premise of self-determinism in consent. For example, when a three-year-old had worked with us, spending over an hour drawing and talking about her ideas, we asked if we could take a photograph or photocopy the drawing to use in our research. She declined stating that she wanted to take it home (MacNaughton and Smith, 2005, p. 119). We did not take a copy of the drawing. This example illustrates our ethical intention of ongoing consent; we asked the participant if she would like to be part of the research at the beginning of the research encounter and then asked for consent when recording data (the child's drawing) at the end of the encounter. A vital aspect of self-determinism is that we listened to the participant and acted when she withdrew consent for us to use her drawing. We refer to this as ethical listening—listening, hearing/seeing, and responding. Ethical listening is a tricky balance woven into the activities of "capturing" or collecting data.

Ethical listening has been particularly important for us when researching with babies. A child's willingness to engage with the research in the moment of data collection can be heard and witnessed in many different ways. Drawing from developmental theories, one way to see if a baby is willing to engage with the research is if he or she makes eye contact. While we acknowledge eye contact is deeply embedded in Western cultures and may not be relevant in every context, for many of our baby participants eye contact is a way to engage and create strong attachments between the baby, family, and researcher. With this noted, for some babies, actions such as avoiding eye contact and strongly moving their head to the side are indication that they are tired. Another baby or toddler may shake his or her head from side to side or pull on his or her ear as a self-soothing exercise. As researchers, if we are not ethically paying attention we can read this, with a developmental frame or ageist bias, as that they are too young to concentrate. If you read the actions in this way, you may try to reengage with the child trying different tools or toys to get the child's attention. A more informed ethical gaze would cause us to reflect and consider whether the child's action signals the need to just pause or acknowledge that the child has withdrawn from the research activity, in which case the researcher would stop collecting data. Working with families and caregivers is important to ensuring young children's consent as these people can help you learn about visual cues in order to understand when the child has disengaged and withdrawn from participation.

Ethical environments

Often researchers strip back the research space or create a specific space that enforces containment of the child by using a high chair or sitting the baby or toddler on an adult's knee or on a chair at a table (Swadener, 2016). The rationale for this can be about not wanting the child distracted by other activities or materials in the environment with a view that young children can be "easily" distracted. We would argue that one way for babies and toddlers to make choices about or consent to participate in the research activity is by creating an environment where there are a number of activities and materials for the child to explore. A baby may reach for other materials as a way to indicate that he or she does not want to participate in the research activity. Toddlers may physically move by crawling or walking from the research activity to another space. This may mean for the researcher that she needs to allocate more time for data collection, to be able to wait and be guided by the interests of the children. It is possible that it may mean that the researcher has to accept that the child has withdrawn. Young children's emerging communication skills mean that the certainty of the child's consent can be unclear.

Disciplinary differences

In a recent piece of research interviewing researchers working with very young children across various disciplines in both the University of Melbourne and several international institutions, we found a large majority of our respondents viewed young children as rights-bearers and made attempts to get meaningful consent from the participating children in their research. Perhaps this was not surprising given that the respondents were self-selected. However, it does contrast with some views expressed by research committees in past decades. Few would now claim that very young children do not have points of view.

As part of this research, we used four levels of informed consent proposed by Alderson and Montgomery (1996): to be informed (level 1), to form and express views (level 2), to influence a decision (level 3), and to be the main decider about proposed treatment or care (level 4). Three-quarters of our participants felt that children be treated as being at level 3 or level 4 in the consent/assent process in their own research. Discipline area seemed to play a part in participants' responses to this question. For example, all three participants undertaking research in medicine selected level 1, while two-thirds of the participants work in education and all but two of these selected level 3 or 4. To gain a more rounded perspective in our research we asked if respondents would be prepared to be interviewed after the survey. Among those agreeing to this were two medical respondents. It was clear from the interviews that those medical researchers shared our view of the CRC, but held very realistically that a child under five would not agree, for example, to having blood taken by needles, though one experienced researcher said she was able to explain her work to the satisfaction of children aged over seven that they would be helping other children.

These examples from medical researchers highlighted some of the issues facing children who are asked for consent. While a little over half of respondents answered that there were negligible or no harms in their research, as Alderson and Morrow (2012) suggest, the harm in social research can be underestimated. Such harm can be as small as wasting the children's time, but as serious as causing the child to feel like an outsider or undermining his or her self-esteem. These harms may not be quite as dramatic as the ones mentioned by one of our medical participants, where anaphylaxis and death were possible, though extremely unlikely, harms of research. Nevertheless, the possible harms of research in education could also be extremely serious and all the more sinister for being harder to spot. This raises challenges for consent as self-determinism and requires vigilance, particularly in ensuring undue pressure is not placed on children to "consent" to participate in research.

Pressures on child to take part

The majority of our respondents believed there were cases where the children were pressured to take part in research. The "culprits" were predominantly parents, but also included teachers, other researchers, and other children. *Sometimes practitioners and parents are keen for their children to participate when the children are unsure.* Several respondents suggested strategies to ensure undue pressure is not placed on the child:

Revisiting key aspects of the consent/assent process, with both adults and children—especially regarding voluntary participation and the right to withdraw.

Ongoing reflective practice from researcher to ensure pressure is not being caused by research practice.

Ongoing monitoring of children's verbal and nonverbal cues.

Building trust and taking time for children to make informed decisions, change their mind, etc.

Conducting research with children separately from adults who are pressuring them.

These responses highlight the different times that the researchers are prepared to spend considering whether the child is consenting. Adults may be too ready to believe that they can easily understand how the children are viewing the research. This harks back to discourses where adults are the decision-makers. Similar discourses maybe evident when acknowledging children's right and capacity to withdraw from research.

The right to withdraw from research

Some writers have suggested that various factors to do with research in institutions and in participatory research make it difficult for the child to withdraw. Gallacher and Gallagher (2008) refer to the "children's schooled docility" (p. 506), which makes children likely to conform to what the researcher or carer wants. One respondent who clearly knew of this argument retorted: *The children in my center are always prepared to say when they don't want to take part.* Most of our respondents believed withdrawing from research was an important right but difficult in practice. There was however some variation in responses:

I don't (ask children). If you give young children the choice to stop all the time it is confusing. I go more on body language.

Choosing instruments and techniques which allow the child to discontinue at any point and observe the child's reactions and also keep telling them regularly that they can opt out if they wish.

Checking-in, even stopping a discussion to check-in and see if they want to continue.

Situational responsiveness: level of interest, open question not to participate if they are "busy" or do not feel like it today.

In all of these responses the experienced researchers were sensitive to the idea that the child has a right to withdraw. This shifts from a traditional assumption that after the initial consent, often from the parent or guardian, the researcher could continue until the data had been collected.

Conflicts of interest in research

The issue of the right to withdraw led us to look at the question of conflicts of interest in research that have the potential to vitiate the consent process where researchers or those consenting on behalf of the child consciously or unconsciously may be less willing to think about the right to withdraw. For example, the researcher may have an interest in getting a Ph.D., a publication, employment, a promotion, or a grant, all of which could be important in the researcher's career, but which could all be threatened if too many participants withdraw. Parents may also be influenced by outside force that impacts decisions about withdrawing their children from research, including feeling they have to cooperate with the management and principals in order to keep their children in what they believe is a good school or childcare center. One of our interviewees experienced in research in many different countries reported that in a number of countries a culture existed where authorities are not to be challenged, and researchers were regarded as authorities whose requests were to be unquestioningly accepted. This example shows how cultural expectations may clash with our understandings of informed consent.

Mitigating conflicts of interest in research

As a way of mitigating the effects of unrecognized or unadmitted conflicts of interest, we asked our respondents whether they would be happy with the presence during the research of a parent or another person who was not connected with the research, who did not have a stake in the research continuing, and who could recognize the cues in the young child of a wish to withdraw. Such a person could support the child continuing or withdrawing from the research and generally make sure the interests of the child were heard. The responses to this were mixed with a slight majority in favor. One of those against the idea saw it as a threat to her professionalism: *that would indicate that I am not a professional and that I don't have the professional knowledge to gauge children's desires to withdraw or if the task is inappropriate.* Another, however, describes her practice in the following way: *Sometimes, in the "busyness" of research, small signs of discomfort can be missed, so I enlist the help of others (parents/teachers, etc.) to let me any discomfort they think may be caused by the continuing research.*

Right to privacy

There are parts of some research that many children may not recognize in advance. For example, they may not realize that photos may be taken in situations which the children are just learning are regarded as private such as the bathroom, and they may be shown in public spaces through the reporting of the research. Most of our respondents were very insistent on the right to privacy. One respondent saw it as related to the right to withdraw:

> *I see children's privacy related to their right to withdraw and not participate. So, if a child seems uncomfortable about a discussion we might be having, I might not probe to find out more. I often wonder what right do I have to know really any of the things I'm asking?*

Others mentioned not videoing in the toilet/bathroom or sleeping area and blurring images to protect the anonymity of the child.

> *We do not use photographs or video data in any research outputs/presentations without explicit consent and we obscure children's faces and any other details that might allow children to be identified.*

This highlights the need for researchers, families, and children to continually communicate throughout the research to gain an understanding of the nature of the research and how data will be gained and later used.

The informed part of informed consent

We have given several examples of, and a caution about, how to inform children under three years about research. It is interesting that in our own survey of researchers, the question that gained greatest attention concerned parents being asked to give blanket agreement to research in designated research institutions; 78.57 percent were opposed to this. Our question concerned a case where the parents have given blanket consent and would not be given detailed information about the research in which their children were involved. They may well agree to this sort of continuing "consent" because they wanted to get their children into a "good centee." But in such a case consent is neither free (because of parents' self-imposed pressures) nor informed.

The dynamic nature of research

One of our respondents referred to *the ongoing nature of consent*. Several respondents advised using *reflective practice*; another says she often *stands back and reflects* in order to assess power imbalances or other ethical issues as the research progresses. These views align with those of Komesaroff (1996), when he used the term "microethics" to refer to the ever-changing relationship between doctor and patient. Guillemin and Gillam (2004) use a similar idea in relation to research. Much qualitative research uses the word "reflexive" in relation to researchers critically examining their data. Guillemin and Gillam go further to apply this idea to ethics:

> Our notion of reflexivity urges researchers to be reflexive in relation to interpersonal and ethical aspects of research practice, not just to the epistemological aspects of rigorous research. (p. 277)

Many of our respondents recognized that ascertaining consent was not a one-off event but continuing throughout the research. However, this recognition presents a problem for the way "ethics" is regulated in many institutions where there is an initial hurdle of getting research ethics approval for beginning the research, followed in some cases by annual reports. While some ethics committees may regard themselves as ethics advisors, many researchers regard research ethics committees as primarily gatekeepers who can allow or disallow their research. Ethical problems that arise in the process of research are often complex and need to be resolved with some urgency, so cannot wait a decision made by committee. This raises questions about how researchers work with committees in relation to young children's capacity to provide assent.

Conclusion

In the belief that ethical dilemmas are better resolved through reflection rather than coercion, we would suggest that researchers seek out trusted peers or consult with the person representing the child's interests, as suggested earlier. One of our respondents regarded having present a person representing the child's interest as a threat to their professionalism. This may be a common reaction to this suggestion. But it should be pointed out, first, that these people would only have advisory roles, not coercive powers, and, second, that many professions are grappling with similar problems and are seeking out nonpunitive ways of nurturing ethical institutions. We can and did learn from other professions and are reassured by the thoughtful and informed responses of our respondents and in particular their often expressed concern to continue examining these issues.

In this chapter, we call for processes and methods that safeguard ongoing informed consent. We pose philosophical and practical safeguards focused on conflict mitigation, minimization of risk, privacy, and independent peer review of consent. We advocate for change in how to think about and plan for dynamic elements of research. This involves adopting a reflexive attitude to the role of the researcher, to the structure of the research design, to data collection methods, and to how we understand and listen with children in research.

References

Alderson, P. (1992). In the genes or in the stars? Children's competence to consent. *Journal of Medical Ethics, 18*(3), 119–124.

Alderson, P., and Montgomery, J. (1996). *Health care choices: Making decisions with children* (*Vol. 2*). Institute for Public Policy Research.

Alderson P., and Morrow, V. (2012). *The ethics of Research with children and young people: A practical handbook* [e-book]. Los Angeles, Calif.; London: Sage. Available from University of Melbourne Catalogue, Ipswich, MA. Accessed July 31, 2018.

Coady, M. (2008). Beings and becomings: Historical and philosophical considerations of the child as citizen. In G. MacNaughton, P. Hughes and K. Smith (Eds.), *Young children as active citizens: Principles, policies and pedagogies* (pp. 2–14). London: Cambridge Scholars Publishing.

Dockett, S., Perry, B., and Kearney, E. (2013). Promoting children's informed consent in research participation. *International Journal of Qualitative Studies in Education 26*(7), 802–828.

Edwards, S., and Cutter-Mackenzie, A. (2011). Environmentalising early childhood education curriculum through pedagogies of play. *Australasian Journal of Early Childhood*, *36*(1), 51.

Eekelaar, J. (1994). The interests of the child and the child's wishes: The role of self-determinism. *International Journal of Law and the Family*, *8*, 42–61.

Eekelaar, J. (2017). The interests of the child and the child's wishes: The Role of Dynamic Self-Determinism. In U. Kilkelly and L. Lundy (Eds.), *Children's Rights* (pp. 129–148). Abingdon Oxon: Routledge.

Gallacher, L., and Gallagher, M. (2008). Methodological immaturity in childhood research?: Thinking through "participatory methods." *Childhood*, *15*(4), 499–516.

Guillemin, M., and Gillam, L. (2004). Ethics, reflexivity and "ethically important moments." *Research Qualitative Enquiry*, *10*(2), 261–280.

Komesaroff, P. (1996). Medicine and ethical conditions of modernity. In J. Day (Ed.), *Ethical intersections: Health research, methods and researcher responsibility* (pp. 34–48). Sydney, Australia: Allen and Unwin.

MacLean, D. (2006). Informed consent and the construction of values. In S. Lichtenstein and P. Slovic (Eds.), *The construction of preference* (pp. 668–681). New York: Cambridge University Press.

MacNaughton, G., and Smith, K. (2005). Exploring ethics and difference: The choices and challenges of researching with children. In A. Farrell (Ed.), *Exploring ethical research with children* (pp. 112–123). Buckingham: Open University Press.

MacNaughton, G., and Smith, K. (2008). Engaging ethically with young children: Principles and practices for listening and responding with care. In G. MacNaughton, P. Hughes and K. Smith (Eds.), *Young children as active citizens: Principles, policies and pedagogies* (pp. 31–43). London: Cambridge Scholars Publishing.

Palaiologou, I. (2014). "Do we hear what children want to say?" Ethical praxis when choosing research tools with children under five. *Early Child Development and Care*, *184*(5), 689–705.

Punch, S. (2013). Research with children: The same or different from research with adults? *Childhood*, *9*(3), 321–341.

Swadener, E. (2016). Foreword. In M. M. Jozwiak, B. J. Cahill and R. Theilheimer (Eds.), *Continuity in children's worlds* (pp. vii–ix). New York: Teachers College Press.

2

Ethics as Play in Aesthetic Encounters with Young Children

Melissa Freeman
University of Georgia, USA

The squiggle game

Child (boy, four years and four months): "Ok, my turn to make, your turn to
    make a squiggle."
I draw a squiggle on a piece of blank paper, a curving line across the middle of
    the page.
Child: "What do you think it could be?"
Melissa: "I don't know."
He draws an oval all around the squiggle by little jagged lines until it has
    surrounded my squiggle, and says: "A boat."
Melissa: "A boat."
Child: "Uh, no, water with a little sna …,[1] with a little worm."
Melissa: "Okay."
A knock at the door and then a teacher comes in.
Teacher: "Hi."
Child: "Just doing a little game, a scribbling game. Then one person tries to
    figure out what, what they want to make it out of, and then the other person
    gets time to scribble, and then the other person, then the other person tries
    to guess what it, what it could look like, but you have to make all different
    kinds of scribbles and all different kinds of pictures."
Teacher: "Sounds interesting." She leaves.
Melissa: "It's your turn."
Child: "Okay, to make … a scribble." He draws.

As an undergraduate student in the early 1980s majoring in psychology and
early childhood studies, I became particularly interested in young children's

---

[1]   An ellipsis in the transcript excerpts denotes a pause rather than an omission.

capacities to interpret their own lives and the world around them. Part of the requirements for the early childhood major included a variety of classes and interning as an assistant teacher in the college's early childhood center, a position that eventually turned into teaching summer camp for six- to nine-year-olds and later getting certified to provide childcare services in my own home while my two daughters were growing up. Part of my coursework in psychology included classes on the Gestalt psychologists, the philosophy of symbolic forms, and psychotherapy with children and adolescents, to name a few. It was in this program that I was introduced to Maurice Merleau-Ponty's (1962) *Phenomenology of Perception* and Donald Winnicott's (1971) *Therapeutic Consultations in Child Psychiatry*, two texts I drew on heavily when writing my undergraduate thesis (Freeman, 1984) that explored what happens when the *squiggle game* is played with young children in nontherapeutic contexts and for nontherapeutic purposes.

Winnicott (1971) describes the role the *squiggle game* plays during his therapeutic consultations with children:

> There is nothing original of course about the squiggle game and it would not be right for somebody to learn how to use the squiggle game and then to feel equipped to do what I call a therapeutic consultation. The squiggle game is simply one way of getting into contact with a child. What happens in the game and in the whole interview depends on the use made of the child's experience, *including the material that presents itself* ... In my cases described here an artificial link is made between the squiggle game and the psychotherapeutic consultation, and this arises out of the fact that from the drawings ... one can find one way of making the case come alive. It is almost as if the child, through the drawings, is alongside me, and to some extent taking part in describing the case, so that the reports of what the child and the therapist said tend to ring true. (p. 3, emphasis added)

My thesis examined Winnicott's use of the squiggle game through Merleau-Ponty's embodied and participatory lens to consider the ways in which children readily move between words and pictures when expressing themselves. As an educational researcher who has always incorporated drawing and other interactive activities when working with children, the invitation to contribute to this book on ethics was an opportunity for me to consider the ethical significance of those practices. Immanent to any encounter is an *ethics-becoming*, an ontological manifestation of a researcher's becoming-with-others, as she makes visible the "responsibility and accountability for the lively relationalities of becoming of which we are all a part" (Barad, 2007, p. 393).

Specifically, I wondered, in what way does the squiggle game, where two or more players take turns making a squiggle on a piece of paper for the other to turn it into an image of their choosing, enact a *participatory ontology* (Ge, 2016) within which we and the things in the world participate in our own and the world's becoming?

Going back to Winnicott's description of the game, psychoanalytic theory played a key role in how he made sense of the "material that presents itself" (Winnicott, 1971, p. 3) during the consultation. In my thesis I argued that it is for this reason that Winnicott talks about this material as mediating between the unconscious and the conscious and places emphasis on the therapist's ability to use this material to move the child forward into an awareness of the situation or conflict that was causing whatever behavior or stress brought the child to therapy. Beyond making the child comfortable by listening deeply, sitting the child on his chair and taking the child's chair, and being small in stature, Winnicott (1971) used psychoanalytic theory to seek ways "to get to the real dream material" (p. 32) and to help children reach their own statements about their current conflict. Winnicott discusses the importance of right timing in making interpretations as essential to their success. In my thesis, I argued that Winnicott sensed that the embodied and visual statements co-occurring with the therapist's interpretation were inherently communicative but still felt it necessary to make these verbal. I concluded that multiple forms of understanding were necessary partners to meaning-making and that prioritization of any one over the other was uncalled for.

Although not part of my thesis, that same year (1984), I had the opportunity to carry out a mini-study looking at how young children (three- to five-year-olds) would engage with the game. To do this, I invited the children to come play a game with me in an adjoining room to their classroom. I sat across from them at a table and because I wanted to compare how different children approached each squiggle, when it was my turn I repeated the same first five squiggles, but would make whatever came to mind when transforming the children's squiggles. I also gave the children two colors to work with, brown and blue, and used the black marker myself.

Returning my attention to these now yellowed drawings and transcripts thirty-four years later, I was not prepared for the uniqueness of each encounter. I wondered: What sense for *ethics* is repeatedly materializing in these encounters? In what way does the game itself as a form of play participate in these ethical configurations? I was provoked by the way the transcripts enacted an inherent meaningfulness even though the game had been played to explore what happened in the play of the game itself. I was also struck by the negligible amount of evaluative talk about either the child or the drawings and was prompted to think about the way our shared focus on the game itself enacted a participatory ethics that furthered its generative effects. However, I was also aware of the way the relational expectations inherent in the transactions between the adult, child, and the game's materials carried within them boundary-making practices (Barad, 2007) or aesthetic regimes (Rancière, 2004) that shaped these encounters in expected and unexpected ways. This chapter is the result of these observations.

Aesthetic encounters as playing-with

Melissa: "Okay, now you do something."
Child: (girl, three years and eleven months). She draws a ghostly looking shape (Fig. 1).

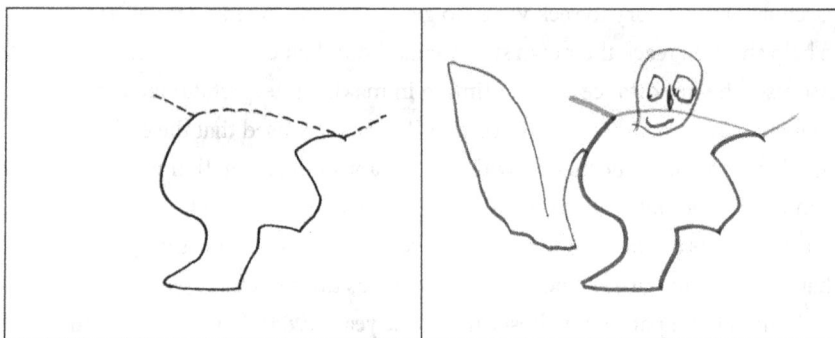

Figure 2.1 Fig. 1 & Fig. 2

Melissa: "Oh, wow!"
While I ponder silently upon the figure, she says: "A person you can make it into."
Melissa: "I think I could."
Child: "Make." She motions two lines near the base of the figure with the bottom of her pen.
Melissa: "If I put two lines like this?" I draw the arms (dotted lines in Fig. 1). She then spontaneously draws the head between my two arms and another squiggle out the side of the body. She does this drawing the person upside down so it is right side up for me.
Melissa: "That's it."
Child: "It's funny. It's a funny kind of house … with a nose and a foot" (Fig. 2).
Melissa: "A house?"
Child: "With a head."
Melissa: "That is funny, isn't it."

What do I mean by aesthetics? Aesthetics as a particular philosophical line of questioning has a long history, but part of its focus has been on the kind of knowledge that is produced when we, as perceiver-receivers (Freeman, 2017), encounter a phenomenon that takes our breath away, causes us to pause, to wonder. Hans-Georg Gadamer (1986) asks: "How do we grasp this truth?" (p. 16). What sense is being made in the particular truths put forth in our affective response to the beautiful in a bird's flight or the joy in a child's laughter? Where does the *meaningfulness* of these encounters come from? For Gadamer, aesthetics as a form of attentiveness to meaning-becoming participates actively "in the movement of a work's constitutive elements" (Davey, 2013, p. 1).

To make sense of this movement, Gadamer (1986) draws on the concept of play. When we think of play, he writes,

> the first thing is the to and fro of constantly repeated movement—we only have to think of certain expressions like "the play of light" and "the play of the waves" where we have such a constant coming and going, back and forth, a movement that is not tied down to any goal … Now play appears as a self-movement that does not pursue any particular end or purpose so much as movement *as* movement, exhibiting so to speak a phenomenon of excess, of living self-representation. (pp. 22–23)

Furthermore, play is participatory and "requires a 'playing along with.' Even the onlooker watching a child play cannot possibly do otherwise. If he really does 'go along with it,' that is nothing but a *participatio*, an inner sharing in this repetitive movement" (Gadamer, 1986, pp. 23–24). For Gadamer, play is our mode of being in aesthetic encounters, and the giving over of ourselves to this movement is a crucial part of this encounter becoming meaning-full. Playing brings us outside ourselves as we are taken up in its flow. Monica Vilhauer (2010) explains: "Being outside oneself, in a very basic way, means opening yourself up to something 'other' than yourself and allowing it to affect you" (p. 39). And this is exactly what the squiggle game does as this longer example demonstrates.

> Melissa: I show him the game with an example. I make a squiggle and turn it into a funny head. The boy (four years and two months) takes his pen, engaging readily.
> Child: "It's also a dinosaur." He draws in the mouth. "See his teeth!" He looks at the drawing. "There he is!"
> Melissa: "Yea, shall we start?"

Child: "He needs a bigger neck." He draws in the neck. "That picture's done."

Melissa: "I'll make one for you." I make the first squiggle (Fig. 3).

Child: "Hm hm." He picks up the paper, looks at it, turns it around several ways. "That's an M just like my name." Then he adds to the picture upside down.

Melissa: "Neat, what's that?"

Child: "A house and a palm tree" (Fig. 4).

Melissa: "Have you seen a palm tree?"

Child: "Yup."

Melissa: "Now you make one for me." He draws a rectangle (Fig. 5). "I know what."

Child: Watching me. "What's that ... a person?"

Melissa: "A person in a boat" (Fig. 6).

Child: "Now you make something." While I write down what the last one was, he fishes out a clean sheet of paper. "Here's the paper." He is impatient to continue and does not like me to spend time writing down titles throughout the game. I make a squiggle for him (Fig. 7). He turns the sheet around, looks at it. "A person," he mumbles. He draws, looking at the picture between adding arms and feet. "That person I made" (Fig. 8).

Melissa: "He looks like he is taking really long steps."

Child: "He's running ... cause he's gonna get arrested. That's why he's running."

Melissa: "He's going to get arrested?"

Child: "Yea."

Melissa: "For what?"

Child: "Cause he drove his car and broke a police car."

Melissa: "Okay, you make one." He draws (Fig. 9). "It's a turtle" (Fig. 10).

Child: "Hm hm. Now you make a copy and I'll copy your copy. Now you go and make something."

Melissa: "Okay." I draw (Fig. 11).

Child: "I know!" Delighted. "I know what it could be!" He adds the eyes. "A ghost!" I laugh (Fig. 12). "A ghost don't have mouths, they don't show the mouth, do they?"

Melissa: "No they don't. Okay you make one." He deliberately draws a certain shape (Fig. 13).

Child: "I know what I'd do with that," he says, before I even look at it.

Melissa: "What would you do?"

Child: "Make a mountain."

Melissa: "It looks just like a mountain. I could just leave it like that but I'll add a house at the bottom so we can see that it is a big mountain" (Fig. 14).

Child: "My turn."

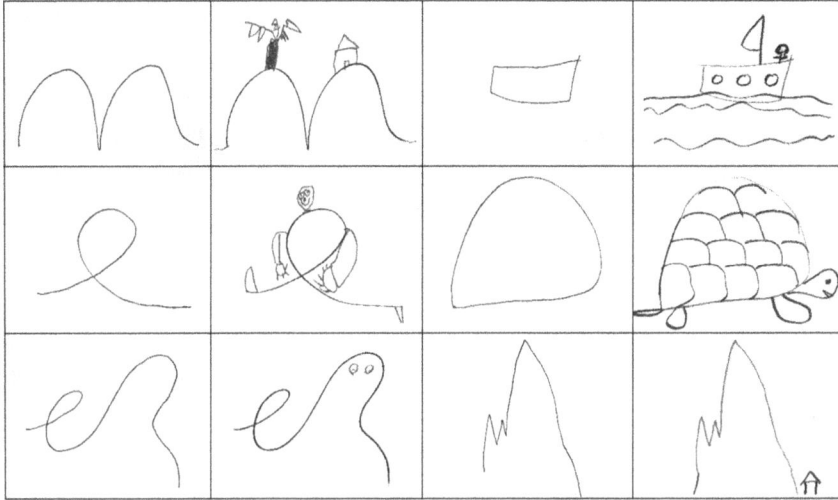

Figure 2.2 Fig. 3 to Fig. 14

Ethics as playful provocations

Aesthetic encounters open up a rift into an unstable flux of meaning within which researchers and research participants make sense of each other's styles of engagement, the spoken and unspoken expectations inherent to the research event, and the multifold becomings of *phenomena* as "specific ontological entanglements" (Barad, 2007, p. 338) with which worlds are created. For Gadamer (1989) "the world that appears in the play of presentation does not stand like a copy next to the real world, but is that world in the heightened truth of its being" (p. 132). In other words, meaning is the material manifestation of ontological entanglements and does not stand for or represent something else. Play best describes this movement of mattering because it works with the generative forces of the in-between. Winnicott understood play within therapy as mediating between unconsciousness and consciousness because it transgressed boundaries between the real, felt, and imagined. Gadamer saw it as transformative because it brought into tension known and unknown configurations opening up the generative capacity of the play of meaning. In this way, sense, non-sense, dissensus (Rancière, 2004, 2010) become entangled in *aesthetic play* (Gadamer, 1989), within which squiggles, language, paper, marker, child, adult, relationships, sense, sensations, and the things of the world perform as partners in the performative event.

Jacques Rancière (2010) argues that aesthetic configurations become political, and thus ethical, when their strategies act

> to change the frames, speeds and scales according to which we perceive the visible … Such strategies are intended to make the invisible visible or to question the self-evidence of the visible; to rupture given relations between things and meanings and, inversely, to invent novel relationships between things and meanings that were previously unrelated. (p. 141)

Although children, like adults, become positioned in particular ways within intersecting discourses and institutional practices, their unique positions in these boundary-making practices (Barad, 2007) and their propensity toward playfulness make them important interpreters of these practices and agents capable of recalibrating their distributive effects. The squiggle game participates as one possible form of engagement where children's capacities to interpret and to create are fostered by opening up new relationships between themselves and others, things and representations, words and pictures, matter and meaning. Patricia Carini (1979) explains:

> Meaning arises through the relationship among things or persons: that mutual reciprocity that occurs in the act of truly "seeing" something. Thus, meaning is not a *thing*, an *object*, or an *entity* itself. Rather, meaning designates the experience of relatedness which enhances and makes more vivid each of the events or persons it joins. For meaning to arise, there must be recognition. (p. 15)

Since I provided the children very little direction except to tell them that this was a drawing game and demonstrate it with an example, the children had to come to some kind of re-cognition of the rules or purpose of the game as it unfolded. This unfolding understanding becomes an important part of the ethical and interpretive matter that manifests in the encounters. And it is in these evident, although often unspoken and uninterpreted, negotiations that play and ethics become together. As the children make their own interpretations of our playing together, of the term "squiggle," or the expectation to "change it into something," and what that "something" could consist of, they offer both new possibilities for meaning-making and respond as capable interpreters and creators of their world. Consider these examples:

While I show one girl (three years and eleven months) an example of the game, she copies it fairly accurately, drawing upside down.

Melissa: "Okay, I'll make a squiggle for you to change it into something." I draw (Fig. 15). "Now you change it into something."

Child: "Okay, this thing, I will."

Melissa: "You will."

Child: "Uh hu." She copies my squiggle above it in blue.

Melissa: "You know what you're going to do?"

Child: "I want to get brown."

Melissa: "That's okay." She adds another line in brown above her blue one.

Child: "Now I want to change it into something else." She points to the blue. "This kind." I did not understand her wanting the blue marker right away and she adds another brown line.

Melissa: "Does that look like something to you?"

Child: "I want black now."

Melissa: "You want to use black now?" I allow her to use the black and she makes the top line in black going off the page (Fig. 16).

Child: "I want to make something for me."

* * *

Melissa: "Okay, I'll start." I draw a squiggle that looks like an M or W depending on which side of the table you are on (Fig. 17). "Now you make it into something."

Child: (boy, four years and one month) connects the two sides of the squiggle with a straight line closing the figure. "Hm."

Melissa: "Does that have a name?"

Child: "What?" Long pause. He is considering the question uneasily. "Hmm … they climb up, um this thing, and then they fall down into a hole," he says as he traces the bumps with his finger.

Melissa: "So that's a hole."

Child: "Yeah, and then they climb up and go around."

Melissa: "So it doesn't really have a name. That's how they do it."

Child: "Yeah!" Relieved (Fig. 18).

* * *

Melissa: "Okay, I'll make one for you." I draw (Fig. 19).

Child: (girl, four years and three months) "I think I'll use brown okay."

Melissa: "Hm hm." She draws.

Child: "There … (very softly) you know what that is?" She traces over it. "It goes like that, so you know what it is?"

Melissa: "What is it?"

Child: "It's … um, a D. It has a squid because it has a little like that, okay."

Melissa: "Is a squid a little mistake?"

Child: "Yea, so it has to be a D-squid, okay?"

Melissa: "A D-squid." I write it down.

Child: "I think that's going to be really long." When I finish writing. "It is really long" (Fig. 20).

* * *

Melissa: "Now I'll make one for you" (Fig. 21).

Child: (boy, four years and two months) "Yup … What is that into?" He says very softly as I draw.

Melissa: "What are you going to make that into?"

Child: "Yea." Again very softly. He connects the two extremities the long way around the squiggle, then adds some marks here and there seemingly matter-of-factly. He does not volunteer a name.

Melissa: "What are you going to name that?"

Child: "Twotee tatoo."

Melissa: "Twoteetatoo?"

Child: "Yea."

Melissa: "That's what you made?"

Child: "Yea."

Melissa: "Is that a real something?"

Child: "Yea, something that's a retat … looks like a retatoo."

Melissa: "A retatoo, what does a retatoo do?"

Child: "He looks, he says 'where's my (board or boy)!' He says that." He laughs. I write it down.

Melissa: "Have you ever seen one?"

Child: "No, so I made it, so I could see one."

Melissa: "You made it so you could see it."

Child: "Yup" (Fig. 22).

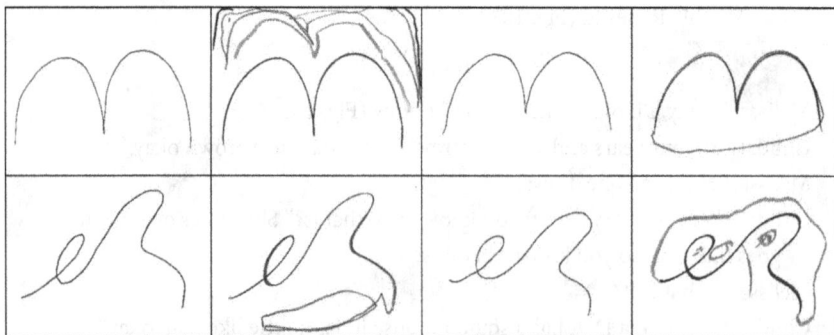

Figure 2.3 Fig. 15–18 top row, Fig. 19–22 bottom row

Cultivating response-ability through play

In *Staying with the Trouble*, Donna Haraway (2016) calls for a cultivation of response-ability, which she sees among other things as a way to train

> the mind and imagination to go visiting, to venture off the beaten path to meet unexpected, non-natal kin, and to strike up conversations, to pose and respond to interesting questions, to propose together something unanticipated, to take up the unasked-for obligations of having met. (p. 130)

Inherent to the idea of response-ability is "becoming-with, not becoming … becoming-with is how partners are … rendered capable" (Haraway, 2016, p. 12). And although the examples provided in this chapter of my playful interactions with children do not, at first glance, seem to rise to the level of making a fuss (Haraway, 2016) or of creating a space "where the relations between sense and sense continue to be questioned and re-worked" (Rancière, 2010, p. 145), I believe their capacity to bring into visibility the capabilities and creativity of those who participate means that they do just that. Furthermore, I believe that play enacts a participatory ontology of becoming-together that develops what Rancière (2004) calls a "political subject," that is, a subject who carries out his or her right to "reconfigure what are given to be facts" (p. 64) in every aspect of life. In this way, making a fuss encourages attentiveness to the effects of our modes of being and doing in the midst of inventive connectedness with known and not-yet-known participating others.

Carini (1979) explains that not only does the mind get better with age at making generalizations and recognizing "the invariant properties of objects in spite of shifts in orientation and perspective" but education generally fosters and values this capacity over the cultivation "to see the expressive uniqueness of other persons … in the interplay and texture of gesture" (p. 38). Contrary to the emphasis on abstraction, the squiggle game focuses on the particular interplay and texture of gesture as it emerges in the visual, verbal, symbolic, textual, and embodied manifestations during the game. There is nothing outside the game that explains the game or gives meaning to the visual and verbal statements made as these are performed. The game is simply there to be played, enjoyed or not, continued or stopped. This does not mean that outside interferences or personal interests do not enter into this flow as well—of course they do. Nor does it mean that all children engaged readily with the game or wanted to play, as several of them chose to simply draw or go back to their classroom. What it does mean, however, is that the capacity of play as a form of engagement that cultivates response-ability and attentiveness to the particular uniqueness of each meaning-making gesture should not be overlooked when we consider how we want to become together as we interact with others and the world we share.

Playing-with as ethics-becoming

I started this chapter to examine the reasons I included drawing and other interactive activities when working with children and conclude with an ethical awareness about the importance of these decisions that is larger than me or my own research practices. To me play, whether we are talking about the squiggle game or playing with toys, words, images, or the world around us, is in need of rehabilitation. Playing-with is ethics-becoming as each event opens for us aesthetic encounters where what matters, and what does not, gets performed anew. Play fosters response-ability because the focus is on the generative capacity of the game itself and the collaborative and interpretive capacities of the players. The openness of the interaction and the focus on form, process, matter, and effect all work together to create awareness of each other's part in the overall performance. This kind of engagement is not something that can be written into an educational system obsessed with outcomes that stand for knowledge removed from the intricacies of its formation, and it cannot be something added to curriculum or, as in my case, research design. Play must be thought of as an overarching mode of participation worth fostering if we take seriously the call by Haraway and others to cultivate response-ability in ourselves and in the practices that give shape to a world-becoming.

References

Barad, K. (2007). *Meeting the universe halfway: Quantum physics and the entanglement of matter and meaning.* Durham, NC: Duke University Press.

Carini, P. F. (1979). *The art of seeing and the visibility of the person.* Grand Forks, ND: University of North Dakota Press.

Davey, N. (2013). *Unfinished worlds: Hermeneutics, aesthetics and Gadamer.* Edinburgh, Scotland: Edinburgh University Press.

Freeman, M. A. (1984). *Explorations of D. W. Winnicott's Squiggle Game.* Unpublished Bachelor of Arts Thesis. Bennington College, Bennington, VT.

Freeman, M. (2017). *Modes of thinking for qualitative data analysis.* New York: Routledge.

Gadamer, H.-G. (1986). *The relevance of the beautiful and other essays* (Trans. Nicholas Walker). Cambridge, UK: Cambridge University Press.

Gadamer, H.-G. (1989). *Truth and method* (2nd revised ed., J. Weinsheimer & D. G. Marshall, Trans.). New York: Continuum.

Ge, Y. (2016). The one and the many: A revisiting of an old philosophical question in the light of theologies of creation and participation. *The Heythrop Journal, LVII*, 109–121.

Haraway, D. J. (2016). *Staying with the trouble: Making kin in the Chthulucene*. Durham, NC: Duke University Press.

Mearleau-Ponty, M. (1962). *Phenomenology of perception*. New York: Routledge.

Rancière, J. (2004). *The politics of aesthetics: The distribution of the sensible*. New York: Continuum.

Rancière, J. (2010). *Dissensus: On politics and aesthetics* (Steven Corcoran, Ed. and Trans.). New York: Continuum.

Vilhauer, M. (2010). *Gadamer's ethics of play: Hermeneutics and the other*. Lanham, MD: Lexington Books.

Winnicott, D. W. (1971). *Therapeutic consultations in child psychiatry*. New York: Basic Books.

3

Drawing Together: Toward a Relational Ethics of Ignorance

Hayon Park

The Pennsylvania State University, USA

"What? You don't know *anything* about Star Wars!" Oliver remarked, while browsing Google images of Darth Vader on my iPhone with Alex, as I responded "I don't know," again, to their question "What happened here?" regarding what type of scene the image was portraying of the Star Wars movie. His expression seemed to convey confusion about how a young adult, who has been around for months, could lack such knowledge of the most frequently mentioned movie on the playground, in block play area, and at the art table. Alex begins to explain, with a high-tone voice, "Well, that's actually when, umm, Darth Vader looks at Luke *very* disappointed, 'cause Luke actually cut his father's arm off, his hand I mean, 'cause he's trying to save his sister." "Oh, that's why ..." I say, as the boys proceeded to discuss other unique features of Darth Vader.

In the kindergarten classroom, where I routinely visited as a researcher, my role developed into that of an artist-in-residence, who at the request of the children assisted in the creation of characters and content related to the children's popular media interests. Faithful to my role as an accessible drawing tool, I carried out most of the general figure drawings without technical difficulty. But when it came to drawing some of the more specialized content from children's contemporary media culture, my status among the children immediately regressed, as I often required assistance in order to sketch the characters desired by the children. As an acknowledgment of my sparse knowledge, drawing requests were often accompanied with detailed descriptions of the characters' unique features, or demands that I search for images on my phone, which could then be used to aid my drawing. The point being that by drawing together, the relationship entailed both the exchange of demands and expertise, as I was reliant on the child's cultural knowledge to deliver my graphic skills and the child utilized my graphic skills while also demonstrating his mastery of a particular media culture for me.

On the one hand, the process of attending to each other's needs involved various forms of questioning, degrees of approval, and practices of negotiation. On the other hand, the process of asking for and attending to such questions, of accepting and resisting approval, and of being in negotiation demanded that each of us, in different ways, establish the will to *un-know* what it is we think we understand about who the other is, about how they work, and the reasons they have for doing so. While the desire to know was ostensibly set forth and communicated, the process of unknowing, however, required that each of us foster the willingness to work against ourselves, against the ideas and attitudes that sustain how we see and think the other. When drawing popular culture figures together, the process often demanded that the child share with me certain understandings about the popular media culture that was in question—a step that was typically unnecessary when Oliver, Alex, and other kindergarteners engaged in drawing with their peers. For me, the experience of drawing with children often entailed having to relinquish the aesthetic principles and methods of drawing that were most familiar. In lieu of these comforts, I found myself having to attend to the subtle shifts and uncertainties that would emerge, changes that made drawing something I was not accustomed to.

In exploring the process of working against oneself to accommodate the other, this chapter discusses "ignorance" in drawing with children, a conceptual orientation that is grounded in the work of French philosopher Jacques Rancière. By introducing a Rancièrian perspective that offers a relational ethics of ignorance, I reconsider the adult–child relationship, which often subscribes to a dominant asymmetrical structure, whereby the adult gets to assume a form of superiority over the child. Rather than making the suggestion to undo these hierarchical relations, I introduce and dicsuss a relational ethics of ignorance that brings to the child's and adult's traditional roles in relationships of inquiry different and unanticipated ethical relations, which enable the child, the adult, and the relationship to become otherwise. In doing so, I bring in a drawing event that emerged in the kindergarten classroom in order to discuss how the presupposition of equality gets produced, but also the ways in which it is negotiated.

The practice of ignorance

In his book *The Ignorant Schoolmaster: Five Lessons in Intellectual Emancipation* (1991), Rancière describes the pedagogical event of Joseph

Jacotot, a university lecturer in nineteenth-century France, who proclaimed that all people, including the uneducated, could learn for themselves without a teacher's explanation and that the teacher could in turn teach himself what he was ignorant of. This claim originates in Jacotot's experience of finding himself teaching a class whose members speak exclusively Flemish; Jacotot did not know their language and the students did not know his. Nonetheless, he organized the lesson around a bilingual edition of the classic French novel *Télémaque*. Through an interpreter, he asks the students to read half of the book with the aid of translation and the other half quickly, and then to write what they thought about it in French.

As the students looked for the French vocabularies that corresponded with those they already knew, they learned to put the words together to create sentences in French by themselves. Having expected regrettable outcomes, Jacotot was surprised by the quality of the students' work, writing: "Their spelling and grammar became more and more exact as they progressed through the book; but above all, sentences of writers and not of schoolchildren" (Rancière, 1991, p. 4). Here, what "schoolchildren" might allude to is the conventional and commonly understood status of students who are seldom considered to be legitimate writers. Nevertheless, as they wrote and learned the language through this unconventional method, it resulted in the production of exceptional literary texts. Although Jacotot had explained virtually nothing, neither the spellings nor conjugations of the language, both the students and Jacotot explored the text and discovered alternative ways to learn by taking the position of unknowing— an act of *ignorance*.

What is the virtue of ignorance, then, that Rancière believes to be the most important quality of a schoolmaster? In response to this question, I illustrate what the ignorant schoolmaster does and chooses not to do. To begin, an ignorant schoolmaster is not a teacher who does not teach but rather "a teacher who teaches that which is unknown to him or her" (Rancière, 2010, p. 1). The schoolmaster does not teach *his* knowledge but instead provokes students to explore what they are able to see, what they think about it, and to then verify it. This suggests that, in practicing ignorance, the schoolmaster intentionally dissociates with his preexisting knowledge about things in order to discover the unknown, of which both he and the students could learn. In doing so, the only knowledge the ignorant schoolmaster activates becomes the "knowledge of ignorance" (Rancière, 2007)—a knowledge that is based in the acknowledgment of one's own incapacities. While this suggests that no direct link is necessary between teaching and possessing knowledge, it is not to suggest that an ignorant schoolmaster relinquishes the authority that they have. In fact, quite the opposite. The ignorant schoolmaster uses this authority to alter the existing dynamics of teaching and learning by empowering students to actualize the range of intellectual capacities they have and that they bring with them to the classroom.

Moreover, an ignorant schoolmaster is ignorant of a particular definition of a schoolmaster and the roles and practices that definition entails. One such role is that of explication. According to Rancière (1991), explication is the "myth of pedagogy, the parable of a world divided into knowing minds and ignorant ones, ripe minds and immature ones, the capable and the incapable, the intelligent and the stupid" (p. 6). To Rancière, explication is an act of stultification: When a master explains, he or she transmits standardized knowledge and exercises power to verify if the student has satisfactorily understood what was explained. It is the mere act of demonstrating incapacity, "to explain that which would not be understood if it were not explained" (p. 3). As the act of explication only confirms the hierarchical order between the one who explains and the other who is being explained to, it indicates that the two reside in distinct spaces, being in distinct forms of intelligence: the inferior intelligence, or "the young child and the common man" (Rancière, 1991, p. 7), and the superior one (e.g., the master). When an ignorant schoolmaster actively refuses the identity predetermined by society (authoritative, explaining knowledge, etc.), it highlights students' will to be ignorant to their expected roles (to listen, follow rules, etc.).

The radical break between two forms of intelligence does not, in fact, remove the schoolmaster's *will*. For Rancière, the method of equality is a method of will. The ignorant teacher may not impose his knowledge but manifests the authority to instigate the intellectual capacity of students. The students learned not by the teacher's explanation; they were "propelled by their own desire" (Rancière, 1991, p. 12). Likewise, the teacher actuated his will to leave his intelligence out of the picture. The only thing that had been established between Jacotot and the students was a will for attentiveness and a decision to conduct a search, establishing "a pure relationship of will to will" (Rancière, 1991, p. 13). The wills operated together to discover the thing in common, which is the intelligence of the book *Télémaque* that served as "the egalitarian intellectual link between master and student" (Rancière, 1991, p. 13). The book, in other words, functioned not only as a primary source of knowledge but also as a mediator between Jacotot and the students, helping the students to activate their already-endowed capacities and the will to learn. Both the teacher and students engaged in learning without a clear vision of the result that might come about. By establishing a stance of ignorance toward their knowledge and common roles, and by highlighting their own will to learn, an emancipatory experience emerged.[1]

Popular culture as *Télémaque*

Similar to *Télémaque,* drawing popular movie characters also served as an intellectual link between the children and myself. In the kindergarten classroom, children's discussions of media culture frequently played a central role in their social activities, which also became integral to their art engagements. However, popular cultural images are not always welcomed by adults, especially in early educational settings. Describing the different approaches and values between adults and children, childhood studies scholar Allison James (1998) introduces the term "ket," a concept derived from children's taste for cheap candies, which they purchase with weekly allowances. Importantly, the kets that children consume are often considered by adults to be rubbish, a lowly and useless indulgence. This iteration of "kets" has expanded to include children's exclusive and prevalent cultural values, such as the toys they play with and television shows or movies that they watch. The aesthetics of kets, in this sense, refers to children's deliberate choices about their own visual cultural worlds and the values they have about how best to construct, use, and maintain the content of these cultural spaces. For children, consuming this cultural content asserts their membership in a generational group that is distinct from other age groups, namely adults. In fact, the media culture images that children choose "provide a common language, pervasive evidence of one's place in the world, and potent motivations of drawing" (Thompson, 2003, p. 143).

When invited to participate in drawing popular culture figures, I disclosed my limited knowledge of even the longest-standing films and TV shows (e.g., Star Wars and Pokémon), as well as the vast and varied forms of contemporary media culture children consume today (Paw Patrol, Vampirina, Super Wings, etc.). When requesting a drawing, for example, children were quick to demonstrate in great detail the distinctive features and strengths of the characters so that I could learn about and utilize this information in the drawing process. Moreover, rather than a mere replication of preexisting images, the children reconfigured

---

[1] For Rancière, a student is emancipated if "obliged to use his own intelligence ... [and] conscious of the true power of human mind" (1991, p. 15). Yet, as Bingham and Biesta (2010) note, Rancièrian emancipation does not connote a move of membership from the minority to the majority, but rather entails a process of one "coming into presence" that generates a rupture in the existing order of things.

particular stories and scenes that were different from the original image references. At times, this required that I search Google images on my phone for photographic reference. However, I also desired to explore how art experiences might eventuate differently when unaccompanied by such technology. In consideration of this, I often suggested to the children that I draw without photo references, to rely on children's visual memories and narratives. In doing so, children partook in the work of drawing by directing me, completing my sketch, or coloring in the outlines. Though unfamiliar, attending to this media content allowed me to demonstrate to the children a certain degree of ignorance toward popular cultural content. Perhaps my endeavor to attain "the least-adult role" (Mandell, 1988) attributed to my experiencing of the ket-aesthetic, as it often "prevails whenever a slackening of adult control occurs" (Thompson, 2006, p. 71). Though my sparse knowledge of children's culture sometimes resulted in miscommunication, my outsider membership allowed me to learn firsthand about the children's interests in certain realms of popular visual culture. To further elaborate my experience of drawing media culture figures with children, the following vignette describes a collaborative drawing event with Alex, wherein we drew Star Wars characters, a process that was primarily dependent on Alex's steady instruction.

Drawing with Alex

On a Friday afternoon, Alex comes to the art table and waits patiently for me to finish my drawing. Upon its completion, he asks, "Now can you get a picture on your phone of Darth Vader and Luke Skywalker?" Having drawn numerous Star Wars characters over the last five months, I confidently declare that I now know how to draw both of them without looking it up. Doubtful, Alex asks, "But can you draw the lightsabers *clinging* together?" In an attempt to reassure him, I say, "I can try." Though Alex's facial expression remained uncertain, his actions seemed to be giving me permission to draw: Alex quietly picked up two Crayola markers, gray and black, explaining, "This [grey marker] is for Luke Skywalker, and this [black marker] is for Darth Vader." After a short pause, he asked, "Can you *please* look it up?" Because I wished to see whether I could draw from memory the image and his description, I suggested that if he dislikes my drawing, he and I can draw again by looking at an image. Without an explicit agreement in place, he begins to describe the scene along with step-by-step instructions: "First, draw Luke Skywalker putting his lightsaber up in the sky, then draw Darth Vader's lightsaber laying in against." My confidence immediately diminishes the moment I begin to draw: "So the lightsaber going this way?" Without answering my question, he asks, "Can you draw this line a little thicker?" To which I respond, "Yes." Noticing that the marker I used was dry, Alex quickly leans toward the marker box, saying, "I'll get a different one. After you're done with Luke Skywalker and Darth Vader, can you look up the dock where they are fighting, and then draw the dock under them?" I agreed. By the time the lightsabers were illustrated, Alex desires to color the lightsabers before Darth Vader's body is drawn. He uses blue for Luke Skywalker's lightsaber, verbally emphasizing that it is *under*. I ask, "Oh … What's the difference between being under and being over?" Continuing to color in, he explains, "Umm, under, if his is under, they will be blue in the middle here, and [if over] they will be red in the middle." He proceeds to diligently fill in both lightsabers.

Meanwhile, as Alex took a turn to draw, I engaged in conversation with other children who also had drawing requests. Completing both blue and red lightsabers, Alex calls me to attention: "Now can you finish drawing?" He then reaches for a thin black marker and places it on the table closer to me, saying, "thin marker." I ask, "Oh, you want me to use the thin markers?" Holding the gray marker close to himself, Alex responds, "Yeah, and you know, grey is only for Darth Vader's gloves, and the rest of him is black. I'll give this to you when it's time." Then, to reaffirm that I am doing the right thing, he says, "You're drawing Darth Vader." Illustrating with the given marker, I ask, "Do you think his arm can come out from his cape?" He quickly responds, redirecting me: "No, his cape goes here." The teacher calls attention to the children who had used the block play area (Alex was one of the children called on to clean up). Before leaving the seat, he looks at me and asks, "Can you keep drawing?"

I proceeded to draw Darth Vader's arm and a part of his cape. Alex returns shortly thereafter and glances at the drawing. He then grabs a thicker black marker to apply additional lines on top of those I had previously drawn. After thickening the lines a bit, he attached the cap to the marker and placed it on the table, near me. Then, looking at me, he says sternly, "You can start drawing." I say, "Okay—what's this?" A short answer returns, "Darth Vader." Pointing at the line next to the arm, I ask, "I mean, this part, what did you draw?" But he only repeated, "Draw the rest of Darth Vader." I still desired to know about the mark next to Darth Vader's arm: "Okay, so, is this part of the cape that you drew?" Alex pauses, and then, fixing his eyes on the paper, sighs. With patience, he then attempts an explanation, "No, that is … that is … now …" Instead of continuing to explain, he takes the marker from my hand and swiftly draws a horizontal line on top of the previously thickened line. He gives the marker back to me with an instruction: "Draw something like the helmet, draw his helmet." I check, "Draw his helmet above this line?" "Yeah, above that line." Still seeking for a satisfactory approval, I ask, "Like this? Does that look like his helmet?" Alex responds, "Yeah, but then draw his face part." I continue to raise multiple questions: "Doesn't it look like this? This could be part of his cape, right? From here?" As his eyes trace my hand's movement, he finally confirms, "Um-hmm." As I asked more questions on the placement of feet and arms, Alex, without answering my questions, again takes the marker from my hand to illustrate as he wished. At this moment, the teacher calls him again to clean up the pieces he had missed previously. Before leaving the table, he gives me an assignment: "Can you make these lines as thick as this?" (see Figure 3.1). I continue to draw during his absence. He comes back in seconds and grabs the thin gray marker to thicken the contours of Luke Skywalker. At this moment we were drawing together—I was working on the left side, adding lines to the figure of Darth Vader, and Alex on the right side of the page.

I finished my part sooner. Alex quietly and carefully continues to draw by leaning close toward the table, often backing up to see the whole picture. After doing so, he looks at me and asks, "Can you look up the dock Darth Vader and Luke Skywalker is fighting?" I inquire how it looks like, and he asserts, "No, you have to type it in. Cause' I don't know how it looks like." Acknowledging that we both needed a reference to continue drawing, I open the Google application on

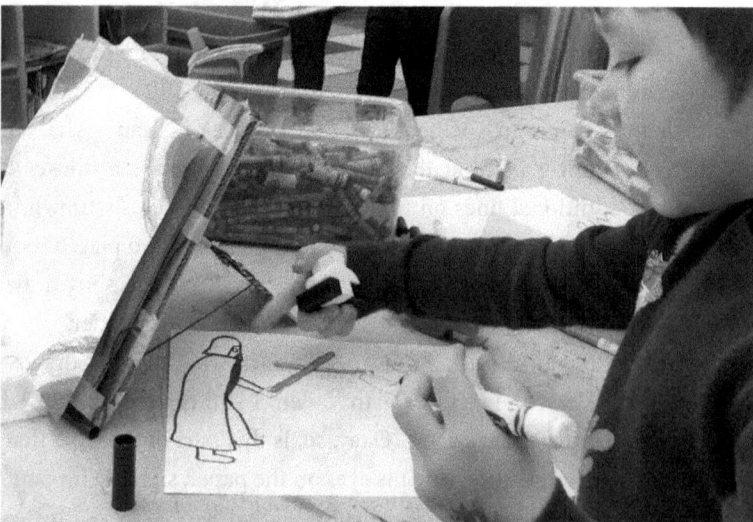

Figure 3.1 Alex asking me to thicken the contour of Darth Vader

my iPhone to search for the fighting scene Alex described. With the help of the photo reference, we completed the drawing by adding the background dock to the fighting scene.

Toward a relational ethics of ignorance

As was described in the previous drawing event, children are the "knowledge holders, the permission granters, and the rule setters for adults" (Walsh, 1998, p. 57). This overturn, of the traditional roles that children and adults occupy in research relationships, closely aligns with Rancière's (1991) elaboration of intellectual equality, in which he argues that one must *assume* equality as "a point of departure" instead of an endpoint, "a *presupposition* rather than a goal, a *practice* rather than a reward situated firmly in some distant future" (p. xix, translator's introduction, original italics). Here, I focus on how these two aspects of equality—presupposition and practice—materialized in my engagements with Alex's production of drawing Star Wars characters.

First, the *presupposition* of equality may not entail achieving an identical peer-status between the adult and the child—insofar as age, physical maturity, and cognitive development remain as apparent differences—but rather aims to minimize these differences by enacting a willful *ignorance* toward the ways in which these statuses center the adult as more-than. In drawing with Alex, a permission to fully disclose my vulnerability was given to myself. On each mark being made, I admittedly exposed how dependent I was on Alex's guidance, and Alex, in turn, tolerated my unusual level of ignorance in media culture that was so familiar to him. My dependency and Alex's tolerance were only possible upon the will to learn through the popular cultural art production. That is, like *Télémaque,* the drawing of a Star Wars scene served as a mediator to narrow the skills and cultural knowledge gap between Alex and I. While Alex brought with him a deep expertise of Star Wars media culture, I was able to offer my proficiency in terms of graphic production. Consider, for example, that in spite of the unsettlement of whether the particular envisioned scene could be precisely illustrated, the child artist willingly took the risk to permit the adult, who knows virtually nothing about the context, to contribute to the production. And I, in spite of having only meager knowledge of Star Wars, proceeded to draw by assuming that I could learn from the child by attending carefully to his patient guidance. We were both knowledgeable of where we were coming from yet ignorant of where we were going.

The collaborative drawing of popular culture figures constituted a *practice* of intellectual equality on the basis of ignorance that both Alex and myself operated. One might easily confuse ignorance with indifference, a detached and static attitude toward what is happening at the moment. However, ignorance invites one to think about equality "actively," as a method of *doing* equality instead of only having equality (May, 2008). It is a matter of what people do, instead of what they receive, particularly what they do that challenges the roles the social structure assigned to them. When Alex and I relinquished our usual logic of action, together we attended to and affirmed the presupposition of equality. We were also *doing* this by an active process that involved a deliberate ignorance to the taken-for-granted identities as well as operating the will to accommodate each other in the production of popular cultural drawing.

In doing so, the process of drawing ignorant entailed what education scholar Bronwyn Davies (2014) elaborates as "emergent listening." Different from "listening as usual," emergent listening seeks for the "not-yet-known" to disrupt one's judgments and prejudices, attending to "letting go of the status quo and of the quotidian lives embedded in that status quo" (p. 28). If listening as usual aligns with Rancière's concept of explication—namely, the practice of repetitive knowledge reproduction without demanding any new thoughts to come about—emergent listening invokes "ignorance" that suspends one's ready-made knowledge to allow critical thinking and the will to unknow to be operated. This method of listening suggests that adults not only listen critically and curiously to children but also preserve ignorance to the already-known knowledge about children's consumption and production of popular culture.

The kind of equality that was produced in drawing with Alex was a negotiated equality, the many potentials of ongoing, emergent negotiations. The process goaded me to know and unknow about children and their culture, and to proceed in spite of the dominant social order that often trivializes children's production and consumption of culture. I learned about children's shared cultural contexts by taking the role of a drawing companion, one who does not—or does not only—impose knowledge but also listen to children's interests and expertise. As such Alex and I were able to produce something other than what Wilson (2007) refers to as an "other than child/other than adult" visual cultural production (p. 11). This production was formed on the basis of a "will to will" (Rancière, 1991) relationship. As such, I have come to believe that, rather than an optional quality, ignorance is an ethical commitment integral to our everyday practices and the relations we share with others, especially children. If one desires to research, draw, read, write, or engage in even seemingly quotidian encounters *with* children, embracing a relational ethics of ignorance may offer new ways of thinking with and about our experiences with children.

References

Bingham, C., and Biesta, G. (2010). *Jacques Rancière: Education, truth, emancipation.* London; New York: Bloomsbury Academic.

Davies, B. (2014). *Listening to children: Being and becoming* (1st edition). London; New York: Routledge.

James, A. (1998). Confections, concoctions, and conceptions. In H. Jenkins (Ed.), *The children's culture reader* (pp. 394–405). New York: New York University Press.

Mandell, N. (1988). The least-adult role in studying children. *Journal of Contemporary Ethnography, 16*(4), 433–467.

May, T. (2008). *Political thought of Jacques Rancière: Creating equality.* Edinburgh, Scotland: Edinburgh University Press.

Rancière, J. (1991). *The ignorant schoolmaster: Five lessons in intellectual emancipation* (1st edition). Stanford, CA: Stanford University Press.

Rancière, J. (2007). The emancipated spectator. *Artforum XLV*, no. 7 (March), 271–280.

Rancière, J. (2010). On ignorant schoolmasters. In C. Bingham and G. Biesta (Eds.), *Jacques Rancière: Education, truth, emancipation* (pp. 1–24). London; New York: Bloomsbury Academic.

Thompson, C. M. (2003). Kinderculture in the art classroom: Early childhood art and the mediation of culture. *Studies in Art Education, 44*(2), 135–146.

Thompson, C. M. (2006). The ket aesthetic: Visual culture in childhood. In J. Fineberg (Ed.), *When we were young: New perspectives on the art of the child* (pp. 31–43). Berkley, CA: University of California Press.

Walsh, D. (1998). Ethics: Being fair. In M. Graue and D. Walsh (Eds.). *Studying children in context: Theories, methods, and ethics* (pp. 55–69). Thousand Oaks, CA: Sage.

Wilson, B. (2007). Art, visual culture, and child/adult collaborative images: Recognizing the other-than. *Visual Arts Research, 33*(2), 6–20.

4

Wool Works, Cat's Cradle, and the Art of Paying Attention

Sylvia Kind

Capilano University, Canada

Introduction

For several months I have been working in the studio with educators and young children at the Capilano University Children's Centre, engaging and experimenting together with long lengths of translucent fabric. The studio is a space of collective inquiry that affords both children and educators time to dwell with materials, linger in artistic processes, and work together on particular ideas and propositions, forming a relational space of investigating and creating together: constructing, making, and composing understandings. It is a space of artistic research and experimental interplay (Kind, 2018). Particularly vibrant are our material investigations where for months at a time we immerse ourselves in extended inquiries with materials, and pay particular attention to collective choreographies and the movements, exchanges, reciprocities, and generative becomings taking place.

The fabric fills the studio as it hangs from the ceiling, is draped over suspended rods creating tent-like structures, and is arranged in colorful bundles and groupings on the floor. The fabric catches the light as the sunlight filters through the large floor-length windows, giving a pulsating luminescent sheen to the room and the hanging panels sway in the softly moving air as the children dance, fly, and circulate among the colors and fibers. The material acts on the child as the child acts with the material, proposing a "motional-relational"

I am particularly grateful to Cristina Delgado Vintimilla, the Capilano University Children's Centre pedagogista, for her insights and engagements with these studio research processes. Her pedagogical promptings and provokings are woven throughout this work.

(Manning and Massumi, 2014, p. 42) responding where, with fabric and yarn, children find a movement and proposition and follow its line of becoming. As the child meets the hanging fabric, fingers its translucent softness, presses her face into its sheen, it leads her deeper into its folds, draping over her, covering, enclosing and she dwells for a while in the midst of the welcoming silky mounds of color. Other children trace their fingers down long strands of green wool, respond to its lure by pulling more of it out from the skein, and twisting and winding bring the strands to intersect with other materials and bodies in the room, and another child, encountering the emerging web of interwoven lines, begins to leap through the fibers.

The studio is alive with fabric, children, inventions, and compositions (Fig. 4.1). And in the studio this morning, the large skeins of thick green wool have a particularly vibrant life as the children pull out the threads and unwind the skeins. The strands trail behind bodies marking movements, trajectories, and intersections. Threads are wrapped around panels of fabric, are knotted in various configurations, are wound around structures, and weave the room together in a maze-like tangle of lines and fabric-yarn bundles. The studio in its entanglements becomes a dynamic dilemma, provoking thought into what it might mean to respond to children's experimentations and create mutual spaces of research and inquiry together.

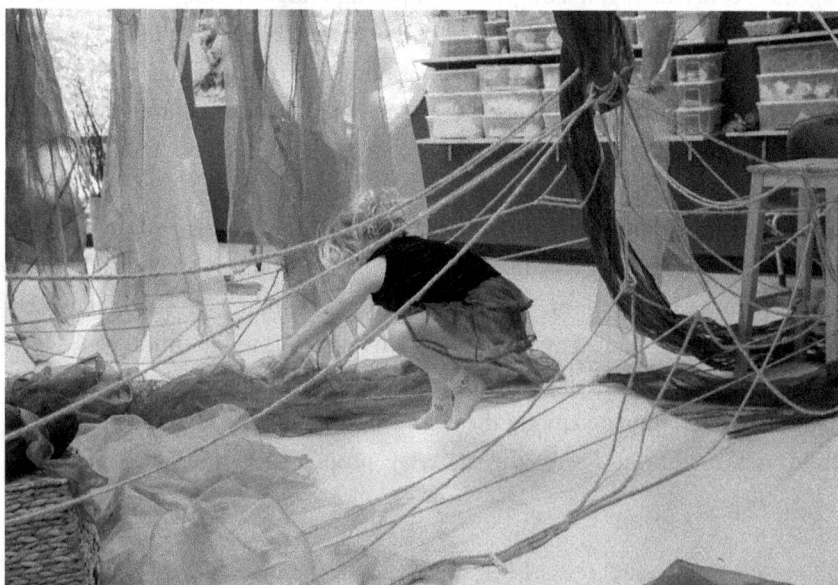

Figure 4.1 Studio entanglements

As in previous projects and investigations, we have spent extended time immersed in experimentations with materials and processes, attending to the play between children and materials, to the ecologies of practices, and to what is generated in and through the material encounters (see Pacini Ketchabaw, Kind and Kocher, 2017). We find that long periods of experimentation are necessary in order to attune ourselves to children's ways of being, to the movements and trajectories of the materials, and to the doings and entanglements. In these long durations we notice the transformability and instability of fabric and yarn, the wrappings, foldings, unfoldings, entanglements, coverings, uncoverings, bundlings, and weavings (see Kind, Vintimilla and Pacini Ketchabaw, forthcoming). We consider the confluence of forces (Ingold, 2013) in an effort to develop a rhythm and feel for the material so that we might more fluidly move with it and with children's inclinations.

Rather than thinking about materials as static bits of matter waiting for children to do something to them, we are interested in the liveliness of materials and how materials are active in shaping our engagements with them. This means getting to know materials by what they can do, what happens when they are engaged with in certain situations and in particular ways, and paying attention to the webs of relation, movements, rhythms, regions of intensity, and to that which is activated and set in motion. We are interested, as Ingold (2013) proposes, in discerning the life and vibrancy of materials so that we might collaborate more creatively with them. Thus, we attend to the relational movements, collective rhythms, and emergent and adaptive processes that take shape through the encounters and exchanges. As Manning and Massumi (2014) describe, we notice how thought is formed *in* the creative act, not just as a precursor to it, and how the children think through materials with ideas and images taking shape in the doing. Rather than primarily using materials to represent concepts that they already have in mind, it is through the making, responding to, and working *with* materials that propositions and ideas take shape and are elaborated on and developed. This resonates with Ingold's (2013) description of making as "a process of correspondence: not the imposition of preconceived form on raw material substance, but the drawing out or bringing forth of potentials immanent in a world of becoming" (p. 31). To attend to this, we embrace a listening that includes listening to the materials themselves, to children's diverse approaches and ways of knowing and being, to the form-taking and making of things, and to "how things dance together with one another" (Vecchi, 2010, p. 15).

Activating possibilities

I am enchanted by the room woven together and take time to linger in the midst of the network of green fibers, and after the children leave the studio, along with Judianne, an *atelierista* practicum student, begin to go through the laborious process of undoing the tangles. We follow the trail of threads and begin to rewind the strands of wool into balls. We retrace the children's pathways over, under, and around structures and fabric, and encounter multiple intertwined points of meeting and co-fabrication. Immersed in the web-like maze of thread and wondering how to respond to these vibrant entanglements, I am drawn to Donna Haraway's conceptualization of cat's cradle. Haraway (in King, 2011) describes cat's cradle as

> a game of relaying patterns, of one hand, or a pair of hands, holding still to receive something from another, and then relaying by adding something new, by proposing another knot, another web. Or better, it is not the hands that give and receive exactly, but the patterns, the patterning. Cat's cradle can be played by many, on all sorts of limbs, as long as the rhythm of accepting and giving is sustained. Scholarship is like that too; it is passing on in twists and skeins that require passion and action, holding still and moving, anchoring and launching. (p. ix)

This helps frame studio processes as a collective exchange of receiving and responding while at the same time altering, inventing, and proposing new configurations that are aesthetic, surprising, and produce variances and difference. This is not a typical search for children's meanings so we can identify, extend, or elaborate on children's interests or theories but a search for joining in the co-motion and co-compositions. These are lived processes of inquiring together with young children, an ethical process that is co-composed, co-constructed, and *made* together where we are learning to move together in a responsive and ongoing exchange. Stengers (in Saravansky and Stengers, 2018), for instance, describes cat's cradle as an event of being *activated* into intervening. As she describes, this means becoming "activated by someone or something into intervening, and produce a motif that is a bit different" (p. 131). In this way, research, like a game of cat's cradle, takes shape as instances of proposing and activating possibilities, offering new shapes and configurations, a back and forth responsiveness, a production of difference, and a symbiotic search for ways of entering into and enhancing children's experimentations and processes. It is an ongoing exchange, always in movement, giving form and shape to things while at the same time engaging in a process that is "forever deferring its own completion in the dynamic form of more becoming" (Massumi in Manning, 2013, p. xii).

While what children say about their inventions and compositions, and their verbalized perceptions and understandings, are significant, most of what is unfolding in the studio during these fabric experimentations can't be adequately expressed in words or even in other symbolic languages such as drawing. To ask children directly what the entangled room is about, what they intended or produced, or to try to elicit reflective insights about their compositions tends to generate surface responses as the insights are not yet fully articulatable, taking shape in the doing, in movement, in multisensory ways, and still need time to more fully find form. Thus, engaging in research and learning from children are much more than gathering insight into children's lives and interests and making space for children's voices, perspectives, theories, and meaning-making. While these things deeply matter in our work with children, it is also necessary to open to other ways of thinking and knowing than privileged through verbal or written language and expressed through representational efforts. More than generating knowledge about something, the effort is to make space for prearticulated (Manning, 2013), gestural, lived, bodied, haptic, choreographic, affective, and enacted speculations and propositions. To add "speculative gestures" (Stengers in Saravansky and Stengers, 2018, p. 134) so that there might be the creation of new possibilities and "attentiveness of a different order" (Manning and Massumi, 2014, p. 11). Research in this context becomes a search for ways of being together, of noticing and mutuality while trying to activate a collective and reciprocal rhythm.

An ethics of attention

Like a game of cat's cradle, in responding to children's experimentations, I hold two strands in tension. One strand gives careful attention to the life, liveliness, and agentic nature of the materials and their dynamic movements, propositions, rhythms, convergences, and mutations, situating children as active participants within a world of active materials (Pacini Ketchabaw, Kind and Kocher, 2017). The other strand holds a compelling concern for encounters of difference. This second strand I hold is woven intimately together with my experiences with my son Nathanial and the rich differences of his life. Born with extensive multiple disabilities, our life together has been colored by long years of illness, where life was tenuous and very fragile and I was never sure if he would make it through the night or next day. Yet always the gift of his life priceless and immeasurable, with much of my life, teaching, and research taking shape in response to him (Kind,

2006, 2008). Learning to walk to his rhythm, to linger a little longer, to consider invented languages and diverse ways of knowing have been his great gifts. To listen to Nathanial is to attune to his ways and his rhythms, to take time to be and to dwell alongside, to know through movement, touch, and song, and to attune to his relations and particular sensitivities to the sounds, textures, sensations of the world. Listening comes through lingering and letting him show me in his time and in his way his particular inclinations, orientations, and delights. He is my constant reminder that listening and responding to children depend on learning to *attune* to multiple ways of knowing and being, to the rhythm of movements and inventions, to the ungraspable, unknowable, unarticulated, and nonverbal: a lingering and expectant listening that gestures toward hands open to receive.

Manning (2013) describes "affective attunement" (p. 7) as a "relational merging" (p. 7) that is a symbiotic "expression-with" (p. 11) and a "preconscious tuning-with that sparks a new set of relations that in turn affect how singular events express themselves in the time of the event" (p. 11). In similar ways I understand attunement as a sensitive reciprocity, a symbiotic orchestration or movement *with*, rather than knowledge about someone or something. To attune to something is to pay close attention, orient toward it, and find a rhythm and synchronicity with it. Ingold (2013) describes this as an event of corresponding *with*, or a process of not seeking to describe, represent, or to gather more information about the world, but "to open up to what is going on there so we, in turn, can respond to it" (p. 7). This opens us to *ways* of knowing, not just knowledge itself, such as attending to children's approaches, pathways, unfoldings, and felt meanings. In my work with children this provokes a search for an alignment *with* children's ways and improvisations, a cadence and modulation, being-with, moving together, in an effort to create a life and way of being together. This situates response-ability, or the ability to respond, as central to attunement. More than the substance of Nathanial's knowledge, or attention to *what* he knows, what is important is how I am changed by his ways and how I take shape in response to him. More than knowledge about children and fabric, what is central is our participation with and response to these encounters. As Rose and van Dooren (2016) discuss, cultivating attentiveness is a "complex mode of participation" (p. 124) and an obligation to "participate in the world in its relational becoming" (p. 125).

From the Latin *attendere*, the word "attend" suggests stretching toward. And so, in seeking to be stretched myself and to nurture deeper attention and attunement to diverse ways of knowing and being in the world, I turn to authors who narrate and write about their "autistic perception" (Manning, 2013, p. 151) such as Amanda Baggs and Tito Mukhopadhyay. I do this not to limit these perspectives to those with neurodiversities or even to understand autism, but in an effort to bring other stories together to intersect, multiply, and enlarge my understandings and field of vision and to open up other dimensions for being in the world and being together with children and materials—in essence, to learn from these perspectives and to enlarge possibilities for ways of being in the world. As Haraway (2016) writes, "It matters what matters we use to think other matters with; it matters what stories we tell to tell other stories with; it matters what knots knot knots, what thoughts think thoughts, what ties tie ties. It matters what stories make worlds, what worlds make stories" (p. 12).

Attuning to ways of knowing

When Nathanial was born, a senior nurse informed me that since he would never walk or talk they would understand if I decided not to take him home. She said others could care for him and it wouldn't matter if I left him at the hospital as he would never be aware enough to know me anyhow. "Does he know you?" is also a common question I get asked by acquaintances who are curious about Nathanial and are trying to figure out the extent of his disabilities and the kind of relationship we have. This question always leaves me at a loss for words and I struggle for a response while feeling the vibrancy of his life, and his many intimate, intangible, and richly lived yet inarticulate relations and perceptions. These instances speak to me of the value of a life based on how much one knows, how one communicates, and a knowing that is understandable and readily recognizable. It assumes an autonomous, independent individual while privileging individual cognitive knowledge. And it measures worth based on expectations of what is typical and conventional such as recognition in a look or spoken words. He does neither of these things, being blind and nonverbal and much of who he is and what he perceives will always remain outside of my grasp. Yet as autism activist Amanda Baggs (in Manning, 2013) argues, too often "personhood is directly associated to verbal interaction, which is then posited as relationality" (p. 9). Not being able to speak is not the same as having nothing to say, and not being able to show one's knowing in conventional ways is not an inability to communicate or an absence of knowing.

What Nathanial proposes to me is the obligation to listen to that which cannot adequately be given form through verbal or representational language and to open to other languages and ways of knowing. This resonates with Loris Malaguzzi's theory of the hundred languages of children, which is based on an assumption of difference (Hoyuelos, 2014). This theory proposes that there are multiple forms of knowledge and ways of knowing, many forms and ways of communicating, different ways of seeing, and a "hundred" modes of representation. In early childhood the concept of the hundred languages is often interpreted as the many ways children *represent* their ideas. Yet language, according to Baggs, is much more than a representation of an already formed idea. For instance, in her video *In My Language* (https://www.youtube.com/ watch?v=JnylM1hI2jc) Baggs enacts and describes a language that is in constant conversation and relation with what is going on around her. As she rocks back and forth and flutters her hands, she is engaged in what appears as a moving-sounding-dancing relation with her environment. Baggs (in Manning, 2012) describes "her language" as one that "feels the world, thinking with it, rather than simply speaking of it" (p. 215). As she describes, "my language is not about designing words or even visual symbols for people to interpret. It is about being in a constant conversation with every aspect of my environment, reacting physically to all parts of my surroundings" (p. 215). It is a language that expresses "the force of a relational environment" (Manning, 2012, p. 215) and articulates "a sensing body in movement, a body-world that is always tending, attending to the world" (Manning, 2013, p. 2). In similar ways Mukhopadhyay (2008) describes how a child becomes-with the world, or when he sees or thinks about the wind, he "is the wind" (p. 118), or when he sees a rolling pencil he becomes so immersed in its movement he "become(s) the pencil" (Mukhopadhyay, 2015, p. 30). He writes poetically and powerfully of these moments of becoming-with:

> I would sit on the swing with a head full of scientific concepts and ears filled with the sounds of the wind. My heart would be filled with happiness as it expanded or contracted perhaps to the rhythm of the swing. What exactly did I perceive while I sat on the swing? I perceived happiness in the colours of the wind. (p. 104)

This bodied, felt, "motional-relational" (Manning and Massumi, 2014, p. 42) perception is not just relevant in relation to individuals with disabilities or neurodiversities but opens rich variances in ways of knowing and being. It prompts me to attend to how we, together with children, might become-with and join with the movements of fabric and fibers.

I notice as well how attuned Nathanial is to the tempo and fluctuations of the wind and how he seems to find a particular synergy with it, particularly when the wind blows in pulses, pauses, and intervals. His way of being is deeply entwined with a sense of rhythmic knowing expressed in his attunement to the wind, to walks with others, in shared song: to the sonority, tonality, and tempos of the world. As we walk outside together, for instance, as his wheelchair bumps over the uneven ground he begins to hum and pauses momentarily, his head slightly turning back toward me in a brief and very subtle invitation for me to join in his singing. Singing and walking together in the wind over the rough path, with musical and sonorous resonances between us, it's not the song itself that delights him but the co-motion and co-being, this sense of being together in the pleasure of this immersion with a song and with the wind and with the textures of the ground. A world that could appear to others as closed and limited is alive with an "intensive relationality" (Manning, 2013, p. 8).

These instances describe a language and way of being and knowing that "feels the world" (Manning, 2012, p. 215), that senses, moves with, and is immersed in its textures and tonalities. As Manning (2012) describes, thought is much more than the "form-taking of words" (p. 215) or even the form-taking of drawings, painting, or sculptural work and children's symbolic representations. Rather, as she writes, "to articulate thinking-feeling is to activate the conceptual work in the prearticulation of the experiential" (p. 215).

The art of attention

As Judianne and I disentangle the studio and wind the strands of wool back into balls the vibrancy of the interwoven room stays with me. A few days later, as a way of wondering about the pleasures of entanglement and children's weavings and knottings and in an effort to work *with* the rhythms and configurations, making them visible in other ways, I gather several balls of the thick green wool and begin to knit. I give tentative and propositional shape to the children's emerging fascinations with the yarn by producing another tangle of lines and threads. I sit on a chair knitting at the edge of the studio and in fluid configurations children gather around, join in, and begin to move with the strands. Children bring in other balls of wool to correspond with the knitting, and wool moves between knitting needles, hands, and children. Rachel holds a ball of wool and its strands extend to Isabelle, who twists and winds it while Graeme intercepts the tangled lines, looping some around his waist. Ava gathers a handful of green yarn and tucks it under her chin, and a paper tube in her hand resonates with the knitting needles. Rachel connects another stray ball of wool, fingers the moving threads, and her weaving gestures echo with my knitting. Wool winds around stools and feet, hands and bodies twist and entangle in rhythmic movements. Lines of traveling wool connect this group of children together and, in this temporary configuration, we become the knitting. For a moment we are the entanglements and are moving with the interconnecting fibers. Like the game of cat's cradle, patterns are re-proposed and we engage in "a gestural dance with the modulation of the material" (Ingold, 2013, p. 26). In doing this I wonder not so much what this means or what children intend, but what kind of responses are necessary. What is being set in motion, how might I participate with this, and what are the ways of receiving and returning this to the children and to the studio not as a repetition of the same but in variances, so difference is enhanced and possibilities enlarged?

As the studio experimentations continue, the children find particular pleasure in settling into, covering, and concealing themselves in the vibrant lengths of fabric. Fabric and bodies become entangled as children immerse themselves in the folds of fabric. Rolling, covering, twisting, tying, knotting, and wrapping, the children are reconfigured into pulsating fabric-bundles. There is intense pleasure in the wrapping, entangling, and immersion and in being together with others in the midst of this. The fabric welcomes, envelops, encircles, and connects. In response to this, and as a way of giving temporary shape to these interweavings, to the tangles of knitting together, and to the wrappings and coverings, I begin to knit a large tubular cocoon that is open at both ends. The cocoon resonates with and reconfigures the ways the lines of wool surround, wrap, enfold, and envelop the children, and proposes another kind of immersive relationality and textural and material knowing. My intention is not to repeat movements or configurations, rather, as Manning and Massumi (2014) propose, to continue to work with the lines of movement in order to activate engagements by offering reconfigurations that work with and offer other possibilities.

In the pauses of knitting when the green cocoon rests on the floor, children step into it and enclose themselves one, two, and sometimes three at a time inside the knit fibers. The wool is soft, thick, and dense and holds them snugly yet it is also elastic and stretches to welcome them. The knit cocoon visually and sensorially offers alliances with the children's fabric entanglements while exaggerating and amplifying the textures, enclosures, felt-experience, and sense of dwelling in the fibers. Noah, for instance, steps into the green form, slowly pulls it over his legs, torso, and head until he is fully enclosed. It holds him, presses into, and gently constricts around his body. Noah settles into it for an extended time, barely moving, then very gradually stretches out and pulling the

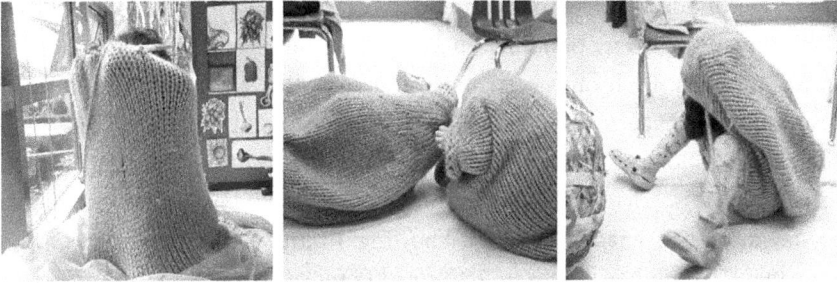

Figure 4.2 In the cocoon

form over his head begins to emerge from the enclosure as if he is morphing into something else. The knit form seems to induce slower tempos and rhythms to children's immersions and entanglements.

In response to this slow hatching from the green cocoon and other emergent becomings and birthings as children cover themselves in fabric and enact eggs hatching, I begin to knit another form, a large enclosure that is shaped like an egg. This form offers more space to rest in than the cocoon, plays with the moments of stillness and cocooning, and offers another propositional configuration. Later in the studio when the form is completed Kaitlyn envelops herself in it, rocks from side to side, feet extending and retracting through the opening, then curls completely inside, gently moving, stretching, and rolling for nearly an hour. Johanna, an educator, wonders with the children what the egg is doing. Maxwell pauses for a bit, stares intently at the egg while waving his hands in an echo of the egg-shape, and replies "I only know what it's *feeling* in there." The bodied, enacted, haptic sense of the egg is alive for him, inexpressible in words but understood through a feeling-knowing. As Springgay (2011) writes of a sensational pedagogy, "knowing always exists as a potential in the space between sensation and cognition. Thus, the body is implicated in the act of constructing new knowings and ways of knowing" (p. 638). To amplify Maxwell's feeling-knowing I knit another smaller egg, adding another multisensory configuration that would emphasize the textures of being in the enclosure, hold children a little more snugly, press in a little more closely, and exaggerate children's sensational ways of knowing.

Through attending to the daily enactments taking shape in the studio and in revisiting the video documentation with the Children's Centre educators during our weekly meetings together, we collectively identify particularly vibrant and repeated fabric-configurations and imagine knit-forms that would resonate and offer textural and textile correspondences. What begins to take shape is a collection of oddly shaped pods and body cocoons, each a visible rendition of the emergent weavings, bundlings, nestings, hatchings, and children's pleasures in togetherness. Each one gives, and will give as this work is still in process, propositional shape to the children's enactments and speculations, returning the configurations to the children as suggestions for further enactment; each an effort to discern the life and liveliness of the children's experimentations, to stay in bodied, enactive, and felt-knowing, to draw others into some of the immanent possibilities, and to activate difference. It becomes a process of searching for altered perceptions and other ways of giving form to the emerging experimentations that are in concert and correspondence with the movements and sensations of the very lively fabric-studio.

Provoked by my life with Nathanial and in resonance with Baggs and Mukhopadhyay's becoming-with and symbiotic conversation *with* their environment, this requires learning to attune to the uncertain and the difficult to articulate. It becomes an effort to open ourselves to the textures, movements, sensations of the world while making, creating, and cultivating situations, spaces, and sensitivities so that we might dwell for a while in intensive relationality and multisensory ways of knowing, producing propositions to sustain the emergences (Manning and Massumi, 2014). Like the game of cat's cradle, it is a search for how we might play along with the materials and the children's studio processes while keeping things in motion and attending to the formation of things in other ways than through words while "producing effects which you cannot dominate but you can learn with and learn from" (Saravansky and Stengers, 2018, p. 131).

References

Haraway, D. J. (2016). *Staying with the trouble: Making kin in the Chthulucene*. Durham: Duke University Press.

Hoyuelos, A. (2014). Pedagogía y política en el pensamiento y obra pedagógica de Loris Malaguzzi. *RELAdEI. Revista Latinoamericana de Educación Infantil*, 3(1), 43–61.

Ingold, T. (2013). *Making: Anthropology, archeology, art, and architecture*. New York: Routledge.

Kind, S. (2006). *Of stones and silences: Storying the trace of the other in the autobiographical and textile text of art/teaching*. Unpublished doctoral dissertation, University of British Columbia, Vancouver B.C. Canada.

Kind, S. (2008). Learning to listen: Traces of loss, vulnerability, and susceptibility in art/teaching. In S. Springgay, R. L. Irwin, C. Leggo, P. Gouzouasis and K. Grauer

(Eds.), *Being with A/r/tography* (pp. 167–178). Rotterdam, The Netherlands: Sense Publishers.

Kind, S. (2018). Collective improvisations: The emergence of the early childhood studio as an event-full place. In C. Thompson and C. Schulte (Eds.), *Communities of practice: Art, play, and aesthetics in early childhood*. New York: Springer Publishing.

Kind, S., Vintimilla, C. D., and Pacini-Ketchabaw, V. (2018). Material choreographies: fabric as a living language of exchange. *Innovations in Early Education: The International Reggio Emilia Exchange, 25*(3), 40–51.

King, K. (2011). *Networked reenactments: Stories transdisciplinary knowledges tell.* London: Duke University Press.

Manning, E. (2012). Propositions for collective action: Towards an ethico-aesthetic politics. *Theory & Event, 15*(3), 1–4.

Manning, E. (2013). *Always more than one: Individuation's dance.* Durham, NC: Duke University Press.

Manning, E., and Massumi, B. (2014). *Thought in the act: Passages in the ecology of experience.* Minneapolis, MN: University of Minnesota Press.

Mukhopadhyay, T. R. (2008). *How can I talk if my lips don't move? Inside my autistic mind.* New York: Arcade Publishing.

Mukhopadhyay, T. R. (2015). *Plankton dreams: What I learned in special ed.* Open Humanities Press. http://www.openhumanitiespress.org/books/titles/plankton-dreams/.

Pacini-Ketchabaw, V., Kind, S., and Kocher, L. (2017). *Encounters with materials in early education.* New York: Routledge.

Savransky, M., and Stengers, I. (2018). Relearning the art of paying attention: A conversation. *SubStance, 47*(1), 130–145. Johns Hopkins University Press. Retrieved August 12, 2018, from Project MUSE database. https://muse.jhu.edu/article/689019.

Springgay, S. (2011). "The Chinatown Foray" as sensational pedagogy. *Curriculum Inquiry, 41*(5), 636–656.

Van Dooren, T., and Rose, D. B. (2016). Lively ethography storying animist worlds. *Environmental Humanities, 8*(1), 77–94.

Vecchi, V. (2010). *Art and creativity in Reggio Emilia: Exploring the role and potential of ateliers in early childhood education.* New York: Routledge.

5

Playing School at Home: Toward an Ethics of Parental Play

Christopher M. Schulte
University of Arkansas, USA

Introduction

In the spring of 2015, shortly after my daughter Sophia turned four, she transitioned to the preschool classroom at her childcare center. Similar to those which proceeded it, this transition was replete with nuances that were exciting and challenging all at once. New friends to get to know, different materials to explore, but also a shift in her daily routine and the demands of having to negotiate different expectations and new personalities. What was especially unique to this transition, though, was the turn that occurred in Sophia's at-home play. From an early age, Sophia showed an enthusiasm for school, often delighted at the chance to play with her peers and to think and learn with those around her. Unsurprisingly, this enthusiasm also manifested at home, in Sophia's play, an endeavor that regularly centered on exploring the daily practices and fodder she'd experienced at school. To this point, Sophia's play was not unlike what you might expect from other children, who, like Sophia, might find pleasurable the experience of contemplating the new, exciting, and sometimes puzzling terrains of school. However, after Sophia's transition to the preschool classroom had officially commenced, her at-home explorations of school underwent a rather dramatic change. As a parent, this shift in Sophia's play—whether it was in fact real (an experience that reflected the lived realities of Sophia's time at school) or imagined (an experience that I was interpreting to have this potential)— generated for me a range of ideas and issues to contemplate, a task for which I felt woefully unprepared.

This chapter, which centers on a short vignette featuring a particular occasion of Sophia's and my experience of playing school at home, explores the complexities of this turn in Sophia's play, and the ways in which my own experience of this shift reshaped the ethics of my relationship to Sophia, of playing school at home, of parenting, and of parental play. Although considerable attention is given to what Sophia did in her play, and how she did it, the issue of why she went about playing in this way is very much a speculative matter. I can't say with any degree of certainty what this experience was truly about for Sophia. Nor is it the case that I can reasonably indicate that my involvement provided the alleviating force that was needed to make Sophia's play-based engagements more desirable, more bearable—for her or for me. What I can speak to is that this experience of playing school at home fundamentally transformed how I think about myself as a parent and about the ethics of playing at home.

As such, in this chapter I narrate this experience in a way that is dialogical, moving back and forth between what I imagine to be Sophia's potential remembrances of a life at school, my own engagements with these possible school-based retellings, and my uncertain and often times anxious meditations on how best to respond. As a way of addressing these complexities, I draw on Simon, Rosenberg, and Eppert's (2000) work on remembrance, a concept that helps to generate a speculative account of Sophia's and my experience of playing school at home. This account, which is both perceived and imagined, and also of the past and in the present, allows me to work against the idea that ethics is always a matter that is given, a code to be followed (Bauman, 1995). As an alternative to this account, I draw on Baraitser's (2008) concept of interruption, both to reveal and disrupt the background of my experience with Sophia, and to "re-personalize" (Levinas, 1987) my own codified bent to think with and about Sophia (e.g., as a child and daughter), and of the relationship between ethics and playing at home.

"Daddy, let's play school."

As her backpack dropped to the floor with a thud, Sophia wasted little time inviting me to participate in what's quickly become an important after-school ritual. In fact, ever since Sophia entered the four-year-old classroom at her childcare center, she has been rather intent to play school at home. "Daddy," she would say. "Let's play school." Of course, I was always keen to play, interested in what might come about as a result of doing so. Indeed, I think that even

Sophia was aware of the fact that our playing together was something that I truly enjoyed. So, it was likely unsurprising to Sophia that I was so quick to confirm: "Sure, I'll play school." I said.

A few moments later, as we both stood in the playroom nook, just adjacent to our kitchen, Sophia provided some additional clarity about our roles. "Daddy," she said. "I'll be the teacher, you be the kid." This too—i.e., the assigning of roles—was something that I had become accustomed to. "Got it." I said, nodding to Sophia in agreement. Satisfied with this response, Sophia turned her attention to the large built-in shelves, which lined one of the walls in the playroom. She then began to rummage through a small basket, which contained some of her "teacher things." Unsure of what—if anything—I should be doing at this point, I decided that it was best for me to stand on the rug and wait for Sophia to provide further instruction. A few moments later, Sophia's rummaging came to an abrupt stop, her hands still buried in the basket. However, this lull in activity was about to take a rather unexpected turn. The instructions that I received next were, well, not exactly what I had anticipated, marking out a rather dramatic break from the ways we usually went about playing school at home.

Turning quickly to face me, I could see that Sophia's eyes were filled with intensity—anger, really. Then, with a noticeably different tone, she said to me: "*You* need to *sit down*." Shocked, and having only begun to process Sophia's initial and—I might add—rather stern directive, she started in again: "*I said, sit down*." Though it was a demand to which I promptly replied, resting my bottom on the rug as quickly and as nondescript as I could manage, I was also completely and utterly flummoxed. Indeed, this becoming-compliant as a student in Sophia's at-home school was a swift and unremarkable transition, one that seemed to *just happen*. Attempting to signal to Sophia that I had something to say, or rather something to ask, I raised my hand. To be honest though, I didn't really have a clear idea of what I was going to ask, only the feeling that I should. More than anything, I just felt compelled to do something, to interject in some way, to intervene. Pretending that my hand was not in fact raised high in the air, and that she had not witnessed it being raised, along with what was very clearly a set of rolling eyes, Sophia turned her attention once again to the small basket in the lower cabinet.

"Miss Sophia?" I said, sheepishly prodding for attention, my hand still raised in the air. Acknowledging that I had spoken, Sophia turned swiftly in my direction, but then raised her right foot and slammed it forcefully into the ground below her, a loud thud filling the air around us. Sophia was clearly angry, her body now trembling as she began to walk over to me. Admittedly, I was nervous. Once she had come to a stop in front of me, Sophia bent down, then grabbed my wrist, her grip tightening and pulling at the hair on my arm. "Ouch," I thought to myself. Then, with her pointer finger just a few inches from my face, she bellowed yet another gruff directive: "*I said, shut up and sit down.*"

After the initial shock of this exchange had passed, and Sophia loosened her grip on my arm, I found myself thoroughly confused about what to do next. I mean, how do I respond? As a parent, I was of course concerned. We had certainly played school before. Many times, in fact. But *not* like this. I was aware too that Sophia's past and current encounters *with* school had included experiences that—by her own admission—were "scary," experiences that had made her a witness to other children's school-based traumas. Moreover, I'm not entirely certain that Sophia's stories about her peers were not also—and perhaps more directly—her own stories, traumas that she herself had experienced. Not that it really makes a difference. I mean, Sophia's experience of school doesn't somehow become less "scary" because, as Hayashi and Tobin (2015) put it, she is a "peripherally participating observer" (p. 58), someone whose involvement and view of these events is situated in the surroundings of "the gallery" (p. 58). The point being she's still involved, entangled with what has been deemed to be "scary." She still occupies a livable, learnable, thinkable, sayable relation to these events.

A difficult return

As a researcher of childhood art, I understood that Sophia's practice of playing school at home—and this instance in particular—was more complex than it appeared to be. I wondered if Sophia's remembering, and the act of re*playing* such remembrances, was, as Simon, Rosenberg, and Eppert (2000) say, a "difficult return" (p. 4)—an experience that "attempts to meet the challenge of what it might mean to live, not *in* the past but *in relation with* the past" (p. 4). So, as a parent who loves and cares deeply for his daughter, and as a researcher who understands the ethical mass of being a witness to children's testimonial practices (Simon, Rosenberg, and Eppert, 2000, p. 18), I made a choice and responded, my eyes fixed on the floor below me: "I'm sorry, Miss Sophia."

By assuming this role, as Sophia's student, and by entering further the milieu of Sophia's at-home school, I found myself wondering if I was doing the right thing. I began to wrestle with whether or not I was abrogating my responsibilities as a father (Gillies, 2005), failing to affirm my own "faith" in the parenting discourses I had come to understand as right and appropriate, as "good" (Jensen, 2010, p. 1). Should I request that Sophia provide an explanation for the play? Should I present to her some alternative versions of school, of teaching? My impulse was to do both. However, deep within the pit of my stomach, running parallel to this sense of uncertainty and the unease that accompanied it, was the instinct to work against my own discomfort and the impulse to figure out the *right* thing to do. But what does it even mean to figure this out, to do the right thing? For me, doing right—at least in this moment—was a matter of attempting to undo what I perceived to be wrong. Or rather, what felt wrong, or at least uneasy, and that in this particular moment registered as a matter in need of attention. Sophia's play was aggressive after all, even violent, her language too. I found myself thinking:

> Children really shouldn't act like this, especially at home ... right? I mean, surely, as a parent, I should do more to put a stop to this, no? After all, what kind of father would I be if I condoned this type of play? And perhaps worse, what kind of father am I to participate in this play, to actively hold space for it to matter?

Although I sensed that my concerns were misplaced, and that the real work of parenting in this moment hinged on my willingness to hold space for Sophia's at-home explorations of school, the feeling of not knowing how best to respond was intense. I was beginning to appreciate that doing the right thing isn't always as clear-cut a matter as I might like it to be. Certainly, not as much as I wanted it to be in this particular moment. Indeed, figuring this out—or so it seemed—was an untidy endeavor, an occasion that masked the ethical recipes that I (as a parent) desired. As Bauman (1995) has written, "Actions may be right in one sense, wrong in another" (p. 5). I certainly felt the weight of this conundrum as I sat on the floor in our living room, confused, searching for some sense of clarity about what to do next. I recognized that doing the right thing—at least in this moment, for me—meant choosing to become an attentive participant in an experience that felt wrong, of having to work against my own attachment to certain "images of the child" (Malaguzzi, 1994), and to some of the "idealized and mythic parenting requirements" (Blackford, 2004, p. 239) I'd come to embody in my own life and practice as a parent.

It wasn't just the problem of being a parent though, of having to negotiate what in these particular moments constituted good and acceptable behavior that made this experience so difficult to parse. Especially challenging was the process of reconciling that this reality, of shame and embarrassment, of abuse, which I now inhabited as a student in Miss Sophia's class, was perhaps a similar reality to the one that Sophia herself was being made to occupy at school. Of course, I couldn't know this for sure, and I certainly don't mean to suggest that school is only ever a place of shame and embarrassment, of pain. Indeed, Sophia seemed to love school just as much as she found it to be scary. Like Sophia's home, and like many other spaces in childhood, school is complicated, capable of enacting relations that are both loving *and* hurtful, curious *and* indifferent, scornful *and* respectful. One attribute or experience does not mean that the other is necessarily excluded or irrelevant. The same should be said about teachers, and about parents too, myself included.

That said, having had some time now to reflect on these experiences, it seems acceptable to suggest, at least in part, that Sophia's interest in playing school at home may have been about learning to live with, and in relation to, the difficult and sometimes traumatic lessons of her past, while at school. Even if the felt reality of these school-based lessons is grounded in the witnessing and remembrance of another's experience, or in the memories that get produced by and routinely memorialized in the cultural worlds that Sophia inhabits, the process of bringing these lessons into presence is important. Doing so, as Simon, Rosenberg, and Eppert (2000) write, brings about "a reckoning" that not only impels us to face the difficult stories of our past, and the past of others, but also obliges us to question and rework the possibilities of who we are, in relation to the past, in the present (p. 8).

A return, to and with the difficult

Certainly, for Sophia, the experience of playing school at home had the potential to be *a difficult return*, an act of remembrance that moved her to explore further the stories of her past *at* school, and the past of others, whose engagements *with* school she'd been a witness to. But I can't speak to this possibility with certainty. What I can speak to is my own experience. For me, playing school at home was "a time of formation and transformation" (Britzman, 1991, p. 8), an experience that prompted me to consider differently my own sense of ethics and responsibility as a parent. The experience of being a student in Sophia's at-home school taught me that parenting is not only a status to uphold, a particular way of being or way in which to be, but also, as Geinger, Vandenbroek, and Roets (2014) say, a "form of 'performativity' … a *doing*, a *becoming*" (p. 490). In playing school at home, there was no parental recipe or protocol to follow, no clear sense of ethics to guide or adequately address the shifting complexities that were produced in these moments of play. Much like Sophia's endeavoring to rework the problem of school, of being a teacher in relation to students, parenting was (and is) an enduring return, both to and with the difficult, a vital act that made me face the need to reorient myself to Sophia, to the experience of being with her at home, to our home more generally, to parenting, and to the problem of playing school or playing anything for that matter.

There's always a remainder

The issue that arises when thinking of parenting as a status, or as a particular way of being, is that it becomes extremely difficult to imagine or embrace anything different, anything more than what it already is. In the moments that followed Sophia's final demand, that I *"shut up and sit down,"* it became very clear to me that being a parent was not enough, that there is always "a remainder" (Adorno, 1973, p. 5), a dimension of activity and responsibility that "exceed[s] our knowledge and control" (Bennett, 2009, p. 14). Indeed, there was always a remainder in the work that I (as a parent) shared with Sophia—worlds of matter and meaning, of purpose and circumstance, that I was simply unable to inhabit, details that would—or so it seemed—remain hidden forever. But because there is always a remainder, there is also always an "opening to learning" (Simon, Rosenberg, and Eppert, 2000, p. 7), an occasion that bubbles up, in which new and different forms of attentiveness become possible. Playing school with Sophia was one of these experiences, an endeavor that always seemed to produce a remainder. It was an occasion that turned me to face my own limits as a father, particularly those aspects of my parenting that needed to be disturbed in order to reposition the experience of parental play as a critical site for learning.

The limiting pressures that I was facing as a father centered on the fact that I was only allowing myself to see parenting as a process that happens to play. But Sophia didn't ask me to parent her play, she asked me to play. The distinction here is important. It not only points to the need to think in more intensive ways about the relationship between parenting and play but also serves as a signal for a much broader issue, about the ethics of parental play, particularly when this play includes or addresses subject matter that is deemed to be difficult, even traumatic, and that reconfigures the child as otherwise to what we might know or expect them to be. Though as a father I have always been keen to play with Sophia, my enthusiasm to do so does not mean that I am necessarily ready or willing to open myself to the intricacies that Sophia's play may materialize.

Nor does it mean that Sophia has an obligation to share with me what these intricacies are, will be, or might become. This lingering sense of ambiguity in Sophia's at-home endeavoring of school challenged what I had become accustomed to as a father who plays at home. As a response to this discomfort and the uncertainty that often accompanied it, I began to contemplate how my position as a parent could be used to adjust the situation.

When Sophia first directed me to sit down, it wasn't the directive itself that was of concern, but rather the tone that Sophia used to give this directive and the implicit complexities that I imagined to be part of it. Sophia's tone generated a remainder of sorts, a dimension of activity that extended beyond my immediate knowledge and control. I didn't understand it, nor did I know what to do with it. But when I really think about it, and if I am being honest, the real issue was that Sophia's actions troubled who I was expecting her to be as a child and daughter, especially at home. Moreover, Sophia's undoing and becoming of these expectations placed on me as a father certain demands that I was ill-prepared to embrace and unwilling to consider. As a parent, it was as if I had disconnected from the ethical positions I held as a researcher, forgetting,

> [That] there is no such thing as "the child" or "childhood", an essential being and state waiting to be discovered, defined and realized, so that we can say to ourselves and others "that this is how children are and should be". (Dahlberg et al., 2013, p. 46)

The implications here are important, especially for those, who, like me, are doing research with their own child(ren), and thus having to negotiate the very real temptation to forget what you know, and what you would do (from an ethical standpoint) in your relationships with other children. In this way, the issue was not only that I was unclear about what to do next, but that I also *felt compelled to do something, to interject in some way, to intervene*. This desiring for intervention, which was in some ways masked by my expressions of wanting to do the right thing as a father, illustrates too the ways in which I was inclined to use my position as a parent to reshape Sophia's play, to default to certain actions that would, again, recast Sophia as the child/daughter I expected her to be and that elided too the ideas and issues that were most pressing for Sophia. Perhaps most important, though, was the extent to which I used my position as a parent to excuse myself from having to say and do certain things that I would do and say for other children.

Of course, as was expressed in the vignette above, I managed to stop myself from doing this, from intervening in this way, from parenting out the details of

Sophia's play that were less amenable to my own parental desirings. Sensing that Sophia's actions were about something more and remembering too that Sophia is always more than one, I made a choice. As a father, I reminded myself that what mattered most was not that I manage to discern in Sophia's play some sense of meaning, that I manage to figure it out, to corral its significance, but that I remain "open and alive to each meeting, each intra-action," so that I might use my capacity "to respond, my responsibility" (Barad, 2007, p. x), to learn with and from the otherness that Sophia presented, and to encounter, welcome, and engage the remainders that this experience of otherness produced.

To remain *open and alive to each meeting, each intra-action*, is based in the recognition not only that our relations to the world are constantly being "disrupted by the other" (Baraitser, 2008, p. 69) but that we have an ethical obligation to take responsibility for these relations, this otherness, and the disruptions that get produced. Here, I find Baraitser's work on the ethics of interruption to be helpful. For Baraitser, who is writing about ethics in relation to the maternal, interruption, "like its close allies, disruption and eruption … reveals the taken-for-granted background of experience through its power to chop it up and intervene" (Baraitser, 2008, p. 68). Playing school at home was an experience that altered the continuum of my thinking about what it can mean to be a parent: disrupting the ways in which I'd come to understand and relate to Sophia, as a child and daughter. It was also a harsh reminder of the ways in which, as a parent, I don't always hold space for Sophia as I do for other children I am working with.

In this way, playing school at home revealed to me the undercurrents of my experience; those deeply rooted theories that were operating within me, orienting me as I talked to Sophia, listened to Sophia, observed Sophia, made decisions about how to play with Sophia and about how—in this play—to be a parent in relation to Sophia and to play. And though the interruptions that I experienced were perhaps, in more general terms, the consequences of my playing at home, particularly this version of school, they were also the outcomes of encountering Sophia in ways that were different from who and how I expected her to be. As Baraitser (2008) puts it, "in the moment in which we are interrupted by the other, something happens to unbalance us" (p. 69). From the moment Sophia's body first turned, pivoting forcefully in my direction, to her final exasperated demand, that I *"shut up and sit down,"* I found myself unbalanced, interrupted by the otherness of Sophia's play and by Sophia, who in these moments was someone other-than the child-daughter I knew and expected her to be. But these interruptions, as Baraitser (2008) says, also have the capacity to "open up a new set of possibilities" (p. 69), to make pliable my ideas about and attitudes toward parental play, and the extent to which such engagements, as ethical forms of practice, might produce a more loving and more contemplative set of relations—to Sophia, to our home, to parenting, and to broader world that we share with each other.

Toward an ethics of parental play

As stated earlier in this chapter, my experience of playing school at home helped me to appreciate that *doing right* isn't always as clear-cut a matter as I would like it to be. Having to make decisions about what is right, and having to also bear "in mind our relationship with and responsibilities to others" (Moss, 2018, p. 57), is an untidy endeavor, an occasion that seldom provides the ethical recipes we (as parents and researchers) might desire. This was especially true for me. Sophia's potential remembrances of school and the experience of replaying these remembrances at home were matters of great concern for me as a parent. Though I was unable to determine with any degree of certainty that indeed this play reflected Sophia's remembrances of a life at school, that this was even a possibility was enough to fundamentally reorient my sense of ethics and responsibility as a parent. Assuming that Sophia's actions were stories from her past, or perhaps the stories of her witnessing the past of others at school, I felt compelled to understand, to learn more, and to contribute in some way to Sophia's negotiation of these complexities. I was deeply concerned that what I was experiencing as a student in Sophia's at-home school was potentially the same experience that Sophia was having at school. The decision to enter further the complexities of this play, and to hold space for its many forms of otherness, was not immediate, nor easy.

In reflecting on the unease of this tension, of having to make a choice about what is right in this particular set of circumstances, I find the work of Zygmunt Bauman (1993) to be helpful, specifically his approach to ethical decision-making. Bauman argues for an ethical position that is postmodern in orientation, meaning, as Moss (2018) described it, a position from which one's sense of ethics "acknowledges that life is unpredictable and messy and that many ethical decisions cannot be clear-cut and certain" (p. 56). By assuming this position, it becomes possible to re-personalize ethics, returning to the individual the uncertain and often difficult matter of having to assume responsibility for the ethical choices that need to be made, as opposed to abrogating this responsibility to a single ethical code (Bauman, 1995). Sophia has a right to consider the complexities of her lived experience and those she imagines or desires to be possible. She also has a right to interpret these experiences—to author what they are, who they serve, and why that matters, and to be able to do so without reproach. And I (as a parent and researcher) have an ethical obligation to recognize this. Essential to this position, then, that ethical decision-making is messy and unpredictable, is the problem of choice and its relationship to responsibility. Because choices are inevitable, the matter of responsibility is unavoidable (Bauman, 1995). It is for this reason that I referred to Sophia's initial invitation to play school as a point of concern. Though I had accepted Sophia's invitation, agreeing to play school, I did not accept (which is to say that I did not understand, nor consider, at least carefully) how the decision to do so, to play, might complicate the ways in which I was, and would become, responsible for grappling with the otherness that Sophia's play presented, and the otherness of Sophia, as Other (Moss, 2018; see also Dahlberg and Moss, 2004).

Here, I find Levinas's (1987) conceptualization of *an ethics of an encounter* to be useful. For Levinas, an encounter is an occasion to meet with and become receptive to difference, an opportunity to be opened to the Other and to the alterity that is produced in one's engagements with the Other. But as Moss (2018) points out, learning to play host to this alterity is about more than simply avoiding the "urge to manage and govern the other" (p. 61), to turn the differences presented by the Other into something that is already known, into something that will remain clear and fathomable, to make it "into the Same" (Moss, Clark, and Kjørholt, 2005, p. 6). In this way, following Levinas (1987), the process of bringing this alterity into presence also entails recognizing that we have an unyielding responsibility *to* the Other and *to* the matter of how to think *with* the otherness of the Other's work.

Playing school at home was an intensive encounter, an experience that not only contained more than I was ready to consider, or that I could reasonably begin to comprehend, but that demanded of me more than I was willing or prepared to give. It isn't that I didn't recognize the potentially serious (and abusive) nature of Sophia's play, that what she was doing was perhaps a *replaying* of her life at school. I did recognize this. Moreover, I reported my concerns about this matter to the childcare center and also requested that Sophia be moved to a different classroom. But this chapter isn't intended to be about this. It isn't a chapter that aims to render a clear determination about what Sophia's play might mean. This chapter is about recognizing the ways in which, as a parent, I needed to craft a broader sense of responsibility for Sophia and for the matter of how to think with the otherness of the Sophia's play. In other words, this chapter is about the ethical relations of parenting to play. Or rather, of parental-play as an ethical practice that generates "an exposure of the self to the Other for whom one is responsible" (Baraitser, 2008, p. 38) and that as a result of this exposure produces a more pliable conceptualization of what parenting might be.

Admittedly, it never became easier for me to be a student in Sophia's at-home school. Each and every time that we played, I found myself sitting on a rug, or in a corner, with my head down, wondering: How do I respond? What do I do? What's the right choice to make here? I always found myself having to renegotiate the tensions between what I *thought* to be right and what I *sensed* to be right. Either way, I had to make a choice, and I also had to assume responsibility for the choices that I was making. I'd like to think that it was helpful for Sophia to put into play certain forms of school that were difficult, and potentially traumatic, and that it was also beneficial for Sophia to witness the felt reality of these forms of school on another body, my own. But I can't say that. I can't suggest in any way that this is what happened or that Sophia was somehow able to remedy these experiences—to soften and resculpt them—because of the play we experienced together at home. What I can say is this: The experience of playing school at home made possible a lingering occasion to grapple with and re-personalize the complexities of being a father, who doesn't always know the *right way* to love and support his daughter.

References

Adorno, T. W. (1973). *Negative dialectics*. New York: Continuum.

Barad, K. (2007). *Meeting the universe halfway: Quantum physics and the entanglement of matter and meaning*. Durham, NC: Duke university Press.

Baraitser, L. (2008). *Maternal encounters: The ethics of interruption*. New York: Routledge.

Bauman, Z. (1993). *Postmodern ethics*. Hoboken, NJ: Blackwell Publishing.

Bauman, Z. (1995). *Postmodern ethics*. Oxford, UK: Blackwell.

Bennett, J. (2009). *Vibrant matter: A political ecology of things*. Durham, NC: Duke University Press.

Blackford, H. (2004). Playground panopticism: Ring-around-the-children, a pocketful of women. *Childhood, 11*(2), 227–249.

Britzman, D. (1991). *Practice makes practice: A critical study of learning to teach*. Albany, NY: SUNY Press.

Clark, A., Moss, P., and Kjørholt, A. T. (Eds.) (2005). *Beyond listening: Children's perspectives on early childhood services*. Bristol, UK: Policy Press.

Dahlberg, G., and Moss, P. (2004). *Ethics and politics in early childhood education.* London: Routledge.

Dahlberg, G., Moss, P., and Pence, A. (2013). *Beyond quality in early childhood education and care: Languages of evaluation.* New York: Routledge.

Geinger, F., Vandenbroeck, M., and Roets, G. (2014). Parenting as a performance: Parents as consumers and (de) constructors of mythic parenting and childhood ideals. *Childhood, 21*(4), 488–501.

Gillies, V. (2005). Raising the 'Meritocracy' Parenting and the Individualization of Social Class. *Sociology, 39*(5), 835–853.

Hayashi, A., and Tobin, J. (2015). *Teaching embodied: Cultural practice in Japanese preschools.* Chicago, IL: University of Chicago Press.

Jensen, T. (2010). Warmth and wealth: Re-imagining social class in taxonomies of good parenting. *Studies in the Maternal, 2*(1), 1–13.

Levinas, E. (1987). *Tie and the other.* Pittsburgh, PA: Duquesne University Press.

Malaguzzi, L. (1994). Your image of the child: Where teaching begins. *Child Care Information Exchange, 3,* (pp. 1–5).

Moss, P. (2018). *Alternative narratives in early childhood: An introduction for students and practitioners.* New York: Routledge.

Simon, R. I., Rosenberg, S., and Eppert, C. (2000). Introduction: Between hope and despair: The pedagogical encounter of historical *remembrance*. In *Between hope and despair: Pedagogy and the remembrance of historical trauma* (pp. 1–8). New York: Rowman & Littlefield.

6

Working with Children in the Spaces Between

Shana Cinquemani
Rhode Island School of Design, USA

Challenging singular positionalities

We were three days into our ten-week Saturday morning art program. After spending a large portion of our second class making art outside, the children requested that we again bring some materials outdoors. As a result, during snack time, we had blocks, yarn, cameras, paper, markers, and other various small materials outside with us. In the middle of the courtyard, Ben and Seth spent time creating a volcano city out of blocks and red yarn. As they worked hard building and filming their volcano city, some of the other children were running around with scarves, pretending to be flying dinosaurs. After Alex accidently kicked over some of their volcano, Ben became anxious about his work being further destroyed during this carefree play and initiated a whole class meeting. He gathered the thirteen other children around him and explained the issue he was facing:

> I want you guys … [to] watch out for what people are building. If you knock it down people will be sad and kids will too. So we don't like building them all again … it's hard to build it all over again. We don't know how to build it all over again. So that's why you have to watch out for people [working] …

The children were attentive as Ben made this speech and agreed to be more careful about the artmaking that was taking place around them.

As I reflected upon this particular moment many weeks later, it proved to be a powerful example of the ways in which the young children I had collaborated with in this research embraced fluid positionalities, resisting singular identities of simply "child" or "student." During this art class, which met for two and half hours each week, the identities of these four- and five-year-old children fluctuated; they lived in the spaces between, becoming artists, explorers, leaders, researchers, curators, and teachers throughout the process. They also made choices that flew in the face of normally accepted artmaking interactions, they pushed back against adult requests, and they challenged ideas about the teachers role in artmaking. In this particular situation, Ben embraced a powerful position among his peers and teachers. Engaged in a meaningful artmaking experience that was at risk for destruction due to the play of his friends, he took the initiative to gather everyone together and problem-solve. He explained the reasons behind his frustration and offered a solution. His peers acknowledged this problem and agreed to be more careful. This was done with basically no intervention by the three adults (myself included) who were present. What was it about this moment and the circumstances that surrounded it, which gave Ben the courage to take action in this way?

Ben was able to embody this position due to the nature and structure of the art class itself. Situated in a Saturday morning art lab school, this particular class was the site of a teacher research inquiry project. As both the lead teacher and researcher, it was my aim to challenge traditional ideas about power, knowledge, and relationships in spaces of early childhood art education. By embracing this "between" space and asking the children I was working with to do the same, I was hoping to create an early childhood art classroom that would challenge existing ideas about relationships in both teaching and research, especially those that reinforce hierarchical understandings, approaches, and practices. I desired to "open up a new space for the reinterpretation and reconstruction not only of the child ... but also of the pedagogue and of the early childhood institution" (Dahlberg et al., 1999, p. 140). Within this context of this research, this new between space begins to reconstruct ideas about the early childhood art classroom and the kinds of identities and relationships that can exist within it (between children and adults, as well as between the children themselves).

Within the remaining portions of this chapter, I will further explore the way in which I came to define and understand the idea of a between space in working with young children and how this conceptualization of space is simultaneously liberating and challenging. The artwork that the children created, the interactions I had with them, and the relationships that developed challenged me to consider my position as teacher and researcher in complex ways that I was not always comfortable with.

Conceptualizing between spaces

Since I began working with young children, I have been preoccupied with ways to create educational spaces that attempt to destabilize traditionally accepted positions of power that teachers and adults often hold. Within this inquiry specifically, I aimed to create a kind of art educational space that resisted traditional teacher–student roles. I desired to create spaces for both children and adults to *be* differently. Inspired by the writing of the postcolonial theorist Homi K. Bhabha (1985, 1990, 1994) this work was conceptualized initially through the creation of a kind of third space that offered possibilities for newness, movement, and negotiation in research, relationships, interactions, teaching, and learning. I had hoped that through the creation of this space, the children and I would both experience fluidity in our positionalities, understanding that we could embrace multiple ways of being within this art classroom.

Bhabha (1994) recognizes the third space as an ambivalent space, or a site of subversion, where those interacting within it create new experiences based on recognition of where original experiences (or ideas) stem from. Within this inquiry, these original ideas were based on an understanding of the roles of both teacher and student, adult and child. I aimed to challenge these traditionally accepted identities in favor of more transparent and fluid ways of being. There are many ways of being teacher, researcher, and student in the classroom; we are always in the act of translation, the act of becoming. These acts of translation allow us to form hybrid positionalities, constructing something or someone new, that is "neither the one thing nor the other" (Bhabha, 1994, p. 49). The hybrid condition is a way to be in-between multiple sources of knowledge or experiences. The third space develops through these acts of translation and experiences of hybridity. It is a space where identity is both constructed and reconstructed (English, 2009) and newness is possible (Bhabha, 1994). Bhabha writes that "these 'in-between' spaces provide the terrain for elaborating strategies of selfhood—singular or communal—that initiate new signs of identity, and innovative sites of collaboration" (p. 2). This space is characterized around production, not simply reflection (Hulme et al., 2009; Richardson, 2006), producing new ideas, experiences, and ways of being.

For me, this between space was reflected in my role as both teacher and researcher, and more often could be described as a desire to be something more: a different kind of adult perhaps. The acts of teacher-research are complex and layered, a way to live the questions one hopes to explore.

Try to live the questions themselves … don't search for answers now, because you would not be able to live them. And the point is to live everything. Live the questions now. Perhaps then, someday far in the future, you will gradually without even noticing it, live your way into the answer. (Rilke, 1984, as cited in Wilson McKay, 2006, p. 48)

To live our questions, to exist in a space between teaching and research, is a way to translate the questions we have into our everyday lives, to integrate them into our practice. Within this space we can begin to redefine the positionalities we hold as teachers/researchers and the ones our students hold as learners (Hubbard and Power, 2003; Wilson McKay, 2006).

Bhabha (1994) argues that "in order for a third space to be created, moments of discursive transparency and ambivalence must occur: epiphanies when the traditional discourses of power and authority are no longer considered a single form of truth" (Cinquemani, 2014). In order for this third space to function within the research, both the children and I needed to stop seeing ideas about classroom behaviors and relationships as absolute or fixed. The classroom needed to function as a site of possibility and ambivalence, where we could engage with each other in new and different ways. By inviting the children to include their own thoughts, ideas, questions, and desires in the classroom, I aimed to create a shared and permeable space where we worked together to plan and negotiate the structure and focus of the time we shared (Thompson, 2009). I wanted to be responsive to the children's interests and desires, even when they conflicted with my own comfort and ideas about what art teaching and learning should look like.

The reality of fluid identities in the classroom

On the morning of our eighth class, Seth came in very excited. He was clutching a bag full of toilet paper rolls and step-by-step instructions for a "toilet paper roll car" that had been cut from a children's magazine. "Can I tell you something? We have toilet paper rolls in this bag and we brought instructions for how to make them [the cars]." He was adamant about wanting all the children in the class to be able to make a car and counted eleven rolls in his bag. I assured him that I could find another three to make sure we had one for everyone. His mother mentioned to me that she "thought they would be fun for the kids to make" and that "it's really easy." I told Seth that after we came back from the art museum, if he reminded me, I would put the materials and instructions out as a choice for the kids.

During the course of this Saturday class, Seth's project enticed a number of children who also wanted to make cars. This experience brought me a great deal of stress, not because the children embraced something that I did not plan but because it was a project that was invented and designed by adults for children. This was not an idea that Seth came up with himself—he simply desired to reproduce something he had already seen. This kind of activity positions children not as creators of their own ideas but as reproducers of a culture created for them (Tarr, 2003).

This anecdote, like the one shared earlier, makes visible the ways in which the children who attended these Saturday morning art classes (and participated in this research project with me) embraced fluid positionalities. Seth, like Ben, challenged the idea that young children are not the ones in control within classroom spaces. He discovered a project that he wanted to work on, brought some materials along to achieve this, and challenged me (as teacher) to help him accomplish his goal of creating a car from a cardboard roll. Additionally, he embraced a leadership role as he attempted to help his fellow classmates create their own cars, working as the expert as he already had a base level of knowledge about the project. This experience was, at its core, the exact kind of encounter I was hoping to foster within this project: the children being in control of what they wanted to make. The structure of the class set up over the previous seven weeks had encouraged Seth to bring his own artistic agenda to class, which in itself is amazing.

However, my own response to Seth's embodiment of his "between" space was complex. While I appreciated the way in which Ben gathered his classmates together to solve a problem he was facing in regard to his own artwork and experience creating art in nontraditional spaces, I (very honestly) hated the project that Seth brought to class. It was exactly the kind of making that I was aiming to reject: cookie-cutter projects with a singular outcome. This experience created an internal struggle for me. I could see the children's desire to create these cars and I wanted them to feel successful and joyful during this process. At the same time, I did not want to encourage this project nor did I have the time and means to help them in the ways they needed. In order to make these cars I would have needed to have all the materials ready (which was impossible given that it occurred for me without prior notice) and walk the children through each step (which was not logistically possible, nor was it something I desired to do). I helped them when they asked for help and offered them all the materials we had for them to use, but without very direct and hands-on assistance they were simply not able to make this project work.

During this time, my own exercise of power and control was clear. I resisted this project at its core. While I helped in some degree, I could have done more. I didn't stop them from engaging in this project, but I quietly resisted this work. During these moments, I visibly rejected the traditional role of teacher the children may have been expecting. But the children, particularly Seth, also resisted their normal role as students: They persisted and engaged in activities that were not offered or approved by their teacher. The nature of this classroom as a between space allowed us all to resist. However, I am not sure that my own resistance was either ethical or respectful. Should I have worked harder to help Seth and his friends create these cars? I am sure I could have found a way to make this project work within the confines of our classroom and the materials available.

Additionally, my dislike for this project clouded my ability to see that Sam and the other children were embracing work that brought them joy, and while I (at the time) saw little value in this project, they were involved in meaningful self-initiated artmaking. This project pushed them to consider how to puncture cardboard in specific ways, determine methods for strengthening and attaching paper, and conceptualize theories on how to make an immobile object move; these are important material engagements. For Sam and his car creating peers, this particular adult-created project had meaning. I was so wrapped up in my own singular interpretation of what these kinds of experiences *should* be like that I lost my way. I might have found a way to be between the kind of teacher the children wished for and the one I thought I should be, but instead I simply resisted. Within this liminal space "neither site, role, or representation holds sway ... one continually subverts the meaning of the other" (Routledge, 1996, p. 400). The between space and my power as an adult allowed me to subvert the larger sense of responsibility that perhaps should have been more obvious to me. In this moment I fear I worked against rather than for the children.

Crafting between spaces to share research

In attempting to live and work in this between space, I was constantly thinking about ways to approach this in both teaching and research. Inspired by the idea of crafting a third voice (Myerhoff, as cited in Kaminsky, 1992) and writing between the two (Mazzei and Jackson, 2012), I wanted to find ways to merge the voices of the children into the products of my research as well. Inherently, this was a desire tangled in issues of ethics. Routledge (1996) describes that "the spaces within which, and from which we speak and write, are imbued with relations of power/knowledge. That we, the intellectuals, are privileged and not without complicity in a variety of oppressive structures and relations" (p. 402). For Routledge, the single voice only represents fragments of the reality it attempts to explore. It is the third voice that is able to articulate the ambiguity of reality. Additionally, in all research with children, adults always hold a position of being more socially powerful (Lahman, 2008), and when we share elements of research enacted with children, issues of responsibility and ownership should be carefully considered (Zeni, 2001).

My interpretation of interactions in the classroom or of the artworks created in this space is simply that—*my* interpretation. I wanted to find a way to intermingle my ideas with those of the children. As a result, I worked to create multivoiced narratives that weaved words and images collaboratively to tell the stories of our time together and of the children's thoughts and ideas. As Lewis (2011) writes, storytelling, "quite possibly, is the principal way of understanding the lived world. Story is central to human understanding—it makes life livable, because without a story, there is no identity, no self, no other" (p. 505). Merging my own narratives with the children's words and images was a way to combine "bits and pieces of each other" together (Mazzei and Jackson, 2012, p. 451), meeting "halfway, in the in-between spaces … [as a] way to move toward justice, equality, and liberty" (Diversi and Moreira, 2016, p. 583).

In attempts to challenge singular ways of knowing or experiencing, storytelling, conversation, and images worked together in this research to create narrative descriptions of classroom happenings that were multivoiced. I embraced ideas of "multivocality" as defined by Farrar and Pegno (2017) as ways to create "complex exchanges … [that reject] speaking *for* another … when speaking for another, we risk presenting underrepresented minorities as objects for a voyeuristic audience" (p. 170). The inclusion of stories and storytelling in narrative research practices works to reject the idea of speaking for another and opens up spaces for voices traditionally marginalized to be heard. Embracing multivoiced approaches that consider multiple perspectives also has the power to make writing "richer, more nuanced, [and] more authentic" (Zeni, 2001, p. 161). Within this inquiry, the children's voices were made visible and deemed important through the use of the multivoiced narratives, thus creating "conditions of possibility" (Ailwood, 2011, p. 29) in these between spaces of research and teaching. I worked to create ways for us to speak in tandem, creating a third space of mingled ideas.

Complicating the between space in teacher research

However, despite my efforts to intermingle my ideas with the children's experiences, this work really only reflects my interpretation of what happened. Without the children's active participation in crafting how and where their own work would be shared, I cannot really argue that we have created a third voice. Is this work even an example of an authentic multivocality practice? These questions are complex and I sit with them even years after this research has taken place. Though I have worked to create ethical relationships *with* children in both teaching and research, I fear that the betweenness that we all occupied further complicated this experience.

Christine Thompson (2009) writes of the idea of *being there* with children in research and artmaking. Thompson notes that it is her recognition of children's artmaking as both intertextual and performative that drives her desire to be there with children in research—to observe, document, respond to, and interact with the young children with whom she works. Schulte (2013) extends this idea and reflects on how *being there* also relates to an ethicality of experience. He describes that in spaces of research, both adults and children enact their own choices about the way in which they wish to be there. These can be moments of uncertainty, as both adult and child consider their level of participation (i.e., to contribute, to contest, to consider). He notes, "Children and adults are invited to participate, but also dared to create difference through this participation. However, not every child or adult dares to enter into, to move, to live, or to think in moments of uncertainty" (p. 2).

Following Schulte (2013), I argue that the children and I crafted our own ways to be there within this space, and the anecdotes shared earlier reflect these moments of collective participation and uncertainty. However, what I remain concerned with is the way in which the children's understanding of *being there* in this fluid space may not have really been their choice at all. Though Schulte argues that children can choose to not enter into moments of uncertainty and make choices about *how* to *be there*, in this case the uncertainty was thrust upon them due to the nature of the class as a space of research. The core ideas that grounded this inquiry (to challenge traditional conceptions of power and authority in work with young children) and the way I chose to enact them (to create a fluid between space) ultimately forced the children in this class to enter into certain kinds of relationships with me and with each other.

I believe that these children saw me primarily as their teacher, despite my efforts to position myself as something more, as a different kind of adult:

Adults doing childhood research should present and perform themselves as an unusual type of adult, one who is seriously interested in understanding how the social world looks from children's perspective but without making a dubious attempt to be a child … It is, however, possible to be a different sort of adult, one who, whilst not pretending to be a child, seeks throughout to respect their views and wishes. Such a role inevitably involves a delicate balance between acting as a "responsible adult" and maintaining the special position built up over a period of time. (Christensen, 2004, p. 174)

Though I made more than one explicit attempt to help the children understand that something larger than just an art class was taking place, that we were exploring questions related to how adults and children could build an artmaking space together, I feel confident that they did not understand what this truly meant. I believe they sensed this was a different kind of space and that perhaps I was a different kind of adult or teacher, one open and eager to integrate their own ideas. However, what I failed to do was help them see the ways in which their artwork, words, and images would live on. I failed to help them understand how *I* would use their work after they left this space behind. I attempted to explore informed consent as a process rather than a "single gesture" (Zeni, 2001, p. 161) but I was, at the core, unsuccessful.

As I reflect on these experiences, I feel that it was this "between" space that created complicated moments for me. All the intricacies and responsibilities attached to more formal roles like "teacher" or "researcher" shifted. Though there were powerful moments that resulted, there were complications as well. The children and I were able to resist singular identities and roles, but I fear all of us sat with moments where this unknown space was uncomfortable. While I can see and interpret Ben embracing a powerful position as he gathered his classmates together and asked them to respect his work and his artmaking space, I am not sure if he really *felt* powerful in this moment. He was clearly emboldened to make this request, but would he have preferred that I (as the adult and teacher) step in and make sure his work was cared for in a respectful way? Did he perhaps feel that I didn't care about his making since I so quietly sat by and let his volcano be destroyed? I am able to say with confidence that I would have intervened had Ben not initiated this gathering, but was Ben sure of my active role of teacher as the enforcer of rules and order in this moment? Or had he already understood that my role as another kind of adult was so fluid that he felt he needed to protect his own work?

The toilet paper roll car project can be interpreted through a similar lens. Was Seth uncomfortable with the way I rejected his multiple attempts to engage me in this making? Did he want me to sit down next to him and help create these cars from start to finish? I can clearly recall his frustration in his inability to bring this project to life, but was this based in my rejection of the project or his own challenges in the process of making (in both the lack of proper materials and the technical skills required that he had not yet developed)? This narrative is further complicated by my interpretations of my own actions, which I see as disrespectful. It was most certainly an uncomfortable space for me at the time and remains one in reflection. As a researcher who defines herself as interested and excited by children's self-initiated artmaking, why was I so quick to reject this making that was clearly important for Seth?

I wish I had created time and space for the children and I to reflect together on the nature of this kind of classroom and how it felt for all of us. Did they like the different kind of adult I was trying to be? Did they feel empowered in their own making and ideas, or were they frustrated with the lack of order and hierarchy to which they were most likely accustomed? I wish we discussed the nature of research and how messy it can be when you try to find answers to complicated questions. I wish we had talked more about what it means to share the artwork you make with adults you have never met. I wish …

When we resist singular ways of being in the classroom (as teacher or student or researcher) we are, in essence, challenging power enacted upon us and embracing more democratic positionalities that allow us to exercise power over others. It is "in creative acts of resistance that the fleeting images of freedom are to be found" (Giroux, 1983, p. 108). Within this inquiry, the children and I both resisted, and it was this resistance that allowed us to confront more typical interpretations of power and knowledge and singular identity construction. However, I am left with questions about how to ethically exist in these between spaces with young children. Specifically, I feel that there is so much more to discover about how children themselves see the idea of "research." As teacher-researchers, we write about our students, children we presumably spend a large amount of time with. Children come to (hopefully) trust us as adults they can rely on. As we engage in research projects aimed at improving both teaching and our students' experiences as learners, are we aware of their experiences throughout the process? These were considerations throughout the course of this inquiry, but they were unexplored with the children. I shared that I was "doing research" but did they really know what that meant? Did they understand how widely their words, images, and artworks would ultimately be shared? How can we more ethically collaborate with children, not just in the process of engaging *in* research but in sharing that research as well? Could we find ways to create new multilayered voices where children speak alongside us in writing? Can they play an active role in presenting their own ideas in public spaces? Is it important to them to be involved in how and where this "research" is shared? Do they even care about this at all? Or would they rather simply play and create, trusting us to meaningfully and respectfully share their work with the world?

References

Ailwood, J. (2011). It's about power: Researching play, pedagogy and participation in the early years of school. In S. Rogers (Ed.), *Rethinking play and pedagogy in early childhood education: Concepts, contexts and cultures* (pp. 19–31). New York: Routledge.

Bhabha, H. K. (1985). Signs taken for wonders: Questions of ambivalence and authority under a tree outside Delhi, May 1817. *Critical Inquiry, 12*(1), 144–165.

Bhabha, H. K. (1990). The third space: Interview with Homi Bhabha. In J. Rutherford (Ed.), *Identity: Community, culture, difference* (pp. 207–221). London, England: Lawrence &Wishart.

Bhabha, H. K. (1994). *The location of culture* (2nd edition). New York: Routledge.

Christensen, P. H. (2004). Children's participation in ethnographic research: Issues of power and representation. *Children and Society, 18*, 165–176.

Cinquemani, S. (2014). Entering the secret hideout: Fostering newness and space for art and play. The Bank Street College of Education Occasional Papers, 31. https://educate.bankstreet.edu/occasional-paper-series/vol2014/iss31/2/.

Dahlberg, G., Moss, P., and Pence, A. (1999). *Beyond quality in early childhood education and care: Postmodern perspectives*. Philadelphia, PA: Falmer Press.

Diversi, M., and Moreira, C. (2016). Performing betweener autoethnographies against persistent us/them essentializing: Leaning on a Freirean pedagogy of hope. *Qualitative Inquiry, 22*(7), 581–587.

English, L. M. (2009). Third-space practitioners: Women educating for justice in the global south. *Adult Education Quarterly, 55*(2), 85–100.

Farrar, C., and Pegno, M. (2017). Multivocal, collaborative practices in community-based art museum education. In P. Villeneuve and A. R. Love (Eds.), *Visitor-centered exhibitions and edu-curation in art museums* (pp. 169–181). Lanham, MD: Rowman and Littlefield Publishers.

Giroux, H. A. (1983). *Theory and resistance in education: A pedagogy for the opposition*. South Hadley, MA: Bergin & Garvey Publishers.

Hubbard, R. S., and Power, B. M. (2003). *The art of classroom inquiry: A handbook for teacher-researchers*. Portsmouth, NH: Heinemann.

Hulme, R., Cracknell, D., and Owens, A. (2009). Learning in third space: Developing trans-professional understanding through practitioner enquiry. *Educational Action Research, 17*(4), 537–550.

Kaminsky, M. (1992). Myerhoff's "third voice": Ideology and genre in ethnographic narrative. *Social Text, 33,* 124–144.

Lahman, M. E. (2008). Always Othered: Ethical research with children. *Journal of Early Childhood Research, 6*(3), 281–300.

Lewis, P. J. (2011). Storytelling as research/research as storytelling. *Qualitative Inquiry, 17*(505), 505–510.

Mazzei, L. A., and Jackson, A. Y. (2012). In the threshold: Writing between-the-two. *International Review of Qualitative Research, 5*(4), 449–458.

Richardson, G. (2006). Singular nation, plural possibilities: Reimagining curriculum as third space. In Y. Kanu (Ed.), *Curriculum as cultural practice: Postcolonial imaginations* (pp. 283–301). Toronto, Canada: University of Toronto Press.

Rilke, R. M. (1984). *Letters to a young poet.* New York: Random House.

Routledge, P. (1996). The third space as critical engagement. *Antipode, 28*(4), 399–419.

Schulte, C. M. (2013). Being there and becoming-unfaithful. *International Journal of Education and the Arts, 14*(1.5), 1–16.

Tarr, P. (2003). Reflections on the image of the child: Reproducer or creator of culture. *Art Education, 56*(4), 6–11.

Thompson, C. M. (2009). Mira! Looking, listening, and lingering in research with children. *Visual Arts Research, 35*(1), 24–34.

Wilson McKay, S. (2006). Living the questions: Technology-infused action research in art education. *Art Education, 59*(6), 47–51.

Zeni, J. (2001). Epilogue: A guide to ethical decision making for insider research. In J. Zeni (Ed.), *Ethical issues in practitioner research* (pp. 153–165). New York: Teachers College Press.

7

Modest Encounters and Engaging Surprises

Christine Marmé Thompson
Penn State University, USA

In these Saturday sessions, I understand that you observe both the children making art and your student teachers, ask questions and, at times, draw with the students to help motivate them during "drawing events" (I love that term! I agree that it adds value to the activity). Do you think your questions ever "break the spell" of children's solitary drawing or discourse between peers? Do you prefer to spend your time mainly observing or do you intend to create dialogue as much as you can? Some kids are more outgoing and become animated when asked to talk about their artwork. How do you proceed with the more reserved students?

(Britta Hyneman, personal correspondence, October 12, 2018)

Just this week, I received an email from a graduate student who is studying in a teacher certification program not far from the university from which I recently retired. She had been reading some of my published work, in a class taught by a valued colleague and friend, and had some questions for me that pertain quite directly to the focus of this chapter. I asked if I could include some of her queries in this manuscript, since they summarize so beautifully the questions that prompt the consideration that follows, of the ways in which we honor children's thoughts and actions, allow ourselves to hear their voices, and share these intra-actions with others. These actions and attitudes cannot be taken-for-granted: In a society so deeply ambivalent about children, it is radical to assume that there is anything to be learned from them.

The intellectual center of the preschools of Reggio Emilia, Loris Malaguzzi (1994) points out that teaching begins in the image of the child the teacher holds in mind, acknowledging that we are seldom able to see children differently, beyond the edges of this template. We assume that children are ours to direct, to divert, and to delight in, as the natural order of things. We talk over their heads and behind their backs. But as Malaguzzi and others remind us, teachers have made a conscious choice to work with children, to serve as "emissaries and anthropologists ... to the child estate," in the words of David Hawkins (2002, p. 45). The same is true of adults who focus upon children as participants or partners in research. There is an obligation implicit in this choice to consider the image of the child one holds and the perspectives and practices that image provides or prohibits.

British sociologists Allison James, Chris Jenks, and Alan Prout (1998) are among those in the evolving interdisciplinary field of childhood studies who recognize children as a minority group, socially constructed by adults who stand in varying degrees of relationship to them. As James and Prout (2015) note, "The immaturity of children is a biological fact of life but the ways in which this immaturity is understood and made meaningful are a fact of culture" (p. 6). In the late 1990s, James, Jenks, and Prout (1998) described varying visions of childhood that were evident in social institutions, the arts, media, and everyday conversations about children. Others have generated similar categories. In the simple dichotomy proposed by art historian Anne Higgonet (1998) as she examined depictions of childhood in painting and photography, we tend to think of children as either innocent or knowing; as dependent or independent; as reliant upon us or unrepentant in their opposition to us; as simple or complex; as charming or cagey, wise, or ignorant.

Like most of those who have elected to stand in a pedagogical relationship (van Manen, 2002) toward children, Malaguzzi (1994) championed a particular image of the child. He envisioned a child with rights rather than a child with needs: a child who is rich, strong, and capable, whose potential is limitless and unknown. Reacting strongly against the prevailing view that children are deficient or incomplete adults, Malaguzzi urged us to see the child as competent and powerful. Yet, at every level—legal, cultural, personal, parental, and pedagogical—we exist in a culture that remains highly ambivalent about its children. We worship and enjoy them; we become incensed on their behalf; we shower them with material possessions and all the advantages we can afford. At the same time, we seem to lack the political will or cohesion to refuse their submersion in toxic educational games played out above their heads by testing and technology companies, or even the everyday indignities that are so much a part of being a child. Consider the things routinely said to children that we would not think of saying—or certainly not in the same abrupt and dismissive manner—to another adult: "Sit down," "Do it now," "Put that away," "What's wrong with you???" "Just mind your own business ..."

Liselott Mariett Olsson (2009) suggests that the field of childhood studies is currently engaged in a struggle to move beyond the image of the child as competent, "to find more and unknown ways of being a child than being defined through one's competencies" (p. 13). As she points out, even the most honorific descriptions of childhood tend to become "a predetermined map, as strongly regulating as the image of the child earlier defined through the workings of developmental psychology" (2009, p. 13). Researchers who are dedicated to the understanding of children and childhood continue to question, refine, and refute prevailing conceptions of childhood, foreshadowing the far more gradual evolution in public sentiment. Evidence of the continuing underestimation of the competencies of children to speak, perform, achieve, understand, articulate their own condition, or testify on their own behalf accumulates daily: Witness, for example, the ease with which we employ "childish" as a reaction to the political misadventures of the moment, the difficulty we experience in finding an alternative term that conveys disparagement quite so concisely. It is a constant battle to demand that children be seen and heard (Carel and Gyorffy, 2014), much less respected in their capacities to know, to experience the world, and to make sense of it.

The complicated relationships among researchers and the children they study are too often influenced by some variation of what Miranda Fricker (2007) has termed "epistemic injustice," a systematic and habitual underestimation of the capabilities of another individual, often due to his or her membership in a particular social group (Burroughs and Tollefsen, 2016; Murris, 2013). This dismissal of the capacities of the child affects the nature of research and the representation of knowledge about children in ways that are too often unexamined, and subsequently unheralded in the stories we tell when we speak for those others. As Malaguzzi (1994) suggested, because our images of the child persist without recognition, we are prone to remain attached to stereotypical, socially constructed views that limit our abilities to respond fully to the individuals we encounter or the collective cultures those individuals construct and participate in.

Cultivating epistemic modesty

One morning, many years ago, I sat on the sidelines of an art class for preschool and kindergarten children as their young student teacher invited the children to point to any lines they might see in the space they inhabited. One chronically wiggly and distracted child raised his hand. The student teacher called on him warily. "Have you ever been to Hardee's?" he asked. The student teacher rolled her eyes (for the benefit of the adults in the room) and responded with noticeable exasperation, "Of course, I've been to Hardee's. But we are talking about lines!" Undeterred, the child made his point: "They have curly fries." He was talking about lines, after all.

I often share this story with university students in order to emphasize the importance of listening to children, not simply to bounce off their responses and move on but to hear them out: No matter how circuitous and off base their comments may seem at first, they almost always have a point to make. Epistemic modesty is called for in our encounters with children, an "emergent listening" (Davies, 2014, p. 25) that allows us to learn from them. And yet, too often, as Davies (2014) warns, we engage in "listening-as-usual," a kind of "repetitive listening, not requiring any thought, and serving to reiterate what is known" (p. 25).

Miranda Fricker (2007) describes the phenomenon of epistemic injustice, in which members of certain social groups are discounted in their capacities to know or to convey knowledge to others. Fricker's analysis focused primarily on gender and race as disqualifying conditions, rendering the testimony of women or members of underrepresented racial or ethnic groups unreliable in the eyes of the dominant class. "A speaker receives an identity-prejudicial credibility deficit when what she says is taken less seriously than it ought to be because of a prejudice on the part of the hearer about a social group to which the speaker belongs" (Hand, 2015, p. 327). Fricker's description fits children's position vis-à-vis the adult world exceptionally well, confronting us with the reality that children are routine targets of discrimination, even at the hands of those who have elected to serve them in some capacity.

The impact of silencing children, distancing ourselves from them in this way, is profound, both for children themselves and for research that purports to describe their experiences (Skrlac Lo, 2018). Writers note the danger of epistemic injustice done to children in their encounters with health care (Carel and Gyorffy, 2014), the legal system (Burroughs and Tollefsen, 2016), and education (Baumtrog, 2018; Hand, 2015; Knezevic, 2017; Murris, 2013), arenas in which children's knowledge and their capacity to articulate their experiences are frequently contested. Skrlac Lo (2018) argues that

> researchers silence young children in research on childhood and that we need to employ methods that hear and recognize contributions children can make to our understanding of childhood in the 21st century. Finding ways to listen to their voices may overcome current epistemic injustices as well as make our collective epistemic resources more robust. (p. 92)

Fricker (2007) locates epistemic injustice in "two of our most basic epistemic practices: conveying knowledge to others by telling them, and making sense of our own social experiences" (p. 1), specifically in instances of what she has termed *testimonial injustice* and *hermeneutical injustice*. Testimonial injustice toward children takes varying forms, to similar effect:

> In cases of testimonial injustice a prejudice (e.g. accent or age) will cause a hearer to give a deflated level of credibility to a speaker's word, and "sometimes this will be sufficient to cross the threshold for belief or acceptance so that the hearer's prejudice causes him to miss out on a piece of knowledge" (Fricker, 2007, p. 17) …. [For example] teachers do not believe a child, because it is a child who is speaking, with typical responses such as: s/he is not telling the truth, or is immature, or at the other (sentimental) end of the scale: endearment: smiling, laughing, or expressions such as 'oh, how sweet'. Credibility deficit is related to age, in that being a particular age has significant impact on how much credibility a hearer affords a speaker, and when and how s/he is silenced systematically. (Murris, 2013, p. 248)

Murris (2013) continues, "hermeneutical injustice is even more difficult to detect" (p. 248). Fricker (2007) defines it as "the injustice of having some significant area of one's social experience obscured from collective understanding owing to a structural identity prejudice in the collective hermeneutical resource" (p. 155). The effects of hermeneutical injustice over time are profound, eroding the speaker's confidence in their own intellectual abilities and the fundamental worth of their contributions to dialogue. Hermeneutical justice leads to and reinforces subservience.

Applying Fricker's concept of epistemic injustice to our relationship with children, then, encourages us to recognize the impact of stereotypical understandings of the child as lacking knowledge, understanding, and maturity on our encounters with young human beings. The impact of this habituated way of thinking on children themselves is considerable; the ways in which it shapes and limits research merit consideration. As Murris (2013) suggests, children are simply not heard as a result of an a priori conviction that those of their kind have little of value to contribute to our collective understanding of the world: "Adults often put metaphorical sticks in their ears in their educational encounters with children. Hearers' prejudices cause them to miss out on knowledge offered by the child, but not heard by the adult. This has to do with how adults view education, knowledge, as much as child, and is even more extreme when child is also black" (p. 245). Children who are members of marginalized racial, ethnic, or gender groups may well be multiply disadvantaged, as Knezevic

(2017) also acknowledges, their experiences dismissed, the value of their own understandings and interests diminished in favor of imposed relevances of the dominant adult culture. As Baumtrog (2018) observes, children do navigate the world with significant gaps in their knowledge and experience, just as all adults do, but children are penalized disproportionately for these lacunae:

> The injustice children face is not that they may lack knowledge in certain domains, as all adults also do, but that they live in a world where epistemic and communicative resources are constructed and enforced by adults by default. They live in an epistemic tyranny of the majority. When they are attributed with being credible knowledge bearers, it is an exception, not the rule. (p. 299)

In addition to the clear frustration experienced by any sentient being whose attempts to articulate their perspectives on the world are regularly dismissed, children's daily lives are circumscribed by the epistemic injustice done to them by unthinking adults. Baumtrog (2018) points out that children are prohibited from making decisions about their lives as a result of taken-for-granted epistemic injustices; they are limited in their capacity to make decisions about the shape of their days, the nature of the problems they construct and pursue, the companions they select, when and where they choose to learn. The enduring impact of these deprivations is even greater. As Knezevic (2017) observes, "those depicted as less knowledgeable are also depicted as morally inferior or unreliable" (p. 471).

Combatting epistemic tyranny

What is the potential impact of epistemic injustice toward children upon research that purports to delve into their lives? As researchers, "our *epistemic obligation* is to hear fully and to recognize others as having epistemic resources that will add robustness to personal and collective understandings of experiences" (Skrlac Lo, 2018, p. 97). Yet laboring under a naturalized undervaluation of the capacities of children to make sense of their lives or to articulate their understandings, it is all too easy to dismiss what children say as insubstantial or to see it, at best, as adventitiously wise or precocious. Carel and Gyorffy (2014) note, "Not only children's testimonies, but also their interpretative frameworks are at risk of rejection by adults, who, with few exceptions, cease to readily understand the child's world. When the two interpretative frameworks clash, the adult interpretation usually trumps the child's" (p. 1256). If we are to avoid imposing our interpretations on children's experiences in ways that distort and diminish, we must make a conscious effort to enter children's world and to adopt their interpretive frames. We must engage in conversation with children in much the same way that we listen to other adults, giving them the benefit of considerable doubt in weighing the plausibility of their accounts.

Research about childhood cannot ignore the fact that children are readily available and ready to be seen and heard. Carel and Gyorffy (2014) consider the implications of the all-too-common practice among medical professionals of speaking over the child's head to their parents, whose accounts of the child's symptoms are treated as necessary and sufficiently informative testimony. A similar situation occurs in research when adult testimony is substituted for the child's, sometimes following the path of least resistance around the demands of ethics boards who make direct interactions with children difficult (Skrlac Lo, 2018). There may be sound practical reasons for relying on adult proxies, as Skrlac Lo (2018) admits: There is

> the perception that young children are less likely to have the literacy or cognitive skills to meet the demands of a research study. Children are not perceived as credible participants because they lack both cognitive and experiential knowledge to understand their experiences and to be able to communicate them to others …. Testimonies gathered directly from children, therefore, are difficult to gather and may be perceived as unreliable due to communication and cognitive barriers between the child and the researcher. Of course, this perspective places the child—rather than the researchers—as having the deficit. (p. 94)

As Carel and Gyoffy (2014) point out, however, the two sources of information are in no way equivalent, and reliance on adult versions of children's experiences exemplifies epistemic injustice toward children: "Denying someone the credibility they deserve is one form of epistemic injustice; denying them the role of a contributing epistemic agent at all is a distinct form of epistemic exclusion" (p. 1257). By circumventing the testimony of children, assuming they are not capable "epistemic agents," we deny them the right to be heard and attribute a passivity to them that, in turn, justifies the need for further adult intervention (Knezevic, 2017), and the ventriloquism that characterizes the "made up knowledge" (Graue and Walsh, 1998, p. xiv) that often guides us in our interactions with children.

A further manifestation of epistemic injustice occurs when adults engage in what Galman (2018) calls "the cult of cute, … the research equivalent of pinching cheeks" (p. 182). This behavior, frequently seen in school hallways, also has a tendency to permit readers to diminish the gravity of the stories told about children in qualitative and post-qualitative research. Murris (2013) explains this well:

When teachers smile knowingly to one another or laugh as children express novel ways of understanding the world, this endearment allows them to avoid any re-examination of their own beliefs and assumptions. Sentimentality and endearment seems to presuppose vulnerability and inequality, the kind we feel when watching a lioness licking her cubs, but only when they are safely behind bars or on television (Haynes and Murris 2013). This laughter is an example of adult distancing from child. Children's speculations are seen as unusual, sweet, perhaps foolish, but harmless. At the same time, in contradictory fashion, child is also often seen as wild, uncontrollable and possibly dangerous. Perhaps adults are afraid to hear what children are saying as worthwhile? (p. 252)

This reaction is frequently seen in public presentations of research conducted with children and featuring their commentaries. Skrlac Lo (2018) ponders the impact of this amusement on children themselves and on our willingness to accept them as contributing members of society:

What does this adult mediation mean in the context of academic research? Since children are not the presumed audience for academic research, why does it matter how children's experiences are recounted? Is there a harm done when children do not know their voices are not necessarily being heard? Here, I offer two responses: first, the child participants in the study suffer very little or no immediate harm since the context of the research is in the "adult" world, separate from their day-to-day experiences, *but*, second, society suffers as a collective by the denied dissemination of perspectives or "limited epistemic resources" (Frank, 2013, p. 266) that could influence the shape of policy and practices. This is where children—as a collective—may endure harm due to misperceptions about childhood that play out in policy and adult behavior. This collective suffering may be difficult to measure, but not knowing whether there is harm in ignoring children's voices does not mean there is no harm occurring. It simply means we cannot measure it. (pp. 96–97)

Reuben's fall

In a 2008 article in the *International Journal of Children's Spirituality*, and in her book published in 2009, Sheri Leafgren describes the incident in an elementary school hallway that prompted her consideration of the ways that children's most positive impulses are constrained by the narrow interpretations of adults:

Reuben fell. A hard smack and muffled grunt signaled Reuben's fall on the hard school-linoleum floor as he moved with his kindergarten class in their silent, gender-based-double-lined trek to the restrooms at the end of the hall. As Reuben lay on the unforgiving floor, Julian—a spirited, full-of-verve, curious, "bad" child—left his place in the back of the line to reach him where he had fallen near the front of the boy's line. Julian gently helped him to his feet, and asked, "Reuben, are you okay?" The other children steadfastly maintained their places in their straight, silent boy and girl lines. Their teacher, Mrs. Buttercup, shook her head, held up two fingers, and said, "That's two, Julian. You are out of line *and* you are talking. You're on the wall at recess." Going "on the wall" is a common punishment in grade school. It means the child must spend all or part of recess standing against the wall of the school building watching the other children play. As the "other" kindergarten teacher in this school building, I had observed that Julian, a lively child, spent most recesses "on the wall" for various infractions of the rules of order in his kindergarten classroom. (Leafgren, 2008, p. 331).

Leafgren continues:

This moment that I witnessed more than 20 years ago was a critical one for me as a young teacher. I clearly saw that Julian's actions were "good"—demonstrating care, empathy, courage, and kindness—and yet, he was punished. For "good" is also defined by teachers and children in school as order, silence, and stillness— in other words, compliance …. In this case, Julian had not complied with classroom rules—*No talking* and *Stay in your place in line*—as he moved to help Reuben and inquire into his wellbeing. As a witness to the event, I was struck by the concomitantly "good" and "bad" nature of Julian's action. (p. 332)

Moments such as these betray the order of things that we have come to regard as natural, to the detriment of children's sense of priorities and our capacity, as researchers and teachers, to see what is happening before our eyes. Seeing fully, listening intensely, and lingering within the situation long enough to avoid quick categorizations and rote response are critical to any interaction that hopes to do justice to the onto-epistemological agency of children. When we substitute predetermined rules, categories, and understandings for presence in the moment, we constrain children and misconstrue their capacities for thought and action and sensitive response to the world around them. The implications are complex, as Skrlac Lo (2018) suggests:

Children are silenced in much research on childhood since the paradigm, theories, and methods are biased against recognizing the uniqueness of childhood from children's perspectives. An examination of these perspective— and a consideration of ways to identify these biases—helps to make clear implicit bias that adult researchers (and society more broadly) may have toward the oft-romanticized but always distanced experiences of early childhood and young children. When reflecting on her work with young children, Davies (2003 [1989]) noted how adult researchers often presume that their adult status provides an objective gaze that allows them to "colour in" the children (p. 150). This "colouring in," the presumption of the right to make meaning of children's experiences on behalf of the children, demonstrates the adult–child power asymmetry that simultaneously positions adults as experts of childhood and children as incomplete or partial knowers. (p. 93)

The questions posed in the email I received not long ago resonate powerfully in dialogue with this quotation. Kate Meyer-Drawe (1986) wrote of the capacity to be surprised by children as an essential attribute of those adults who choose to work with them, and the truth of this statement is reinforced daily in encounters with children and the representations made of them. It is too easy to assume that we know, and they don't. It is tempting to indulge in the hubris that comes with age and experience, seldom stopping to realize that, just like every child, we adults navigate the world with partial knowledge of some things, none of others, stumbling through the lacunae, making our way more or less successfully in a world that we will never fully comprehend.

And sometimes, even with the best of intentions, we stumble, interfere, disrupt, intrude, and break the spell. I do so far more frequently than I would like when interacting with children engaged in drawing events (see, for example, Thompson, 2017, and, for corroboration, Schulte, 2012). Children's spaces, and the events that occur within them, are fragile ecologies, and yet they are resurgent and robust. In these diffractive assemblages, we are as much a part of their experience as the markers that are available (and the condition they are in), the friends at hand, the cleanliness of the drawing surface, and the temperature of the room. Children are remarkably tolerant of adult intrusions, and yet sometimes they clearly wish we would just go away or stop being so very dense. A considerate adult will retreat or adjust as needed. Children's capacity to tolerate lapses does seem to depend, however, upon their overall judgment that the blundering adult is generally and genuinely interested in them, in their ideas, and their productions. A preexisting relationship of trust is an essential prerequisite of such forebearance.

The correlative phenomenon of "coloring in" children's intentions, of seeing only what we already believe that we know, of jumping to foregone conclusions, is equally as detrimental, if not as immediately felt by children themselves. Ultimately, arguably, it is more harmful to children, present and future, to fail to see what is happening around us, to see things only as "instances of …" things we already know, and to continue to pass on these flawed representations as valid observations. Epistemic modesty demands that we be present and persistent, that we "stay with the trouble," as Haraway (2016) advises, and that we remain open to the possibilities and pleasures of being surprised by children.

References

Baumtrog, M. D. (2018). Navigating a necessary inequality: Children and knowledge-based injustice. *Alternate Routes, 29*, 294–306.

Burroughs, M. D., and Tollefsen, D. (2016). Learning to listen: Epistemic injustice and the child. *Episteme, 13*(3), 359–377. https://doi.org/10.1017/epi.2015.64.

Carel, H., and Gyorffy, G. (October 4, 2014). Seen but not heard: Children and epistemic injustice. *The Lancet, 384*, 1256–1257. Retrieved September 14, 2018, from *www.thelancet.com*

Davies, B. (2003/1989). *Frogs and snails and feminist tales: Preschool children and gender.* New York: Hampton Press.

Davies, B. (2014). *Listening to children: Being and becoming.* London: Routledge.

Frank, J. (2013) Mitigating against epistemic injustice in educational research. *Educational Researcher 42*(7): 363–370.

Fricker, M. (2007). *Epistemic injustice: Power and the ethics of knowing.* New York: Oxford University.

Galman, S. C. (2018). *Naptime at the O.K. Corral: Shane's beginner's guide to childhood ethnography.* New York: Routledge.

Graue, M. E., and Walsh, D. J. (1998). *Studying children in context: Theories, methods, ethics.* Thousand Oaks, CA: Sage.

Hand, M. (May 2015). What do kids know? A response to Karin Murris. *Studies in Philosophy and Education, 34*(3), 327–330. https://doi.org/10.1007/s11217-015-9464-5.

Haraway, D. J. (2016). *Staying with the trouble: Making kin in the Chthulucene.* Durham, NC: Duke University Press.

Hawkins, D. (2002). *The informed vision: Essays on learning and human nature.* New York: Algora.

Haynes, J., and Murris, K. (2013). The realm of meaning: Imagination, narrative, and playfulness in philosophical exploration with young children. *Early Child Development and Care, 183*(8), 1084–1100.

Higgonet, A. (1998). *Pictures of innocence: The history and crisis of ideal childhood.* New York: Thames and Hudson.

James, A., and Prout, A. (2015). *Constructing and reconstructing childhood* (3rd edition). London: Routledge.

James, A., Jenks, C., and Prout, A. (1998). *Theorizing childhood.* New York: Wiley.

Knezevic, Z. (2017). Amoral, im/moral, and dis/loyal: Children's moral status in child welfare. *Childhood*, *24*(4), 470–484.

Leafgren, S. (2008). Reuben's fall: Complicating "goodness" ad schoolroom disobedience. *International Journal of Children's Spirituality*, *13*(4), 331–344.

Malaguzzi, L. (March 1994). Your image of the child: Where teaching begins. https://www.reggioalliance.org/downloads/malaguzzi:ccie:1994.pdf.

Meyer-Drawe, K. (1986). Kaleidoscope of experiences: The capability to be surprised by children. *Phenomenology + Pedagogy*, *4*(3), 48–55.

Murris, K. (2013). The epistemic challenge of hearing child's voice. *Studies in the Philosophy of and Education*, *34*(3), 327–330.

Olsson, L. M. (2009). *Movement and experimentation in young children's learning: Deleuze and Guattari in early childhood education.* London: Routledge.

Schulte, C. (2012). *Being there and becoming unfaithful with children through art: Deleuzoguattarian embodiment, subjectivity, and the production of difference.* Unpublished doctoral dissertation. University Park, PA: The Pennsylvania State University.

Skrlac Lo, R. (2018). Changing childhoods: Using queer theory and intersectional methods to reconsider the epistemic resources of children with gay and lesbian parents. *Global Studies of Childhood*, *8*(1), 91–104.

Thompson, C. M. (2017). Listening for stories: Childhood studies and art education. *Studies in Art Education*, *58*(1), 7–16.

Van Manen, M. (2002). *The tone of teaching: The language of pedagogy.* (2nd edition). London, Ontario: Althouse Press.

8

"Don't Forget to Show Them This One!" Post-Qualitative Potentials of Arts-Based Research with Young Children

Marissa McClure

Indiana University of Pennsylvania, USA

Introduction

In this chapter, I will share narratives I have written from arts-based participatory research projects with young children in several Reggio-inspired art studio spaces in public schools, childcare centers, and community-based programs. My hope is to create a map that makes visible some of the potentials and ethical considerations of post-qualitative, collaborative research approaches as they are held in tension with traditional conceptions of ethics in research with children. Throughout a timespan of more than ten years, the paradigms under which young children and I worked together shifted from qualitative methodologies, which were radical for their time, to arts-based approaches to a post-qualitative perspective. The shift that we experienced mirrors the movement that Karen Murris described from the psychological to the sociological to the philosophical study of childhood (2016, p. xiv). These paradigms swirled about us and brought descriptions of our work in research dialogues into a greater ethical focus.

Throughout this chapter, the intersection between feminist new materialist thought and decolonizing methodologies (Tuhiwai Smith, 2012) grounds my theorization of the ethics of our post-qualitative work together and the ways in which I position this work in relationship to more general assumptions about doing ethical research with children. To situate research with children as decolonizing, I share three guiding principles of decolonizing work: It is community-defined, the research process is collaborative, and the outcomes are meaningful to the community. Linda Tuhiwai Smith's description of *whānau tupu ngātahi*, or families growing together, provides further inspiration for the ways in which I would like to conceptualize possibilities in research with young children who are members of vulnerable and historically excluded groups. In that initiative in New Zealand, elders reconstituted indigenous languages by teaching them to young children in early childhood centers. It was an intergenerational and systemic approach to reclaiming knowledge that had been all but erased by colonization. Could research with children follow a similar path, whereby adults and children co-construct research knowledge together in order to reconstitute intergenerational ways of knowing and making that may be devalued by the colonizing practices of education?

In particular, I would like to address the ethical questions that arise when a teacher, artist, and researcher is working with very young children and within an institutional context that itself prescribes adults' and children's roles within embedded and historical power relationships that exist as part of traditional conceptions of research ethics. In these contexts, I place special ethical emphasis on working with young children who are members of populations considered to be particularly vulnerable and historically excluded and who are generally defined as being unable to legally consent to their participation in research (Alderson and Morrow, 2011). These groups include children of color, children living in poverty or experiencing homelessness, children in the US context who are not first-language English speakers, and children who are undocumented immigrants. Here, there are significant intersectional connections between being both a child who is already defined as being a member of a vulnerable group and also a member of an historically excluded group. I believe that the intersecting societal constructions of these social and cultural spaces inhabited by young children augment the level of rigor necessary in working with young children who may face danger if their work is exposed in particular ways: even in those venues that might be considered ethical within a traditional research paradigm. I consider the question of whether or not processes are, can be, or should be research if they are not shared within traditional or emergent research venues but only between participants in the making of and interacting with the work together. Throughout the chapter, I present an underlying framework in which I question the ways in which children are seen as "Others" both in descriptions of research practices and in the sharing and research consumption of the visual work they create during research projects. I additionally consider how the researcher's presence becomes hidden in such accounts and how the researcher's intra-active contribution to the work that is created in collaboration remains shrouded to emphasize the work of the other and to ascribe a meaning to shared work that may be greater than the meaning that children themselves assign to the work. Further, I implicate my own presence as a white adult working with young children who are members of historically excluded groups. Research and artmaking with children are never neutral practices. It is, in fact, the possibilities in a robust acknowledgment of this very intra-action that creates shared meanings and decolonizing potentials.

To highlight this, I address the impact of particular art media upon collaborative research. Since 2007, my collaborative work with young children has focused upon our shared use of digital technologies and new media—specifically digital photography and video. Using new media for both documentation of process and the process itself poses important considerations that might be obscured by more traditional media and that might exist outside of discussions focused paradigmatically on photography. Photography has especially varied social histories in both the documentation and exposure of children's lives and the lives of marginalized peoples that ranges broadly beyond the scope of this chapter. In the narratives that I share here, the video pieces, in particular, allow for a seepage between the process of artmaking and its documentation, between intended and unintended outcomes, and between the social and temporal processes of artmaking and art viewing and re-viewing. They disclose my adult role in ways that are both pertinent to and sometime interfere with the presentation of the research from the perspective of the children who created it. Seeing myself on video with children as an actor and not the adult making the video forces me to confront a presence that is often hidden, even in work done "in collaboration" with young children and the way in which such work is presented within formalized research dialogues. Throughout the chapter, I position young children's digital photographic and video practices as new media artmaking from a feminist new materialist perspective. As Kate Mondloch shares in her account of feminist new media art, "For feminist new materialists (...) knowledge production (...) is a material-semiotic relation that is emphatically *relational, embodied, and embedded*" (2018, loc. 261 original emphasis). I would like to connect these ideas to our contemporary understandings of the posthuman child. Children's bodies, like women's bodies, are sites of political and biological contest. In this way, like feminism, childhood can never be theorized without a consideration of the ways in which children's bodies function in political ideology, society, biology, and culture.

Because our work together confronts the assumptions that underlie many traditional qualitative approaches to research, especially in the roles of researcher and participants, I turned to post-qualitative, feminist new materialist, and decolonizing perspectives to map the movements that were happening and the potentials of these intimate and shared spaces with a particular emphasis on the possibilities inherent in intergenerational collaborative work.

"Don't forget to show them this one!"

As I sit with a group of sixteen four- and five-year-old children enrolled in a Parent and Child Education (PACE) state-funded preschool program in a public, Reggio Emilia-inspired school in southern Arizona, R* jumps up to exclaim "Don't Forget to Show Them This One!" He's pointing to a portrait made by one of the children of an older man at the neighborhood free kitchen where the children regularly volunteer as part of their long-term Hunger Project, *No Más Hambre*. In that project, the children recognized and worked to combat food insecurity within their school and neighborhood not only by creating and maintaining an intergenerational community garden but also by cooking and bringing meals regularly to the free kitchen. The man is wearing a stiff black mesh cap with the expression "$&t^ happens" screen printed in large white letters on it. It's a sunny Monday morning, and I am packing up some of the children's digital photographs and video pieces to share at an upcoming international conference in childhood studies. I've invited the children to participate in choosing some of the images that I will share. I've made choices about others: This is a practice that I will interrogate later throughout this chapter. The pieces that I find intriguing often differ from those to which the children return. These visual pieces themselves, despite their magnetism and their fixation of a particular research gaze, often function as mere artifacts of the work that exists between us. Of course, this image of the man with that word on his hat is funny: It can be read on so many levels, and I am not sure if or how the children might understand that. In this instance, I decide it is inappropriate for me to make at least one of these meanings clear. Instead, I invite a question about "what makes this piece particularly interesting to you?" The children talk excitedly about meeting the man in the photo and about returning to the free kitchen to present him with the very special gift of a glossy 8x10 of his portrait. In these uncharted moments, I am especially mindful of the unique ethical challenges working with young children and digital technologies pose. As Patricia Tarr and Sylvia Kind (2016) explain in their discussion of digital photography, I practice continued gratitude for the "gift" of children's images and voices in our work together, and seek to represent our shared power in making as it intra-acts throughout our initial experiences and my sharing here.

I share this narrative because writing narratives has long been one of the most crucial aspects of research with young children for me. Through writing narratives, I hope to map some of the questions that I will consider further throughout this chapter. I acknowledge that I am creating this focus around my own intentions. If presented with the same research record as me, the children would undoubtedly have concerns that differ from mine. My questions surround the ways in which we can invite children's voices into the process of creating art together as research; how children represent themselves within the representations we create of them; reflections on the nature of time and its impact upon research ethics; and the responsibility of the researcher in using their power in overlapping and often contradictory situations where their position is inherently privileged.

Traditional research ethics in tension

There are a number of useful texts that share practical concerns when undertaking research with children (e.g., Alderson and Morrow, 2011; Harcourt and Sargeant, 2012). As a qualitative, post-qualitative, and decolonizing approach, research *with* children is a relatively recent development that might be traced, in part, to the turn of the twenty-first century. In their putting forth of a post-qualitative possibility, Lather and St. Pierre (2013) confront the inadequacy of qualitative research approaches in mapping the complexities of affective interactions and intra-actions between human and material worlds. Inspired by the philosophies of Deleuze and Guattari and Derrida, the post-qualitative turn has resonated with early childhood scholars and art educators who work in the messy and intimate margins of life with young children (e.g., Davies, 2014; Hackett, Procter, and Seymour, 2015; Murris, 2016; Olsson, 2009; Pacini-Ketchabaw, Kind, and Kocher, 2017; Schulte, 2017; Trafi-Prats, 2017).

I have conceptualized my work with young children within a framework inspired by my own implication within the work (e.g., Walkerdine, 1990). This implication includes not only my current intra-active positioning but also the "afterlife" (Mitchell and Reid-Walsh, 2002) of childhood and specifically white girlhood that coexists within the me that I now present as an adult and as a researcher. Jacqueline Reid-Walsh and Claudia Mitchell's conception of the idea of "kitchen" research has long appealed to me as I attempt to frame my work with young children. While they refer to the specificity of parents researching with their own children, I might claim an equivalently affectionate relationship with not only the children in my own classrooms but also the cultural works that they create in our shared spaces. I have often felt that my fondness for the children with whom I worked created our work together in a way in which would differ from adults with a more distanced relationship.

Here, I would like to acknowledge that while the objective kinds of questions that researchers should ask while undertaking research with children are of great significance, they might also obscure or render experiences "objectively" ethical when they in fact are not. In fact, I would like to situate this space as the very nuanced place in which we might sit with young children in our work together: in these everyday moments of intra-action that are not accounted for in an Institutional Review Board (IRB) approval and in a research design and that include our words, our gestures, our immediate and unplanned intra-actions of support and empathy. This is work that demands a purposeful and intentional delicacy. In fact, the very design of post-qualitative and decolonizing approaches to participatory arts-based research with young children defies the possibility of a fully rendered ethical research proposal, design, or questions because the research itself is generated collaboratively within a moving community. With the absence of a broad, overarching framework, the researcher herself is left to continually navigate and constitute ethical encounters with young children that fall outside of a predetermined script. This is where $&t^ happens.

A question then arises of how the researcher herself might, with the absence of an institutional framework or the inappropriateness of framework to situation, make ethical decisions in relationship with children as she is always cognizant of her own positionality. Here is where the principles of decolonizing work provide a possible map—where I might continually ask myself if our work together is communally defined, if we are sharing the research process, and if the work is meaningful to us as we constitute an intergenerational research community through our intra-active work.

Where traditional ethics falter

In the narrative with which I opened this chapter, I was a teaching artist and researcher within a preschool classroom in a Reggio-inspired neighborhood school in urban southern Arizona. In demographic terms, 90 percent of students at the school qualified for the free lunch program, 87 percent were Hispanic, and 10 percent were Native American. There was one student who spoke English as a first language in the classroom of sixteen four- and five-year-old children.

My study proposal was to document young children's making with new media including digital photography and digital video. Supported by a university grant and approved by the IRB, the school district research office, and the building principal, the project already had multiple levels of stakeholders and oversight before it reached the children and their families. IRB approval took nine months with multiple revisions, as the IRB was unaccustomed both to arts-based research and to research in which young children as participants generated the research questions. I took required general research ethics training, as well as a special training module for the Native American populations with whom I would be working. I created parent informed consents, which I translated into Spanish, and both English and Spanish verbal minor Assent forms. In the US context, very young children are legally unable to consent to their participation in research, so assent is a contested term that some researchers prefer not to use. This takes on additional urgency when a researcher does not share the same first language with her participants. However, the IRB required verbal assent for the approval of this research. Even though not legally binding, talking with children and their families about our work together was a necessary part of modeling the process by which they would have voice in our work together. I held an informational meeting with families in which I introduced the project and distributed the consent forms. All families except for one signed the forms in full. The Native American family that chose not to fully consent cited religious beliefs that prohibited their child from being depicted in photographs. They then later chose to fully consent because their child expressed a great interest in the work. In this case, the child did not know that his family did not fully consent, as he was offered full inclusion in the work in the classroom with the caveat that his works not be publicly shown or exhibited. This is an example of an ethical question whereby I decided that it was most fully inclusive for the child to create work with his classmates, even if that work could not be shown in a traditional format. In the end, his collaborative work was exhibited with his family's full consent. This is an example, as well, of a situation in which a child's work sits in the intersection of multiple identities, the ways in which researchers must remain attuned to practices that colonize already vulnerable groups, and the ways in which members of these groups actively negotiate the research process as it intersects with and in some cases might alter their beliefs and practices.

Despite these multilayered precautions, ethical considerations arose in every aspect of our work together and its sharing. These ranged from teachers' concerns about exposing images of children online to my concerns about the children's ongoing documentation of people experiencing homelessness in their neighborhood and of undocumented immigrants who could only consent verbally to have their photographs created by the children. On our many outings in the neighborhood, children photographed and recorded many of the people who they met and who intrigued them. The children asked for consent to photograph each of these people: However, because our group itself was large and diverse including myself, other teachers, student teachers, and family members including young siblings and infants, many others who did not directly consent appear in the research record. The very nature of the diverse spaces in which we worked together created ethical uncertainty when placed within a traditional framework or within static conceptions of place and time. For example, this work was created during a climate in which surveillance of difference was both a pressing and immediate danger: During the course of the project, Arizona passed the controversial Senate Bill (SB) 1070 that at the time of its passage was the broadest and strictest anti-immigration measure in the United States (2010). SB 1070 allowed officials to stop anyone suspected of illegal status, which in reality meant profiling based on appearance. The neighborhood where I worked with the children had been Mexico not even a century prior and bordered both the sovereign Pasqua Yaqui and Tohono O'Odham nations. The widely contested bill was partially upheld by the Supreme Court in 2012.

Additionally, because of the highly collaborative and play-based nature of the work, it was sometimes difficult to discern which children should be credited as the authors of the work. For example, the children often chose to photograph and to video record play scenarios and playscapes. In these instances, some children would be playing or "acting" in the scene, some would be observers but still full participants, while others would be documenters. In our work together, I made several visual attempts at discerning the children's various roles in these actions (e.g., McClure, 2013). I created a password-protected bilingual blog that families could access daily to see what the children had created together and to share in the movement of the work. However, in many cases, accurately sharing our work together proved increasingly complex, and my attempts to "make sense" of it perhaps obscured the social meaning of the pieces for the children as a whole because I did not interrupt during the play to involve them in questions about its meaning in time. Because I did not have an omnipresent record beyond the children's photographs, video pieces, and my own field notes, I was not able to access the children's reactions in the moments except through what was captured in the pieces themselves and in the children's re-viewing of them. This lack of a verbal/audible research record generated several questions from other school adults about whether or not children's "voices" were present in the work. Their questions caused me to wonder whether or not children's visual voices could be granted the same status as their spoken voices in participatory work together; why the spoken voice was privileged as more meaningful or ethical; lingering effects of the privileging of traditional forms of literacy upon children from historically excluded groups; and the temporal questions of revisiting work that exists in a particular moment and how meaning grows in repeated relationships with the work.

Research ethics in tension with time

There are two questions that I would like to explore in this concluding section. First, in working together with very young children who may not remember their participation in the research, how might it be, or is it possible, to assess the impact of the work upon children in the moments in which they were intra-actively creating it. Next, when the work together only exists in the memories and experiences created intra-actively between the researcher and participants and it is not shown beyond this, what might its impact be, and how or why is it worth doing?

In order to conceptualize time, I would like to adapt a framework originally proposed by Karen Barad (2007) that has been adopted and adapted by a number of contemporary researchers working with young children or writing about young children's work (e.g., Davies, 2014; Murris, 2016). In Barad's conception, the times that we perceive as linear and one way in actuality coexist with one another. In his work as a theoretical physicist, Barad described the theory of agential realism in which phenomena and objects are created in intra-action with one another and in which agency is relational rather than a fixed attribute of an entity. In a physical sense, this very close reading frees moments from a fixed sense of time. In this case, the young children about whom I am writing today are no longer young children, yet our shared work together might in some way exist within all of us at this moment. In this way, the ethical nature of our relationship together may very well be what remains of a research record whose visuality may be forgotten.

In terms of that visuality, when I first was asked to refrain from sharing the children's digital images, I felt a great loss. I had imagined that the value of our work together would be illustrated by the beauty of the images, many of which were so arresting that the adults who saw them would wonder how young children could have created them. The photographs, in particular, had an immediately charismatic power, as they fit so nicely into a photographic gaze and printed so lushly when exhibited. I had hoped to harness this magnetism in order to illustrate that young children—especially those who are members of vulnerable or historically excluded groups—should be afforded the respect of being offered high quality and response art media, a supportive expanse of time, and a response educator in which to indulge their ideas. I wondered whether I could communicate this message without visual evidence: How could I adequately and ethically share the sensitivity of our interactions? Showcasing the children's visual work has been a hallmark of early childhood art education and in particular, the Reggio-inspired practices that inform my own work with young children. So, now I was left to question not only this message but also the purposes of our work together if it could not be ethically shown in traditional research venues such as publications, conferences, and exhibitions.

This caused me to consider how I might talk about our work as it existed only between us, in relationship, in a particular space and time that likely had much greater meaning for me as a researcher and as an artist than for the children with whom I worked. How might I honor the gifts that they had given to me? My initial impulse was to contact children with whom I had worked in the past to get a sense of what, if any, meaning the work had for them. Because of social media and digital tools, I am still in communication with a few of these children and their families. I have watched them grow from preschoolers to preteens. They have taken the record of our work together with them, even as they remain young children in my memories and in the artifacts that are housed in my hard drive and papered on my office walls. In this case, I have taken the purpose of our work together not only to be an advocate for the deep meaning of young children's work and its place as a central component of a serious, ethical and moral, and meaningful curriculum but also to model and to challenge myself to continually interrogate my research methodologies and to practice socially just ways of interacting with young children. This is the work that Barad and Tuhiwai Smith have identified as untangling the colonizing, racist, sexist, and nationalist practices that are embedded not only in research practices but also in some traditional conceptions of research ethics. Therefore, my research narratives are not the authentic representations of the research record that I initially sought (e.g., McClure, 2013) but more accurately my own memoir: a novella always-in-progress that I am using to highlight the apertures within these processes and to propose alternatives.

References

Alderson, P., and Morrow, V. (2011). *The ethics of research with children and young people: A practical handbook*. Thousand Oaks, CA: Sage.

Barad, K. (2007). *Meeting the universe halfway: Quantum physics and entanglement of matter and meaning*. Durham, NC: Duke University Press.

Davies, B. (2014). *Listening to children: Being and becoming*. London, UK: Routledge.

Hackett, A., Procter, L., and Seymour, J. (2015). *Children's spatialities: Embodiment, emotion, and agency*. London, UK: Palgrave Macmillan.

Harcourt, D., and Sargeant, J. (2012). *Doing ethical research with children*. London, UK: Open University Press.

Lather, P., and St. Pierre, E. (2013). Introduction: Post-qualitative research. *International Journal of Qualitative Studies*, *26*(6), 629–633.

Laura Trafí-Prats (2017). Learning with children, trees, and art: For a compositionist visual art-based research. *Studies in Art Education*, *58*(4), 325–334, doi:10.1080/00393541.2017.1368292.

McClure, M. (2013). The Monster and LoverGirl: Mapping complex relations in preschool children's digital video production. *Studies in Art Education*, *55*(1), 18–34.

Mitchell, C., and Reid-Walsh, J. (2002). *Researching children's popular culture: The cultural spaces of childhood*. London, UK: Routledge.

Mondloch, K. (2018). *A capsule aesthetic: Feminist new materialisms in new media art*. Minneapolis, MN: University of Minnesota Press.

Murris, K. (2016). *The posthuman child: Educational transformation through philosophy with picture books*. London, UK: Routledge.

Olsson, L. (2009). *Movement and experimentation in young children's learning: Deleuze and Guattari in Early Childhood Education*. London, UK: Routledge.

Pacini-Ketchabaw, V., Kind, S., and Kocher, L. (2017). *Encounters with materials in early childhood education*. London, UK: Routledge.

Schulte, C. M. (2017). Possible worlds: Deleuzian ontology and the project of listening in children's drawing. *Cultural Studies? Critical Methodologies*, *16*(2), 141–150.

Tarr, P., and Kind, S. (2016). The gaze and the gift: Ethical issues when young children are photographers. In J. Moss and B. Pini (Eds.), *Visual research methods in educational research* (pp. 251–266). Berlin, Germany: Springer.

Tuhiwai Smith, L. (2012). *Decolonizing methodologies: Research and indigenous peoples* (2nd edition). London, UK: Zed books.

Walkerdine, V. (1990). *Schoolgirl fictions*. London, UK: Verso.

9

Becoming a "Mutated Modest Witness" in Early Childhood Research

Jayne Osgood
Middlesex University, UK

Doing research differently

This chapter aims to reconfigure some entrenched ideas about early childhood research by considering the possibilities that are generated when attention is turned to the everyday habits, ordinary routines, and mundane materials that make up life in early childhood contexts. Following Haraway (1997), I want to argue for a "successor science" that reworks ideas about observation and researcher objectivity, and that recognizes (and celebrates) a researcher's place as entangled and implicated. For the "mutated modest witness" (Haraway, op, cit.), matters of concern are encountered, sensed, and produced through haptic moments in early childhood. Researching in this mode insists that we go beyond re/presentation or "giving voice" toward being in the thick of things and actively participating in world-making processes.

This marks a relatively recent departure in my research practice, for over a decade I was concerned to critique, problematize, and deconstruct policy and other textual accounts of early childhood education and care (ECEC). Through critique I identified a troubling set of discourses that discursively positioned women and children in marginal and problematic ways (e.g., Osgood, 2006, 2009). Through qualitative research (interviews, focus group discussions, observations) I gathered rich accounts of life within nurseries and through exercises of critical deconstruction I was able to tell alternative (feminist) narratives about the gendered, classed, and raced nature of work in ECEC (Osgood, 2012). Despite my convictions to identifying counter discourses from within, claiming to give voice to a marginalized, feminized, workforce, and exercising researcher reflexivity to ensure reciprocity and ethical research relationships, my research nevertheless had the scent of being done to or done on (Osgood, 2012). Troubled that despite my best, feminist efforts, I was still somewhat at a distance from my research participants and dislocated from the difference that my research might make in the world. As Taylor and Ivinson so eloquently express it:

> By properly recognising that we have no birds-eye position from which to look back or down at our world, we have to take seriously our own messy, implicated, connected, embodied involvement in knowledge production. (2013, p. 666)

These feelings of discomfort and dis-ease at the limitations of critique were further compounded by the acknowledgment that my researcher subjectivity was encountered as both a resource and a problem (see Osgood, 2010 for discussion). I needed other ways to undertake research with and within early childhood education (ECE) contexts. Here the promises offered by feminist new materialism beckoned me to consider how else research might be undertaken, in more socially engaged, generative, and hopeful ways. Over the past seven years or so, I have become more deeply immersed in feminist new materialist philosophy. Consequently, what counts as research (Rhedding-Jones, 2005), what counts as valid knowledge (Lather, 1993), and what gets included within frames of enquiry (St Pierre, 2004) have become considerably rethought.

Putting feminist new materialism to work has invited a more entangled and immersed approach to research, one that insists that I recognize my relational entanglements in early childhood contexts and that the concern is not to capture accounts that re-present what I think I see and know but rather, by embracing uncertainty and (k)not-knowing, new knowledges and ECEC practices are given opportunities to emerge. I have been grappling with what going beyond the human subject (and bringing materiality and affect more forcibly into the frame of my investigations) might mean for politically motivated research (see Osgood and Guigni, 2016; Osgood and Robinson, 2019). As a feminist researcher I remain troubled by inequalities exacerbated by classism, racism, sexism, male privilege, and the persistence of patriarchal systems—all (humanist) issues that have a very real bearing on experiences of childhood and therefore concerns that I want to keep central to my work. But such a humanist framing fails to take account of the ethical dilemmas that are present for children of the Anthropocene. Feminist new materialism makes clear the limits of human exceptionalism—it is not enough to only attend to human(ist) matters of concern, we have an ethical response-ability (Haraway, 2016) to recognize and take account of our entangled place in the world. We can bring this sensibility into our everyday lives and the research that we undertake with children (and their entanglements with spaces, materials, memories, affects, bodies, sounds, and smells) in a quest for more liveable worlds (Haraway, 2008).

In my most recent research I endeavor to put feminist new materialist methodologies to work (see Osgood and Guigni, 2016; Osgood et al., 2016; Osgood, 2019a, 2019b, 2019c; Osgood and Robinson, 2019). For the purposes of this chapter, though, I report on a current and ongoing study that I am undertaking that seeks to reconfigure approaches to studying "diversity" in early childhood, one that involves putting feminist new materialist philosophy into practice (Osgood, 2015). I offer an account of the affordances that are made available by taking up Haraway's figure of the "mutated modest witness" (Haraway, 1997) and keeping in play one of the most significant concepts in feminist epistemology, that of "situated knowledge" (Haraway, 1988). Together these figures work to heighten my ethical responsibility—a worldly responsibility (Haraway, 2008), as researcher I must be attuned to so much more than only the human actors in any given scenario. This approach celebrates the conceptual elasticity that feminist new materialism offers in a quest to neither find nor seek solutions, but rather generate new ways to think about and be in the world.

Taking a small number of embodied, material-affective events and haptic moments from one London nursery, and starting from materiality, I offer a generative account of seeking to work with Barad's (2007) conceptualization of ethics as onto-epistemological. As she states:

> Ethics is about mattering, about taking account of the entangled materialisations of which we are part, including new configurations, new subjectivities, new possibilities—even the smallest cuts matter. (p. 384)

Reconfiguring research as "mutated modest witnessing"

For Haraway modest witnessing is about reworking and mutating established ideas and practices about how to do science. Her figure of the mutated modest witness is a practice of critical scholarship that involves our own as well as other bodies, materialities, knowledges, politics, ethics, and truths, and, crucially, it is a hopeful practice. In her groundbreaking essay *Modest_Witness@Second_Millenium. FemaleMan©_Meets_OncoMouseTM* (Haraway, 1997), she playfully attempts to refigure science's *masculine* modest witness. She is committed to reworking polluted histories and practices, namely claims to objectivity, achieved through the embodied presence of scientist as witness, as bearing testament to truth/knowledge production, what she terms the "god trick." In *Modest_Witness*, Haraway presents a robust critique of modern experimental science as it was performed in laboratories at the Royal Society in London, in the mid-seventeenth century, and that leaves indelible imprints still upon dominant modes of knowledge production.

At that time experimental science was built upon a form of modest witnessing that was open to only a very narrow selection of people (namely white, upper/middle-class English gentlemen) "of social standing and with quality of mind" and therefore deemed well qualified to establish matters of objective fact. This mode of modest witnessing produced specific gendered subjectivities, i.e., powerful *masculine modesty* and an associated and very specific version of *masculine objectivity*. Objective scientific knowledge rested upon boundaries and standards and central to these was the scientist: an impartial, embodied, present being who could see, hear, record events that took place within the laboratory (Fig 9.1), without sullying or impacting upon the knowledge that was produced. Scientific events were considered nothing more than the materialization of the objects, and as such valid, truthful representations. This mode of enquiry established that the testimonies of qualified modest witnesses would ensure that matters of objective fact were discovered and secured. These scientific practices set up distinctions between insider and outsider, where insider science is characterized by careful empirical observation, meticulous record-keeping, high seriousness, and reasoned argument. By contrast, outsider science is shaped by culture, society, politics, religion, ideology, imprecision, intuition, desire, and common sense—all of which act to degrade and pollute true knowledge. The privileging of insider scientific practices produced a peculiar kind of modesty framed by a commitment to remain at a distance, to work objectively and transparently within experimental processes, and to allow objects of nature to speak through the scientist as if uncontaminated by culture.

The lab then becomes the "theatre of persuasion" (Haraway, 1997, p. 25) animated by a politics of representation; knowledge becomes a representational practice that presents scientists as apolitical, detached, masculine, modern meanwhile everyone else is marked as other—as engaging in outsider science. The spaces where science experiments took place were restricted, so who could be a modest witness was gendered, raced, and classed:

Figure 9.1 The civil man of science

Source: https://daliennation.wordpress.com/2014/03/17/the-history-of-science-in-society-the-royal-institution-19th-century/

> Coloured, sexed and labouring persons still have to do a lot of work to become similarly transparent to count as objective modest witnesses to the world rather than to their "bias" or "special interest". To be the object of vision, rather than the "modest", self-invisible source of vision, to be evacuated of agency. (Haraway, 1997, p. 32)

Accepting this model of scientific practice permits a limited version of objectivity, as beyond question, since it is both universal and given to nature. Haraway (1988) is at pains to deconstruct this narrative in order to imagine a more critical science committed to situated knowledges and where the practice of credible witnessing remains in place. For Haraway, situated knowledges enable partial perspectives that produce strong objectivities—these are features of the successor science she argues for, a science framed by feminist politics. She imagines situated knowledges to be built collectively, from partially shared perspectives, that are constantly reworked, negotiated, and reviewed, but that can be called truths by those building them. She undertakes a reworking of partiality:

> Instead of hearing "partial" as an insult … as an accusation, I'm using it to deliberately grind against the meaning. I'm talking about how you never have the whole truth. When I talk about partial knowledges, the privilege of partial

perspective, it's because a very particular notion of partial—the relentless relationalities and knottings and connectings, without ever having an illusion that you can finish it. (Haraway, 2018, p. 21)

Haraway's mutated modest witness is a project of reworking each of the polluted categories central to scientific practice: knowledge, perspective, objectivity, and truth. She contests how science is framed, practiced, and its relevance in the real worlds from which it emerges and to which it is always connected:

The point is to make a difference in the world, to cast our lot from some ways of life and not others. To do that one must be in the action, be finite and dirty, not transcendent and clean. (Haraway, 1997, p. 36)

She argues that witnessing and modesty are practices too important to leave out of science projects but the point is to figure out what each might mean in a successor science that would take democracy, freedom, partiality, location, and accountability more seriously. A *feminist* modesty then requires asking difficult questions about race, class, gender, and sex with the goal of making a difference in the world. Haraway's successor science and figure of the mutated modest witness work against the "god trick":

A true modesty is about being able to say that you do have certain skills. In other words, being able to make strong knowledge claims. Not giving into stupid relativism, but to witness, to attest. The kind of modest witness I call for is one that insists on situatedness, where location is itself a complex construction as well as inheritance. It is a figure that casts its lot with projects of those who would not or could not inhabit the subject position of the laboratories, of the credible, civil man of science. (Haraway, 2000, p. 160)

She argues for *feminist* objectivity characterized by situated knowledges that is about knowing, seeing, witnessing, attesting, and speaking as a particular body that is located in a particular time and place, both literally and relationally. This reworked, remodeled conceptualization of objectivity is never innocent or unproblematic because it is always partial, situated, located, and therefore accountable. Our seeing, sensing, and being in the world is always located, active, and specific, and recognizing this allows for more truth-full knowledge of worlds to emerge: "We are not in charge of the world. We just live here and try to strike up non-innocent conversation" (Haraway, 2004, p. 327). Haraway's concept of worldling (Haraway, 2008) stresses that worlds are multiple, partial, located, contradictory, overlapping, messy, and always in process, and they only become more visible as "a world" when they are fabricated through stories that can then be partially shared and collectively lived as truths, albeit momentarily. We can do this, she argues, by exercising loving care and response-ability that involves paying careful, loving attention to how others see, hear, and know—all of which is central to a better way of doing science.

Putting Haraway's successor science into practice

With this theoretical framing in place, I seek to illustrate how the figure of the mutated modest witness and practices of feminist objectivity can find expression in early childhood research to stretch and rework ideas and practices surrounding "multiculturalism" in early childhood. As Haraway (2018) states of her SF philosophy, "SF is a methodological proposal ... it is a toolkit for thinking, feeling, storying, relating, to be taken up, used, modified, offered, shared, whatever" (p. 43). Take up this methodological proposal as a means to attempt research differently, in a way that allows for feminist objectivity, partial perspective, and situated knowledges to generate other stories about childhood. The partial, situated location of this investigation unfolds within the toddler room, in a north London nursery, on a damp and drizzly Wednesday afternoon in December. Ladybird Room is an otherworldly space, a dwelling, a pedagogical home occupied by three- and four-year-old children, adult educators, and a host of nonhuman and more-than-human agents. A look around Ladybird Room reveals it to be an all-too-familiar environment to the early childhood researcher. However, engaging practices of mutated modest witnessing refigures it as a sensorium rich with possibilities to tell otherworldly stories about childhood. Through its familiarity, the space and all its inhabitants become extraordinary and offer endless possibilities to reimagine early childhood education and how "multiculturalism" and "diversity" might be encountered differently through a process ontology. Observing the routine, everyday material discursive entanglements unfolding and enfolding within the room creates space for other stories to emerge in unexpected and unanticipated ways. Through socially engaged practices of deep hanging out and a willingness to venture off the beaten path (Haraway, 2016), I am presented with multiple sticky-knots with which to reconfigure ideas and practices about "multiculturalism" and early childhood. Exercising an open-ended, speculative approach to research in ECEC is difficult to explain to the staff, I am immediately taken to wall displays: a map of the world with photos of children's faces superimposed upon the country from which their families originated; then a chart displaying all the languages spoken; and various photo displays of children engaged in "learning about other cultures"; then I am gifted a copy of the (outstanding) Ofsted report that provides further evidence of the ways in which the nursery facilitates and embraces "multiculturalism" and finally an information sheet prepared by a Chinese parent about festivals and celebrations "at home." While these artifacts and accounts volunteered by staff are interesting re-presentations, my concern is to engage in practices of mutated modest witnessing so that I might sense, hear, smell, see "multiculturalism" as it manifests through everyday encounters and microscopic events.

Here I share an excerpt from my fieldnotes, where my own as well as other bodies, materialities, knowledges, politics, ethics, and truths unfurl and interweave to produce other ways to encounter "multiculturalism." I then conclude by endeavoring to pull at strings that offer a speculative account of *what else* is going on when we allow ourselves to ask *what if* and so work beyond the limitations of recognition and representation:

HAIR & CHAIR
Within seconds of settling onto a too-small-chair in Ladybird Room two children (let's call them Ana and Elsa) have introduced themselves to me. Ana begins stroking my hair in an inquisitive way. Both girls are black-British and have their hair in braided cornrows—they seem preoccupied by the texture, colour and length of my hair and continue lifting and stroking it whilst engaging me in enthusiastic conversation. They tell me their names, that they understand I am an "expert about Christmas" and that they were expecting me and really pleased that I have come.

MACDONALDS, CHURCH, SEQUINS & DISNEY PRINCESSES
The whole time the girls are making star collages they talk busily, telling me about their lives, their likes. Elsa tells me that she goes to Christ's Church where they sing and are getting ready for Christmas but the best thing about going is the trip to MacDonald's on the way home. I am asked if I like MacDonald's more than Christmas? Do I have a MacDonald's near my home? The questions are in quick succession that I barely have a chance to answer—which is a relief as I don't like MacDonald's and actively avoid ever going there or taking my children there—but I don't share this with them rather offer that I think there is a MacDonald's somewhere near where I live. Elsa then shows me where artwork goes to dry (on a rack in the corner) then she is back at the table gluing another star and talking avidly to me about Disney Princesses (they are illustrated on the beakers that hold the sequins they are gluing).

A DINNER INVITATION: HOMECORNER, CHAIRS, MIRRORS, DOMESTICITY

A little while later Ana takes my notebook and decides that she is a waitress and takes my food order. Then Elsa comes over and takes the notebook and my pen and begins to "write" asking me what day it is. The girls then take it in turns to write on my notebook and appear to have no intention of returning it.

Then I am invited to come to dinner. I am taken over to the home corner and I quickly realise that I will not fit in the dining chairs placed around the round table that have arms on the sides and are not intended for adults. So, I pull up one of the stacking (still too-small) chairs and sit at the edge of home corner. My seat is opposite a mirror above a wash basin and to the side of a makeshift wall with a reflective surface. I catch sight of myself and my ridiculously long legs, my knees are almost at my ears as I attempt to fold myself into this other too-small-chair. I think of Alice in Wonderland as I am offered a plastic chicken to eat—Ana has consulted the food order in my notebook and determines that I ordered cake as well, but we will need to "make that from scratch." She brings over a large lump of the green sparkling playdough and jams it into the metal teapot. The cake-making and sharing goes on for some time and I am required to sample it—again I catch sight of the scene in the reflective surfaces … struck by my adult body in a simulated miniature otherworld—a world of domesticity and make believe; familiar and strange at the same time.

MAGICAL REALISM: CAKE, CANDLES

Ana and I are regularly consulting about what is real, pretend, magic (I don't have to really eat the "cake") but I do have to blow out the make believe candles but not yet because they are not alight ….Without verbalising it is clear that Ana has a bright idea as she springs up from her chair, eyes wide, brows raised—she purposefully scampers off and returns with the empty shaving foam can and applies the foam remaining on the nozzle on to each of the pipe cleaner candles—she can't find the right word (lighter, match?) but knows instinctively what the can has become but soon the foam/fire is used up but not all the candles have been lit. She instructs me to light the rest of the candles— reminding me it is Christmas cake—it may have candles, but it is not a birthday cake but a magical Christmas cake. I ask what is magic about it and I am told that it disappears.

TALKING "GOBBLE"

Elsa then re-joins us—she is wearing a purple conical party hat as a unicorn horn and has two boggly eyes still attached to her cheeks. In all seriousness she begins to chat with me again, asking questions about my home, and whether I have a

Christmas tree and which decoration is my favourite. Then the conversation moves to her grandparents (2 nanas, 1 grandad) in the few spaces left for me to answer I attempt to keep up with the shifts in her questioning.

They both begin to snort and giggle "Why do you talk like that?" Elsa asks. "Like what?" "Different, just different" … "You talk gobble! That's it, gobble!" I ask what gobble is and it seems that my accent is not like hers, or any of the children, or the educators (my "Queen's English" intonation is unfamiliar in this north London nursery with its "multi-cultural" population—It's gobble! And it's funny!).

DRINK ME! EAT ME!
Elsa flits off again and Ana has decided that we need a drink to go with our cake. She takes a plastic bottle from the shopping basket which was once a bottle of nail varnish remover, I have another fleeting Alice-like thought about the potential dangers of drinking toxic substances—but it is clear that this is water, to pretend-drink ….

Ana moves over to the hand basin and looks around her using the mirror to scan the room—as if to check the coast is clear—I suspect she might be breaking certain rules (playing with water in a non-designated water playing area?) but she is confident and comes back to the table and begins to pour the water in to the Disney Princess beakers in which small dollops of play dough sit—I am instructed to drink—and I pretend to do so. Ana returns to the basin several times—and then she is caught in the act, as she overfills the metal teapot with water it trickles over the table and the play dough floats on top of a puddle of water that shouldn't be there—an educator comes over and begins to rehearse the rules about not playing with water in home corner. What a mess! I feel that I am being included in the gentle reprimand, the brimming teapot is taken away and its contents poured down the sink. I can spy a concealed look of exasperation in the mirror above the basin. Meanwhile, Ana and I take paper towels from the dispenser and begin absorbing the puddle—the structure of the towels is transformed from stiff, crisp, dry rectangles to soggy, disintegrating, cold, mushy balls. We both sense that this signals the end of the game.

What else?

My intention is not to offer a deconstruction or interpretation of what these moments from research might mean or to identify evidence of "multiculturalism" in early childhood contexts. Rather, my concern is to grapple with what else gets produced through practices of mutated modest witnessing. While there are clearly human actors within these scenes (Elsa, Ana, myself, and the educator) the other (nonhuman and more-than-human) actors worked together to produce affects that linger still: confusion, judgment, thrill, and musing (Stewart, 2007). I want to argue that such ordinary affects can be productive in how we come to figure with materiality and affect so as to think more intensely and act more responseably (Haraway, 2008). Within these scenes the liveliness of matter (Bennett, 2010) is sensed, and it is possible to trace how various agents (chair, hair, playdough, water) together with researcher and child bodies, space, and time activate multiple intensities and forces, unpredictable fault lines, and energetic currents.

Through these entangled encounters resonances were provoked, memories agitated across and within bodies. For example, "gobble" transported me back to previous research situations where social class signifiers, such as accent, hairstyle, choice of clothes, produced uncomfortable affects (Osgood, 2010). In that "gobble" moment I was transported to other points throughout my own childhood into adulthood that have been marked by uncomfortable affective processes of social mobility; further, "gobble" worked on me to dwell upon the privileged, white, middle-classness that my own children inhabit.

These strange encounters with routine and everyday happenings in Ladybird Room interrupted and fractured the familiarity of being in a nursery, having undertaken research in nurseries for over twenty years there is a predictability and easy recognition of the organization of space, furniture, and materials. Yet, taking up the figure of the mutated modest witness made the simple, mundane acts of talking and sitting something else. When bodies are out of place, out of time, and excessive it becomes possible to encounter ECE differently. The too-small chairs contort adult bodies and therefore insist that researcher sensibilities become reconfigured (as mutated modest witnesses) in nursery spaces. Sensing and noticing "ridiculously long legs" while embarking upon a feast of plastic chicken generate discomfort and awkwardness. Such sensations insist that I must recognize my emplacement, that I am infected and affected by the (extra) ordinary in ECEC:

> The ordinary can turn on you ... it can flip into something else altogether. One thing leads to another. An expectation is dashed or fulfilled. An ordinary floating state of things goes sour or takes off into something amazing and good. Either way, things turn out to be not what you thought they were ... The ordinary is a thing that has to be imagined and inhabited. (Stewart, 2007, p. 105)

In these encounters, matters of fact (including those relating to chairs, accent, playdough, and the texture/length/color of human hair) intra-acted with matters of concern and matters of care that generated resonances and dissonances. This mode of enquiry demands that the researcher be open to the queerness that resides in spaces where habits, magic, and fantasy comingle with regulation, containment, and surveillance. This was acutely felt in home corner, a deeply familiar zone in early years settings. It has been the subject of feminist critique for reinscribing gender stereotypes, yet being open to what else might unfold in this simulated space of domestication offers interesting surprises. The vital materialism (Bennett, 2010) of the various objects within this space created opportunities for surging capacities to affect and to be affected. Within these micro-moments something was released, a ceaseless motion of relations, scenes, contingencies, and emergences unfolded. Sensations, expectations, wonderings, memories, and habits were set in motion. To be affected in this way provokes endless questions, questions about children, childhood, and life in the Anthropocene and the significance of our worldling practices (Haraway, 2008) as they unfold within the everyday scenes of Ladybird Room.

These observations raise important questions about what spacetimemattering (Barad, 2007) does to our human embodied encounters and therefore our conceptualizations of the child and childhood. It is striking what children are affected by, and in turn, how this calls into question what is magic and what is real. The constant doing, making, and playing that customarily unfolds within early childhood contexts provide rich opportunities to attend to the affective that can shift our investigations. As Hickey-Moody (2018) reminds us, materials work to prompt us to remember experiences and "to have emotional, sensory, intellectual and memory-based responses that are quite specific to the material assemblages of making practices" (p. 2).

Practices of mutated modest witnessing demand deep hanging out and a willingness to be immersed and infected by life in a child-sized world. Taking up an *Alice in Wonderland* sensibility, working with the affects of discomfort, awkwardness, excess, and being out of place is generative and provides a portal through which to unsettle established ideas about childhood and "difference" (Fig 9.2). Such deep immersion unsettles and expands ideas about the ways in which policies, curriculum frameworks, and pedagogical practices play out. By focusing on the seemingly unremarkable and routine everyday it becomes possible to attune to our ethical-response-ability. Rather than being positioned as "agents in hot pursuit of something definitive" we instead "become attuned to what a particular scene might offer" (Stewart, 2010, p. 5). Close attention to

Figure 9.2 An Alice-like researcher sensibility
Source: http://ilonareny.com

what unfolds in early childhood contexts can tell us so much about children's place within the world and their participation in world-making practices. Taking up a child-like inquisitiveness and curiosity in our research practices involves a willingness to create alternative (otherworldly, magical) stories that are corporeal, sensory, and haptic. Affective methodologies, such as that offered through mutated modest witnessing, recognizes our entangled place:

> The material self cannot be disentangled from networks that are simultaneously economic, political, cultural, scientific and substantial … what was once the ostensibly bounded human subject finds herself in a swirling landscape of uncertainties. (Alaimo, 2010, p. 20)

Recognizing that the researcher is always active in processes of production opens up possibilities to delve into the significance of matter, time, place, space, and context and the ways in which they are interwoven, and to consider what they produce. The mutated modest witness is not an innocent bystander gathering representational accounts of the world out there, rather she is implicated and invested. It is to the productive potential of the everyday, ordinary, habitual, routine, and otherwise unremarkable (Stewart, 2007) that we must pay attention. As my observations attest, early childhood contexts are extraordinarily ordinary, excessive, and affectively charged. We need to attend to close examinations of what these extraordinary moments, objects, materializations, and entanglements make possible when we consider childhood and how childhoods get produced. As Stewart stresses (2007), the project then becomes one of experiment rather than judgment:

> Committed not to the demystification and uncovered truths that support a well-worn picture of the world, but rather to speculation, curiosity, and the concrete, it tries to provoke attention to the forces that come into view as habit or shock, resonance or impact. Something throws itself together in a moment as an event and a sensation; a something both animated and uninhabitable. (p. 1)

References

Alaimo, S. (2010). *Bodily natures: Science, environment and the material self.* Bloomington, IN: Indiana University Press.

Barad, K. (2007). *Meeting the universe halfway: Quantum physics and the entanglement of matter and meaning.* Durham, NC: Duke University Press.

Bennett, J. (2010). *Vibrant matter: A political ecology of things.* Durham, NC: Duke University Press.

Haraway, D. J. (1988). Situated knowledges: The science question in feminism as a site of discourse on the privilege of partial perspective. *Feminist Studies, 14,* 575–599.

Haraway, D. J. (1997). *Modest_Witness@Second_Millennium.FemaleMan_Meets_OncoMouse: Feminism and technoscience.* London: Routledge.

Haraway, D. J. (2000). *How like a leaf: An interview with Thyrza Nichols Goodeve.* London: Routledge.

Haraway, D. J. (2004). *The Haraway reader.* London: Routledge.

Haraway, D. J. (2008). *When species meet.* Minneapolis: University of Minnesota Press.

Haraway, D. J. (2016). *Staying with the trouble: Making kin in the Chthulucene.* Durham, NC: Duke University Press.

Haraway, D. J. (2018). *Modest_Witness@Second_Millennium. FemaleMan_Meets_OncoMouse.* (2nd edition). London: Routledge.

Hickey-Moody, A. C. (2018). New materialism, ethnography, and socially engaged practice: Space-time folds and the agency of matter. *Qualitative Inquiry,* 1–9. https://journals.sagepub.com/doi/abs/10.1177/1077800418810728.

Lather, P. (1993). Fertile obsession: Validity after poststructuralism. *The Sociological Quarterly*, *34*(4), 673–693.

Osgood, J. (2006). Deconstructing professionalism in the early years: Resisting the regulatory gaze. *Contemporary Issues in Early Childhood*, *7*(1), 5–14.

Osgood, J. (2009). Childcare workforce reform in England and the "early years professional": A critical discourse analysis. *Journal of Education Policy*, *24*(6), 733–751.

Osgood, J. (2010). Narrative methods in the nursery: (Re)-considering claims to give voice through processes of decision-making. *Reconceptualizing Educational Research Methodology*, *1*(1), 14–28.

Osgood, J. (2012). *Narratives from the nursery: Negotiating professional identities in early childhood*. London: Routledge.

Osgood, J. (2015). *(K)not-knowing "diversity" in early childhood education: Putting feminist new materialism to work*. London: Middlesex University Press.

Osgood, J. (2019a). Queering understandings of how matter comes to matter in the baby room. In L. Moran, K. Reilly and B. Brady (Eds.), *Narrating childhoods across contexts: Knowledge, environment, and relationships*. London: Palgrave Macmillan.

Osgood, J. (2019b). You can't separate it from anything!: Glitter's doings as materialised figurations of childhood (and) art. In M. Sakr. and J. Osgood (Eds.), *Post-developmental approaches to childhood art* (pp. 111–135). London: Bloomsbury.

Osgood, J. (2019c). Materialised reconfigurations of gender in early childhood: Playing seriously with Lego. In J. Osgood and K. Robinson (Eds.), *Feminists researching gendered childhoods* (pp. 85–108). London: Bloomsbury.

Osgood, J., and Giugni, M. (2016). Reconfiguring "quality": Matter, bodies and becomings in early childhood education. In G. S. Cannella, M. Salazar Perez and I. Lee (Eds.), *Critical examinations of quality in early education and care* (pp. 139–155). New York: Peter Lang.

Osgood, J., Giugni, M., and Bhopal, K. (2016). Reconfiguring motherhoods: Transmogrifying the maternal entanglements of feminist academics. In K. A. Scott and A. S. Henwood (Eds.), *Women education scholars and their children's schooling* (pp. 54–70). London: Routledge.

Osgood, J., and Robinson, K. H. (2019). *Feminists researching gendered childhoods*, Feminist Thought in Childhood Research Series. London: Bloomsbury.

Rhedding-Jones, J. (2005). *What is research?: Methodological practices and new approaches*. Evanston, IL: Northwestern University Press.

St. Pierre, E. (2004). Deleuzian concepts for education: The subject undone. *Educational Philosophy & Theory*, *36*(3), 283–296.

Stewart, K. (2007). *Ordinary affects*. London: Duke University Press.

Stewart, K. (2010). Atmospheric attunements. *Rubric*, *1*, 1–14.

Taylor, C., and Ivinson, G. (2013). Material feminisms: New directions for education. *Gender & Education*, *25*(6), 665–670.

10

The Cucumber Party: For a Posthumanist Ethics of Care in Parenting

Laura Trafi-Prats
Manchester Metropolitan University, UK

Introduction

This chapter considers relations between parenting, care, and the everyday through a posthumanist ethics of care, which thinks parenting as being situated in concrete matters involved in the maintenance of forms of life that are messy, carry tensions, and raise questions (Puig de la Bellacasa, 2017). A posthumanist ethics of care seeks to undo the individualization and normativization of care in which care is seen as a moral obligation that can be rightly done. Puig de la Bellacasa (2017) affirms that care is "everything we do to maintain, continue and repair our world so we can live in it as well as possible" (p. 3). A posthumanist ethics of care conceives this *as well as possible* as a "speculative opening about what a possible involves" (Puig de la Bellacasa, 2017, p. 6). Care is thought as a problematic where the question of how to care is not resolved with a set of idealized meanings but encountered as a situated provocation. A posthumanist ethics moves care toward a *critical ontology* in the sense formulated by Foucault (1984), as a philosophical ethos that not only examines the limits of anthropocentric ethics where care is something that only humans do but develops "experiment[s] with the possibility of going beyond them" (p. 50).

I want to stop for a moment on this concept of critical ontology (Foucault, 1984) to note the work done so far by the emerging field of parenting studies. I want to examine how this work relates to the two parts of this ontology, which are historical analysis and speculative experimentation. In the UK, parenting studies constitutes a small field situated in the intersection of social theory, policy analysis, and childhood and family studies. It emerges and articulates in the context of an increased individualization of social life. This individualization goes back to cutbacks to the welfare state that began in the Thatcher years and continued through the governments that followed (Jensen, 2018). In this respect, parenting studies methods have relied on the critique of hegemony and the analysis of neoliberalism as a historically formed discourse in which the family is considered the central unit over which the governance of the state is deployed (Jensen, 2018). Parenting studies has dedicated efforts to criticize the politics (McRobbie, 2013), policies (Burman, 2007; Clarke, 2006; Jensen, 2018), and public discourse (Rose, 2018) that repeatedly deliver a paradoxical understanding of the family, as both a resource and a danger for social renewal.

Going back to the argument that a critical ontology involves considering care not only as a project of historical analysis but as one that involves experimentation, I note that parenting studies still lacks a theorization of parenting as an experiment in living—that is, a thinking-doing of parenting as a speculative exercise that can offer a glimpse of what life in the care of/with others might be beyond the excruciating limits of neoliberal governance (also see Rousell and Cutter-McKenzie, 2019). With the intent to experiment with parenting, I mess with one of its limits: the assumption that parenting is a human-to-human relation that centers on becoming human. My questions are: What else can be thought and done in parenting by the troubling of the human and animal binary through the lens of feminist science and technology studies and a posthumanist ethics of care? Will this troubling allow for both an examination and an experimentation with different orders of relations? (Foucault, 1984).

In the sections that follow I review but also experiment with different orders of relations between care, parenting, the everyday, the animal, and image technologies. In the first order of relations, I look into the human–animal binary operating in the discourse of human exceptionalism and how it renders some instances of humanity, for example mothers and children, close to the animal. I connect this to an examination of parenting policy exposing how the human–animal binary is active in the ways vulnerable parents living in poverty in the UK are both targeted and othered as less than human. Second, I turn to microethnographic work that I do as mother with my daughter, Ingrid, and my partner, Eric (see also Trafi-Prats, 2018, 2019), to experiment with other *possible* orders of relations that conceive parenting as a lived and situated practice that perhaps could be imagined *alongside* the animal. Latimer (2013) describes the notion of being alongside animals as a way of experimenting with other concrete and collective ways of being-with "that can throw us into a world beyond ourselves" (p. 79). In the final section, I continue thinking with this concept of being alongside other kinds by examining the role of video and photo technologies in intensifying our awareness of how we (Ingrid, Eric, and Laura) cared vitally and in situated ways, through doings and undoings, attachments and detachments with other kinds that eventually made and remade the worlds we dwelled in/with more-than-human others.

The animalization of parenting

Human exceptionalism defines the human as separated from worldly matters. In human exceptionalism, reason, consciousness, and morality are considered key human attributes, which are asymmetrically situated against the realm of the physical (Frost, 2016). Body, animals, but also women (mothers) and children are constituted as *knowable* and available to mastery. By being associated to the physical world animals are seen as resources for knowledge, work, and food. Animals are only perceived as valuable for what they do and afford (Latimer, 2013). As Grosz (2011) has pointed out, identical mechanisms to those of othering the animal appear in certain discourses around femininity strongly associated to the body and nature. Also, Burman (2007) has described how developmental psychology was forged by a confluence of practices stemming from biology, ethology, anthropology, and the medical sciences, which constituted the child as an object of study. In this order of relations, the animal is at the center stage of a process of othering where multiple others are rendered as less than human, objectified and situated closer to the animal. As Latimer (2013) affirms, "The asymmetrical power relations between the human and the animal means that humans themselves can be figured as too animal; that is, as insufficiently cultivated or not civilized enough" (p. 85).

I want to consider the power of the human–animal binary in shaping contemporary parenting policy. In the UK the policy discourse around parenting follows the global trend of associating parenting to social opportunity, the reduction of inequality, and economic growth via the ability to work and compete in the global market. Parenting behavior and life style have become a matter of public concern that permits government intervention in what could otherwise be considered an invasion to the fundamental right of privacy (Dermott and Pomati, 2016). Very specific techniques such as looking directly at the child when you speak, reading to your child, supporting her homework, attending school parent evenings are featured in government reports, but also on popular parenting websites, as measures of good parenting directly associated to academic outcomes and future success in life (Field, 2010).

In the second decade of the 2000s, the increase of the inequality and poverty provoked by the financial crisis was followed with a move toward an individualized explanation of poverty (Dermott and Pomati, 2016) and a more intense targeting of underprivileged families who were often portrayed as the cause of social conflicts (Jensen, 2018). In 2010, the Field Report offers a strategy to address childhood poverty through good parenting roles. The concept of good parenting is based on the disassociation between material conditions and techniques of so-called good parenting (Dermott and Pomati, 2016). Field (2010) writes, "Something more fundamental than the scarcity of money is adversely dominating the lives of these children" (p. 17). This separation of wealth, class, ethnicity, health from practices of parenting continues at the center of later policies of early intervention (Allen, 2011) and workless families (DWP, 2017). The language of these policies is of an intense negativization with a vocabulary that is othering and vile, and that renders parents living in difficulty as national burdens and solely responsible for making their life conditions challenge the chances of their own children. Everything in these policies aligns with the discourse of human exceptionalism: the treatment of families and children as disposable resources, the disdain for the material life conditions of parents, and the belief that parenting is a mental state that could be practiced regardless of situated experiences, as well as the reduction of good parenting to specific logocentric practices around language, rationality, and human-to-human interaction.

The rematerialization of parenting through attention to care

In critical opposition to human exceptionalism, feminist science technology studies (from here on FSTS) articulates around a relational ontology in which the question of how connections are made and how connections matter is put at the center. Haraway (2016) writes, "It matters what thoughts think thoughts. It matters what knowledges know knowledges. It matters what relations relate relations. It matters what worlds world worlds. It matters what stories tell stories" (p. 35). FSTS considers knowledge-practices not as a source that provides reality but as multiple situated practices embedded in concrete worlds and how these practices carry consequences by contributing to the sustenance or decay of these worlds. The concept of care is central to FSTS, not as a normative framework such as *quality care* or *good parenting* but as a speculative question of how to care for worlds made of more-than-human assemblages of bodies, technologies, things, places, affects—that is, how to care for worlds that keep life going in a damaged and impoverished planet, where concrete, mundane but critical practices of care have little recognition and provoke considerable struggle (Puig de la Bellacasa, 2017). Differently, from the parenting policies discussed earlier, this posthumanist ethics of care focuses on situated knowledges:

> [It] cherishes insight for alternative relatings to be found in the worlds of the domestic, petty ordinariness, the difficult and playful, the joyful and aching mediations of caring affection, crucially involved in everyday experiences of interspecies intimacies in contemporary natureculture worlds. (Puig de la Bellacasa, 2017, p. 88)

Puig de la Bellacasa (2017) more than proposing a universal idea of care that applies to all situations affirms care's partiality. Taking part is needed in care to "think from and for particular struggles, [which] require from us to work for change from where we are, rather than drawing upon other's situations for building theory, and continue our conversations" (p. 87). Puig de la Bellacasa's ethics of care offers important provocations to realign parenting with care as a way to return materiality and situatedness to cultural understandings of parenting, but also to see parenting in worlds of relations that are more than human to human as a way to practice the critical ontology discussed earlier (Foucault, 1984), which requires possible experiments of going beyond the assumed limits of how to care. These could be worlds of relations that enable parenting to be positively articulated through embodiment, affect, curiosity, and the multiplicity of unconnected and random experiences involving being a mother that resist cohesivity and grand narratives of parenting but that still speak of care-doings and care-knowings (Baraitser, 2009).

A situated story of care in parenting

Bodies of/in care are done in mundane everyday practices. Considering this, Lisa Baraister (2009) defends an *anecdotal approach* to parenting that foregrounds the raw materiality of parenting (sensations, intensities, moods, encounters) where something extra is issued provoking an ethical movement toward difference, "between what it is and what is ought to be" (p. 152) between "pleasure and obligation" (p. 152). Paying attention to the materiality of my everyday world, I cannot think in it as just made of human-to-human relations. I don't have a car, so I walk to many places. Often Ingrid, my daughter, walks alongside. In our walks we encounter, observe, and become committed to urban animal species with which we share and compose territories over iterative and prolonged time periods of being alongside.

Latimer (2013) affirms that being alongside animals is ethically and politically relevant because it permits imagining and practicing other forms of sociality based on being-with other kinds "that helps us escape the worst consequences of human exceptionalism and its ordering of relations" (p. 93). Latimer (2013) differentiates her notion of *being alongside* from Haraway's (2003) notion of *companion species* that completely eradicates the prior figures of human and animal and focuses exclusively on patterns of interspecies relationality. As Latimer (2013) affirms, Haraway "goes beyond the individual and the divide" (p. 92) and in doing so her theory is more about hybridity than thinking in terms of "partial connections alongside partial division" (p. 93).

Being alongside is a concept that argues against the idea of blurring differences between human and animal. While Latimer values the radical onto-epistemological affordances mobilized by Haraway's concept of companion species, she nevertheless considers key to think with the tensions and "the irreducibility of parts that can never settle into a whole" (Latimer, 2013, p. 93) in human and animal relations. Being alongside other kinds seems close to a posthumanist ethics of care that enacts both attachment and detachment, connection and division, while avoids producing a comparison human-animal. I explore this idea of connection in partiality a bit further through an anecdote featuring Ingrid, Eric, I, multiple snails, a rat, walks, and the backyard of the apartment building where we currently live.

Our first Spring in England was characterised by long days deploying a mix of periods of rain and sunshine. In our walks to the school, Tesco or the park Ingrid and I were enchanted by encountering numerous snails traversing the narrow sidewalks in Monton Road. We would look at their slime tracks, their slow movements through impossible surfaces, their striking shells and sensing antennae. But we would also see many of them crashed by feet and vehicles. We soon felt affected by the repeated slaughtering of snails that we saw day after day of rain and sun. "Mama, Google why they don't know that they are going to die if they walk in the street" I Googled this topic and we learnt about the unsophisticated nervous system of the snail and how it cannot communicate danger to other snails. Ingrid soon began a practice of picking up the snails from the middle of the street and situating them back in nearby bushes. We continue today doing this practice if the suctioning/attaching powers of the snail allow us. Also, back in Spring of 2016, Ingrid discovered that a number of bushes in our

apartment building in their shady areas hosted numerous sleeping snails. We
began spending time visiting and perusing the bushes some evenings after school.
Ingrid would carry a spray bottle and would try to wake up the snails, hold them
in her hand and observe them moving. She also initiated a collection of empty
snail shells that she encountered in her walks. One of the shells that she picked up
during an excursion to a nearby forest by the Liverpool coast was not empty at
all. As it was drying over a kitchen towel we noticed that a hole appeared in the
paper and that a snail was eating it. Ingrid was ecstatic and wanted to keep the
snail, now named Banana, in the house. Eric and I convinced Ingrid that Banana
would be better off living outside and that we could do a cucumber party and
help Banana meet some of the snails in the bushes. From this followed that for a
number of evenings Ingrid would be cutting slices of cucumber, going downstairs
and hosting cucumber parties for/with snails, Eric or I would go alongside. One
of the mornings that Ingrid and Eric went down to clean the cucumber remains,
they found a dead rat with a hole near the head and pellets around. Ingrid invited
me to go down and see it, but I couldn't follow this time. Eric collected the rat
with a plastic bag and deposited it in the garbage. I was horrified, not only for the
rat but because the cucumber snail parties may have attracted the rat, and also
attracted the person that lived in our building who shot the rat. "Mama, Google
if rats eat snails." Effectively they do. There is even a blog that explains that one
sign that points to the existence of rodents is finding around your building empty
and perfectly clean snail shells. The cucumber parties got cancelled. That same
morning, I washed again the collections of snail shells contained in our house and
the boxes and surfaces where they sat.

I think that this anecdote illuminates well Puig de la Bellacasa's (2017) idea
about the situatedness of care. Being in zones of contact where people, snails,
rats, garbage, and, and, and live alongside provoked us (Ingrid, Eric, and Laura)
to think of worlds that are ongoing, done and undone, and made of an excess
of bio-historico-cultural layers. Such zones of contact emphasize the lure of
closeness and touch, but also the awareness of alterity marked by the unexpected
of being alongside with other kinds. While these worlds may not always feel
"pleasant or liveable, they have something situated to teach us about caring
proximities" (p. 116).

Care is always partial. Ingrid, Eric, and I could care for the snails in some
ways, like not stepping on them and being sensitive and complementary to the
powers of their nervous system. However, we failed to care in other ways. By
organizing cucumber parties we left them exposed to their predators. Eventually,
we stopped caring so intensively, especially when we understood that snails and
us were interdependent with rodents, and that rodents and other humans who

hate rodents could be a threat to our livelihood. In care we became affected and responsive to some matters and not others.

Care, writes Puig de la Bellacasa (2017), needs "reciprocal exposure and vulnerability, rather than speeded efficacy or appropriation" (p. 116). Efficacy and appropriation are precisely at the center of good parenting and the assumption that there are a number of universal practices that can be abstracted from context and appropriated by all parents, and that such practices will correlate with educational success (Dermott and Pomati, 2017). As Hackett (2017) has discussed, these correlations are often presented with a positivist rhetoric that feels scientific and right. Their effects in pathologizing the lives of poor families are profound (see also Burman 2007).

Using the language of Clarke and Haraway (2018) in *Making Kin Not Population*, possibly, a posthumanist ethics of care propels an understanding of parenting that is less a project toward the economization of populations in need of governance (e.g., parents living in poverty) that objectifies and dehumanizes, and is more a project of making kin across multiple and various worlds. Making kin connects species and environmental reproductive justice by affirming that forced models of child development are not disconnected from other models of forced development that concern the environment such as plantation regimes, mono-cropping, industrial animal generation, and their lethal consequences including species extinction, loss of refuge, deforestation, genocides, and pathologization of the poor, to name some (Haraway, 2018). Clarke (2018) describes making kin as "daily actions that transform partial relations into deeper ones, kinship crafted through the exchange of things, sharing activities, and other practices" (p. 33). Thus, making kin with snails reintegrates affectivity, bodily attachments, material creativity, and passionate observation, in a form of knowing as care that avoids abstraction and distance. In this onto-epistemology, attending to care seems to be in the opposite pole of good parenting understood as a universal protocol of practices. As Puig de la Bellacasa (2017) affirms, it is by delving into the materiality, partiality, and embeddedness of care that we can become more ethically aware about its material consequences.

Intensifying ethics of care with photo and video matterings

I want to take a step further in grappling with the materiality and partiality of care-knowings in parenting by suggesting that issues and dilemmas of care can be intensified by technology and uses of technology that problematize both vision and what is to be in closeness with other kinds (Puig de la Bellacasa, 2017). It has been central to FSTS to recognize the agency of artifacts and the mediation of technology in the production of knowledge and worlds (e.g., Barad, 2007; Haraway, 1997). FSTS has actively questioned the anthropocentric, colonial, and positivist understanding of technology as a form of human enhancement and human progress. It has defended an ethical approach that connects specific uses of technology to its matterings and consequences toward other human groups, species, ecologies, and planet (Haraway, 2016). At the same time, FSTS has been generative in thinking radically and playfully with technology, and has argued for feminist ways of composing technology with bodies, places, and philosophical concepts that propel experimentation with alternative ways of living (Braidotti, 2013). Following this legacy, Puig de la Bellacasa (2017) affirms the need to make everyday technologies a matter of care, not of enhancement, by thinking in the consequential and situated matterings as well as overlooked possibilities of specific technological compositions. I want to consider this framework of ideas in order to think about how a phone camera was generative of care-knowings connected to our (Ingrid, Eric, and Laura's) walks and encounters with snails in the neighborhood.

I (Laura) often participated in the encounters with snails via practices of looking, talking, approaching, sensing through the lens of my phone camera. I have copious pictures of things that attracted my attention when being alongside snails. Figure 10.1 contains four photographs that reflect a small representation of this collection. The top left photograph depicts a snail moving in the middle of the street close to Ingrid's toes. It is an image captured after repeated experiences of finding snails detoured in the sidewalk after a short rain. In this case, I felt attracted to the fleshiness of Ingrid's skin in strange co-presence with the snail, both abstracted from the surroundings. The top right photograph is a close-up of a snail that Ingrid detached from the concrete as it retreated inside its shell. Again, it is a picture of what became a common gesture during our walks after learning that snails couldn't sense or anticipate danger. The bottom left photograph is of a cucumber slice and snails with what Ingrid described as "a loopy shaped snail poop." Ingrid quietly observed the animal defecating and appreciated the shape of its excrement. The bottom right photograph relates to the moment when Ingrid brought Banana to his first cucumber party and expected that Banana would instantly set direction toward the fresh cucumber slices. The acts of making these photos were situated in an ecology of sustained relational action between Ingrid, Eric, I, the snails, and the neighborhood. Although the

Figure 10.1 Composition of four individual photographs showing different encounters and interactions with the snails, Summer 2017

Photographs by Laura Trafí-Prats with iPhone camera app

pictures were authored with the orientations and gestures of my (Laura's) body, aesthetic choices, and the technical affordances of the phone camera, the act of making them brought group responses and connectedness. Ingrid and Eric often stopped with me and looked at what I was picturing. Sometimes this initiated a conversation about it or provoked further related actions. Making pictures made us notice things in the snails and the neighborhood that otherwise we would not had paid attention. In doing all this we (Ingrid, Eric, and I) progressively built an interest and knowledge on the snails and attuned toward their movements and presence.

Looking back at the pictures on our digital devices at home made us aware that the lure of being close and in contact with the snails combined with an increased awareness of their alterity (Puig de la Bellacasa, 2017). Looking and casually talking about the images unintendedly implicated us (Ingrid, Eric, and I) in the ontology of being alongside other kinds (Latimer, 2013) and its partial knowing made of connections and disconnections. For instance, in a conversation that Ingrid and I had around the top right photograph, Ingrid enacted a sense of connection with the snail by noting the tenderness of her hands holding the snail quite carefully. She explained that different from other snails who had retreated quite quickly inside the shell after being picked up, this one was especially unique because it lingered on. She valued how as a result of this, we could see its body in movement, partially contracting. Additionally, Ingrid pointed at a sense of disconnection by noticing how her body marginally fitted in the frame. This disconnection intensified when Ingrid asked me why I had not captured her face, which she remembered being quite close to the snail. This made her appreciate that in the picture the snail's eyes were facing away. This informal conversation seems to reveal that Ingrid intuitively felt that the image performed both a sense of connection and disconnection between human and animal. At the same time, the perception and recollection of the event did not produce a comparison human–animal where Ingrid emerged as sovereign but enacted a moment of mutuality in difference (Latimer, 2013), which the making, looking, and conversing with the aforementioned picture intensified. Cinema scholar Laura Marks (2002) argues that close-up bodied images, like Figure 10.1, generate a desire for closeness. It is in the specificity of this closeness that we (Ingrid and I) could recognize the unknowability of the other and the impossibility of knowing wholly. What is ethical in the practice of making-viewing images that mobilize both connection and unknowability is that such unknowability brings the possibility to stretch perception toward what resists being seen, sensed, and represented. Parenting with a posthumanist ethics of care needs experimental practices of "inhabiting the potentials of neglected perception, of speculative commitments that are about relating with, and partaking in, worlds struggling to make their other visions not so much visible but possible" (Puig de la Bellacasa, 2017, p. 118).

I want to stop on this idea that image-making could help us develop speculative and experimental commitments to worlds. I do this by considering Ingrid's growing interest and practices with a chest-mounted GoPro camera. In the context of the snail anecdotes, Ingrid wore this GoPro during the cucumber party when we (Ingrid, Eric, and Laura) returned Banana to the outside. At that point, Ingrid had already experimented wearing the GoPro on other walks and around the house and enjoyed the wide-angle lens: how it rendered unusual perspectives of her long hair propelled by the movements of her body, her arms and hands moving or holding something from the inside, and the exaggerated length of her legs when viewed from above. In an ethnography concerning the use of GoPro cameras in a primary school computer club, Caton and Hackett (2019) have described children's behavior with the chest-mounted cameras as one that dislodges the axis of perception from the height of adult eyes to the varying heights of children's chests, forcing a less adult-centric intimacy with the world—a world that is seen from a different perspective that raises aesthetic connection with environments and objects through novel and unexpected views.

Certainly, the video generated by the chest-mounted GoPro produced a different perspective from the ones embodied in Figure 10.1 made with a hand-held phone camera and Laura's point of view. As Elwick (2015) suggests, we may perceive and sense an event differently when seen from two different cameras, used in different ways and by different bodies. Elwick's (2015) proposition of perceiving an event from different perspectives contributes to the idea of a speculative stretching of perception argued above. It denaturalizes the adult's gaze that populates narratives of care and education, where images are used to speak about children's worlds objectively without questioning their mediating and materializing forces (Kind, 2013). It brings an ethical orientation in which Ingrid, Eric, and I have felt propelled to see images as relational fields where it is possible to feel connectedness while at the same time discuss the tensions and bifurcations that our different perspectives and perceptive modes enact (Puig de la Bellacasa, 2017).

Figure 10.2 showcases different frames extracted from video footage of the first cucumber party, where Ingrid wore the chest-mounted GoPro. Multiple bifurcations can be perceived in these images. There is an ongoing contrast between human bodies and how these bodies act around the cucumber party. I (Laura) am holding my phone camera in active practices of looking through and outside of it while tending my arms sometimes toward the snails, other times toward Ingrid, but I am never too far from the cucumber site. Ingrid's body, the peripheral parts that we can see through the GoPro (arms, legs, feet, hair), moves vividly along the perimeter of the building and occasionally returning to the cucumber site. She walks, runs, stops to observe, picks, walks, deposits. While moving, she projects long shadows, blocks and unblocks the low sunlight at dusk. The video captures the modifications of light, atmosphere, and space that Ingrid's movement materializes.

Figure 10.2 Selection of video-stills from the first cucumber party, Summer 2017

Video by Ingrid Caudill-Trafí with chest-mounted GoPro Hero 5. Manipulated and reproduced with kind permission of the videographer.

The GoPro images also deploy striking differences in scale, awkward framings, and the deformed optics that render the snails marginally visible, when in principle they were the motive of all this activity. The video emerges as a diagram of the embodied, fragmented and decentered gestures and actions (bodies walking, bodies standing, fingers holding, arms tending, torsos bending, eyes looking, phones capturing), and the movement (lines, forces, energies) that materialize the technologically mediated vision of environmental relational activity. A diagram is not a figure that represents or tells but one that maps fluctuating and incorporeal processes happening between bodies and static structures as pure abstract forces in a coextensive ongoing field (Zdebik, 2013). Perceiving this video diagrammatically permits to think it as more than a capture and closer to a complication where what is visible can only be articulable as expressive ways of collective being, occupying, making, and remaking the territory of the cucumber party. This productivity cannot be abstracted to form a cohesive sign. In this respect, the video footage as a diagram links to the mundane and to an ethics of care where vision does not correspond anymore to a humanist metaphor linked to clarity and unmediated access to a distinct world. As Puig de la Bellacasa (2017) argues, this is another way of thinking vision, where the experience of seeing touches us. More specifically, she calls it a *touching-vision* or a vision that *is moving* and felt in the body. What moves us, makes our body act, is to understand that our ways of seeing and knowing the cucumber party cannot be separated from our bodily engagements and interdependence with worlds. Touching-vision propels us to think speculatively with sensorial impressions and how our bodies can issue further action in our future engagements with these worlds. As Puig de la Bellacasa (2017) writes, "what we do in, to, a world can come back, reaffect someone somehow" (p. 115), and this is ethically compelling.

Watching for the first time the footage of the cucumber party filled me (Laura) with estrangement, struggle, and not-knowing. However, Ingrid enthusiastically reacted toward a section of the video that she described as "I am entering the sunbeams with my head." Ingrid enjoyed seeing her body moving toward the light projected by the sun and the visual effect of some sunbeams passing across streams of her long hair while darkening the rest of the image. From my perspective, the fact that part of the visual field had blacked out was an undesirable disturbance in the flow of action. Ingrid's thoughts made me consider Marks's (2000) point about film and video-images as mimetically sensed in the body, that is, the possibility of thinking in video images not as a transmission of signs to be read but as a mimetic experience, where "video bears witness to an object and transfers the presence of that object to viewers" (p. xvii). Connecting with Deleuzian (1989) cinema-philosophy, Marks (2000) considers that in images, like the one of "entering the sunbeams with my head," the body is freed to its own gestures that at the same time frees perception from the expected flow of action. Hence, it forces us to think. The image brought Ingrid to an unexpected moment of contemplation, which rather than propelling an intellectual response produced a body response that continued issuing and resurfacing over time. Time passed after the viewing, and one day Ingrid created a drawing, which featured us (Ingrid, Eric, and I) with very tiny bodies and extra-long shadows with extensive legs. Ingrid noted the connection of this feature with the GoPro wide-lens and how she recalled our shadows being rendered. The video-mediated experience of being alongside the snails affectively arose in Ingrid an interest for continuing the use of the chest-mounted GoPro in later neighborhood walks, as well as a motivation for further activation, perception, and thought around atmospheric and bodied interventions. This derivative activity attests to the incorporeality of the video-diagram as an abstract machine whose way of production operates in the indeterminate space between the visible and the articulable (Zdebik, 2013). What was done in/with the cucumber party came back and continued re-affecting our bodies, life, and movement in the neighborhood (Puig de la Bellacasa, 2017).

Repeatedly watching the video, sometimes by myself, and sometimes with Ingrid, intensified my awareness of how in the activity of the cucumber party, Ingrid, Eric, and I were not the only agents who saw, touched, acted. The video as a vision-touching technology deployed reality as an intra-acting more-than-human process of aliveness. The practices in, with, and after the video were "entangled with the very matter of relating-being" (Puig de la Bellacasa, 2017, p. 114) and displaced the anthropocentric idea of the human as "master subject-agent that appropriates inanimate worlds" (p. 115). The video, as embedded in the series of mundane anecdotes with the snails, is generative of a view of care in parenting that does not depend on reproductive practices: making babies, successful school test performers, and eventual competitive workers within global capitalism. As Haraway's (2018) thinking seems to suggest, care-in-parenting is an issue of *composition* or making kin not of reproduction. Making kin involves the building of situated patterns for learning to live and die with other-than-human others. Kin are not species, but assemblages made in daily and situated ways where parents, families, communities become more aware, learn, support, imagine, experiment with non-accumulative, non-extractive, non-individualizing ways of living as an ethics, aesthetics, and politics of decolonization and de-exploitation of parenting.

References

Allen, G. (2011). *Early intervention: The next steps*. London: HMG.

Barad, K. (2007). *Meeting the universe halfway: Quantum physics and the entanglement of matter and meaning*. Durham, NC: Duke University Press.

Baraister, L. (2009). *Maternal encounters: The ethics of interruption*. New York: Routledge.

Braidoti, R. (2013). *The posthuman*. London: Polity Press.

Burman E. (2007). *Deconstructing developmental psychology*. London: Routledge.

Caton, L., and Hackett, A. (2019). Head mounted, chest mounted, tripod or roaming?: Ontological possibilities for doing visual research with children and GoPro cameras,. In N. J. Kucirkova, Rowsell and G. Fallon (Eds.) *The Routledge international handbook of playing and learning with technology in early childhood* [Kindle version]. http://www.amazon.co.uk.

Clarke, A. E. (2018). Introducing making kin not population. In A. E. Clarke and D. Haraway (Eds.), *Making kin not population* (pp. 1–41). Chicago: Prickly Paradigm Press.

Clarke, A. E., and Haraway, D. (Eds.) (2018). *Making kin not population*. Chicago: Prickly Paradigm Press.

Clarke, K. (2006). Childhood, parenting and early intervention: A critical examination of the Sure Start national programme. *Critical Social Policy, 26*(4), 699–721.

Deleuze, G. (1989 [1985]). *Cinema 2: The time-image* (Trans. H. Tomlinson and R. Galeta). Minneapolis, MN: University of Minnesota Press.

Department for Work and Pensions (DWP) (2017). Improving lives: Helping workless families. https://www.gov.uk/government/publications/improving-lives-helping-workless-families.

Dermott, E., and Pomati, M. (2016). "Good" parenting practices: How important are poverty, education and time pressure?. *Sociology, 50*(1), 125–142.

Dermott, E., and Pomati, M. (2017). The cost of children: parents, poverty, and social support. *Poverty and social exclusion in the UK: Vol. 1: Volume 1-The nature and extent of the problem, 1*, 155.

Elwick, S. (2015). "Baby-cam" and researching with infants: Viewer, image and (not) knowing. *Contemporary Issues in Early Childhood 16*(4), 322–338.

Field, F. (2010). *The foundation years: Preventing poor children becoming poor adults*. London: Cabinet Office.

Foucault, M. (1984). What is enlightenment? (Trans. C. Porter). In P. Rabinow (Ed.), *The Foucault reader* (pp. 32–50). New York: Pantheon.

Frost, S. (2016). *Biocultural creatures: Towards a new theory of the human*. Durham, NC: Duke University Press.

Grosz, E. (2011). *Becoming undone: Darwinian reflections on life, politics and art*. Durhan, NC: Duke University Press.

Hackett, A. (2017). Parents as researchers: Collaborative ethnography with parents. *Qualitative Research, 17*(5), 481–497.

Haraway, D. (1997). *Modest_Witness@Second_Millenium.FemaleMan_Meets_OncoMouse: Feminism and technosience*. New York: Routledge.

Haraway, D. (2003). *The companion species manifesto: Dogs, people and significant otherness*. Chicago: Prickly Paradigm Press.

Haraway, D. (2016). *Staying with the trouble. Making kin in the Chthulucene*. Durham, NC: Duke University Press.

Haraway, D. (2018). Makin kin in the Chthulucene: Reproducing multispecies justice. In A. E. Clarke and D. Haraway (Eds.), *Making kin not population* (pp. 67–100). Chicago: Prickly Paradigm Press.

Jensen, T. (2018). *Parenting the crisis: The cultural politics of parent-blame*. Bristol, U.K.: Polity Press.

Kind, S. (2013). Lively entanglements: The doings, movements and enactments of photography. *Global Studies of Childhoo*d, *3*(4), 427–441.

Latimer, J. (2013). Being alongside: Rethinking relations amongst different kinds. *Theory, Culture & Society*, *30*(7/8), 77–104.

Marks, L. (2000). *The skin of the film: Intercultural cinema, embodiment and the senses*. Durham, NC: Duke University Press.

Marks, L. (2002). *Touch: Sensous theory and multisensory media*. Minneapolis, MN: Minnesota.

McRobbie, A. (2013). Feminism, the family and the new "mediated" maternalism. *New Formation*, *80*, 119–137.

Puig de la Bellacasa, M. (2017). *Matters of care: Speculative ethics in more than human worlds*. Minneapolis, MN: Minnesota.

Rose, J. (2018). *Mothers: An essay on love and cruelty*. London: Faber & Faber.

Rousell, D., and Cutter-Mackenzie, A. (2019). 'The Parental Milieu: Biosocial connections with nonhuman animals, technologies, and the Earth'. *Journal of Environmental Education*, *50*(2), 84–96.

Trafí-Prats, L. (2018). Mothering as an aesthetics of existence. In C. M. Schulte and C. M. Thompson (Eds.), *Communities of practice: Art, play and aesthetics in early childhood* (pp. 197–212). Cham, Switzerland: Springer.

Trafí-Prats, L. (2019). Thinking childhood art with care in an ecology of practices. In J. Osgood and M. Sakr (Eds.), *Postdevelopmental approaches to childhood art* (pp. 177–191). London: Bloomsbury.

Zdebik, J. (2013). *Deleuze and the diagram: Aesthetic threads in visual organization*. London: Bloomsbury.

11

Pondering the Pond: Ethical Encounters with Children

Bronwyn Davies
University of Melbourne, Australia

Introduction

I will ponder, in this chapter, the *matter* of ethical encounters between adults and children, where matter, in Barad's words "does not refer to a fixed substance; rather, *matter is substance in its intra-active becoming—not a thing, but a doing, a congealing of agency. Matter is a stabilizing and destabilizing process of iterative intra-activity*" (Barad, 2003, p. 822, emphasis in original). The concept of intra-activity refers to

> relationships between multiple bodies (both human and non-human) that are understood not to have clear or distinct boundaries from one another: rather, they are always affecting or being affected by each other in an interdependent and mutual relationship. (Barad, 2007, p. 152)

The matter and mattering of ethical encounters, then, in this conceptualization involves multiple relationships among humans, and among humans and more-than-humans.[1] Further, in a new materialist analysis of intra-active encounters, the automatic dominance of one group over another, or of one individual over another, and the automatic assumption of human dominance over the nonhuman world are called radically into question. Even dominance over oneself and one's own matter, of mind over body, demands further thought.

Adult domination is integral to usual modes of interaction between adults and children, where adults are likely to approach children with the intent of managing

---

[1] In new materialist analyses when we first extended our thinking to include beings or matter other than human we indicated our newfound inclusivity by writing about "humans and nonhumans," thus inadvertently setting up a binary. More recently there is a preference for "human and more-than-human," which avoids that linguistic trap.

and mastering them, and children's activity is often construed as learning mastery over their own bodies and their emotions. Such an ethics is based on a moral judgment about what we should each become, and it imposes "from a superior vantage point a definition of Being that presumes to judge and find lacking" (Wyatt and Davies, 2011, p. 107).[2] Ethics, if framed in terms of moral judgment and mastery, will most likely be focused on curbing adult violence and maximizing children's development of mastery over themselves, rather than an opening up of creative strategies and engagement with the not-yet-known.

I want to explore here this different kind of ethics, a new materialist ethics, focused on intra-active encounters among people, and among people and things. *Things*, in Bennett's analysis, are what we encounter when we give up our epistemological domination of objects, where "objects are the way things appear to a subject—that is, with a name, an identity, a gestalt or stereotypical template ... Things on the other hand, ... [signal] the moment when the object becomes the Other ... when the subject experiences the object as uncanny" (Bennett, 2010, p. 2).

Figure 11.1 The pond and the ibis

---

[2]   For a full discussion of this version of ethics, and contrasted with a Deleuzian ethics, see Wyatt and Davies (2011).

In that encounter the subject recognizes the impossibility of objectifying the Other and searches for ways of knowing that which is rising up toward it (Cixous, 1976; Mitchell, 2005). In such encounters with the unknown/unknowable Other, Barad advocates "the ongoing practice of being open and alive to each meeting, each intra-action, so that we might use our ability to respond, our responsibility, to help awaken, to breathe life into ever new possibilities for living justly" (Barad, 2007, p. x).

This chapter is an exploration of that intra-active practice of being open and alive to each meeting. I will ask: How might we put such an injunction to work with children by generating ethical encounters that are open and alive to both human and more-than-human others, to affecting and being affected by the other, in the joint project of finding ways to live justly?

The story I begin with is of a boy, his mother, a pond, and the intra-actions among them. I was sitting by a pond in the Botanic Gardens, near my home in Sydney, when this small drama began to unfold (Fig 11.1).

A small boy picked up a large palm frond, much bigger than himself, and threw it into the pond. Just before he threw it, his mother, sitting nearby, yelled "no!" He then picked up a very large stick and glanced at her. She shouted "no!" again, and he threw it into the pond. The third time, he picked up a smaller stick, and when his mother yelled "no," he hid it surreptitiously behind his back, glancing at me, as if to say, "see how cunning I am, she doesn't know I am still holding it." The mother turned her face away from the boy and the pond; her body registered futility and exhaustion. The boy threw his smaller stick and then began looking for a larger one. He continued to throw sticks while his mother looked away, but his game seemed to be less fun, once the edge of danger, that her shouts had given to his game, had ceased.

Quite apart from the fact that my own peace by the pond was shattered, I was distressed at the harm that the boy's game was potentially doing to the pond and to its inhabitants. I wondered if the pond was able to accommodate the boy's careless play. Perhaps the gardeners would clear up after him. And what of me, I wondered, as the bystander? Could I have intervened and what might that intervention have looked like?

One readily available reading of the stick-throwing is that the boy was positioning himself as the active agent, the dominant one, a (male) positioning so ubiquitous it is barely noticed and not at all remarkable (Davies, 2008). As Bennett points out, cultural forms like the gender binary "are themselves powerful, material assemblages with *resistant* force" (Bennett, 2010, p. 1, emphasis in original). The boy's accomplishment of himself as a boy is, in this sense, a material assemblage of normative masculinity, that is, of a body capable of throwing objects larger than himself and of resisting opposition to the performance of his masculinity. Such material assemblages

> are not simply objects or things, but qualities, speeds, flows and lines of force. Their character is defined not by what they are, but by what they can do, or become. And they are always in the process of becoming, not through an intention to arrive at a pre-determined end-point, but through multiple encounters with emergent multiplicities. (Bansel and Davies, 2014, p. 41)

As I pondered the speeds and flows of this particular assemblage that the boy's game was generating, I realized, with a start, that there is a giant phallic symbol, an obelisk, in the middle of the pond (Fig 11.2). It had, in fact, taken me a long time to see the pond and appreciate it, as the obelisk had blocked any desire to linger; for months I had walked straight past it. At the time of my story I had so thoroughly learned to ignore the obelisk that I had forgotten it was there, thrusting up into the pond and dominating it.

Is it too fanciful to think of this phallic object, this thing, as having excited the boy into displaying his masculine strength and domination over the sticks, the pond, and the mother? Is the thing-power circulating primarily between the boy and the obelisk?

The history of human domination over this particular waterway is at least 230 years old. The freshwater spring in Sydney Harbour made it an ideal place for the First Fleeters, in 1788, to set up the British Colony of New South Wales.[3] Until the arrival of the British colonists, the local indigenous people had taken very good care of this and other sources of freshwater. The colonists, by contrast, set up their houses along the stream, then threw all their rubbish and excreta into it, polluting it so thoroughly that they eventually had to abandon it and search for another water supply. The bounty of the natural landscape was there, in their minds, for their use and presumed to be inexhaustible. It is curious to think about the acts of domination first played out right here by this pond that stretch back 230 years.

My ancestor, David Collins, was among those First Fleeters. He was eager to be recognized by his British masters as a worthy (masculine) subject. In responding to published eulogies offered to British soldiers, victorious in battle in other parts of the Empire, David Collins asked why he and his fellow officers, who were building the colony of New South Wales, might not also be recognized as British subjects who were contributing to the glory of Empire. Surely, he argued in his

---

[3] New South Wales at that time was conceived as the entire east coast of the continent, stretching from the northern tip of Cape York to the southernmost part of what is now Tasmania and stretching as far inland as the British could as yet imagine.

Figure 11.2 The obelisk

journal, bringing British civilization to savages, and transforming the convicted British outcasts into decent men and women, was a glorious enterprise?

> Though labouring at a distance, and in an humbler scene, yet the good, the glory, and the aggrandizement of our country were prime considerations with us. And why should the colonists of New South Wales be denied the merit of endeavouring to promote [British values], by establishing civilization in the savage world; by animating the children of idleness and vice to habits of laborious and honest industry; and by shewing the world that to Englishmen no difficulties are insuperable? (Collins, *Account*, p. 55)

The stream of freshwater, which came to be known as the Tank Stream, after the tanks they built to contain its water, was fed by wetlands that now lie underneath King Street in the middle of the city. In establishing the glory that was to come, axes rang out on the forests that surrounded the stream.

> The spot chosen for this encampment [he wrote] was at the head of the cove, near the run of fresh water, which stole silently through a very thick wood, the stillness of which had then, for the first time since the creation, been interrupted

by the rude sound of the labourer's axe, and the downfall of its ancient inhabitants; a stillness and tranquillity which from that day were to give place to the voice of labour, the confusion of camps and towns, and the "busy hum of its new possessors." (Collins, 1798, p. 4)

Two hundred and thirty years later, the sticks and branches were mobilized by the boy to continue the history of this colonial *spacetimemattering*.

But moral judgment of my ancestor, or of the boy, or of the exhausted mother, is not relevant here. Moral judgment serves as a self-protective measure, placing a barrier between the one who judges and the one who is judged. It abjects the other, spitting them out as if they are foul and not part of oneself "(which is never one or self)" (Barad, 2014, p. 182). If I engaged in such judgment, as I confess I did for some minutes after I witnessed the boy-stick-mother assemblage, I would effectively reinforce my self-righteous borders, shutting myself off from the entangled intra-actions of the assemblage and to any understanding of the spacetimemattering it was part of.

Deleuze suggests that instead of moral judgment, we ask of the other "What is it to be this? What makes the just-thisness of you, in this moment?"

> You ask yourself how is that possible? How is this possible in an internal way? In other words, you relate the thing or the statement to the mode of existence that it implies, that it envelops in itself. How must it be in order to say that? What manner of Being does this imply? You seek the enveloped modes of existence, and not the transcendent values. (Deleuze, 1980, np)

To ask that question, how is it possible, in an internal way, I want to go back in time a little, to a day by the pond before the boy-stick-obelisk assemblage formed itself, in order to bring the thing-power of the pond more clearly into my story, as another *actant* in the assemblage. An actant, or source of action, "can be human or not, or most likely, a combination of both" (Bennett, 2010, p. 9): "An actant never really acts alone. Its efficacy or agency always depends on the collaboration, cooperation, or interactive interference of many bodies and forces" (Bennett, 2010, p. 21).

The concept Bennett works with, similar to Barad's intra-action, is "a shared, vital materiality" (Bennett, 2010, p. 14) that opens up among humans and among humans and Others, and which, she argues, puts the violent hierarchy of anthropocentrism and essentialist subjectivities under erasure. She asks, "Why advocate the vitality of matter?" and she answers:

> Because my hunch is that the image of dead or thoroughly instrumentalized matter feeds human hubris ... by preventing us from detecting (seeing, hearing,

smelling, tasting, feeling) a fuller range of nonhuman powers circulating around and within human bodies. (Bennett, 2010, p. ix)

And so I turn to my own story of intra-action, or shared vital materiality, with the pond:

> I was lying on a bench beside the pond. It has lavender colored water lilies, a family of dusky moorhens and two brown ducks. There are ibis, too, who fly in to enjoy the shade at the edge of the pond, sheltered as it is by an overhanging giant water gum and a vast weeping lilly pilly. The ibis migrated to the city decades ago when there was a severe inland drought and, like me, they never went back. Nearby there is a coffee shop and there are chairs and tables outside.

> Lying on my bench, looking up through the canopy of leaves (Fig 11.3).

> I feel enveloped and restored by the pond. It is alive with its own life, its own means of staying alive and supporting the life of the birds, and the life of the pond. That life-sustaining energy laps out and envelops me. I become, for the time I lie there on the bench, a member of the pond, partaking of its life, the affect flowing in between one body and another—an uncanny exchange, so subtle that it lies before awareness, and resists representation.

Figure 11.3 The Giant Water Gum canopy

There is a seeming difficulty, even absurdity, in trying to find words for the thing-power or vital materiality of the pond. I have no doubt that the matter of my body was affected by the pond, but I don't have the concepts to adequately "acknowledge the obscure but ubiquitous intensity of [its] impersonal affect" (Bennett, 2010, p. xiii). It is through the work of artists and writers who use syntax, lines, and colors to "raise lived perceptions to percepts and lived affections to affect" (Deleuze and Guattari, 1994, p. 170) that the intra-action might begin to be put into words, making legible the intensities and flows in between the materiality of my body and the vital materiality of the pond. For now I must depend on the images and small videos I have made on my iPhone and some help from new materialist thinking.

As I sat by the pond, I was emergent with the pond, in my openness to being affected by it and its vital materiality. In my openness to being affected by the pond I came to know it, and myself, differently—without borders, without ascendance, without mastery, and without words. I began to know what the pond could do by entering into composition with it. As Deleuze and Guattari say: "We know nothing about a body until we know what it can do, in other words, what its affects are, how they can or cannot enter into composition with other affects, with the affects of another body" (Deleuze and Guattari, 1987, p. 257). In this reconfigured assemblage of shared materiality with the pond, what comes to matter?

Barad (2007) argues that "intra-acting responsibly as part of the world means taking account of the entangled phenomena that are intrinsic to the world's vitality, and being responsive to the possibilities that might help us and it flourish" (p. 396). In becoming aware of my shared vibrant materiality with the pond, I came to understand that the pond is a vital materiality, and that it matters. Together, we became part of the "entangled phenomena that are intrinsic to the world's vitality" (Barad, 2007, p. 396). I was not separate from the pond, but "of the world in its ongoing intra-activity" (Barad, 2003, p. 828). As such, my responsibility toward the pond became more than a bunch of idealistic words, but a will to care for the pond as being of me and me of it.

I wonder, then, how might the boy-stick-obelisk assemblage shift from the re-citation of mastery and dominance to one of interdependence and shared material vitality? How might the boy "cultivate the ability to discern nonhuman vitality, to become perceptually open to it" (Bennett, 2010, p. 14)? In trying to answer that question I run into my own epistemological limits; my existing language is inadequate and may even work against me, because of the way "conceptualization automatically obscures the inadequacy of its concepts" (Bennett, 2010, p. 14). The task I have set for myself (and this is my response to the boy-stick-obelisk assemblage) is one of envisaging what an ethical encounter in the boy-stick-obelisk assemblage might become while remaining aware of the limiting force of the concepts I, or he and his mother, might draw on.

Emergent listening

Habituated ways of thinking about the boy and his sticks involve listening-as-usual, which relies on repetition. Listening-as-usual picks up on and lodges itself within the striations that make up the orderly, everyday world. Listening-as-usual to the boy–mother encounter is to hear, for example, a willfully naughty boy and a negligent mother, and to conclude that the boy needs to be taught to obey his mother and the mother needs to acquire some parenting skills. Both mother and boy can be exposed to moral judgment and found to fall short. Listening-as-usual can ask questions only in terms of already laid down concepts, and in mobilizing them, cement both their certainties and their limitations. To interrupt those certainties and their limitations, Bennett suggests, "what is also needed is a cultivated, patient, sensory attentiveness to nonhuman forces operating outside and inside the human body" (Bennett, 2010, p. xiv). Such an attentiveness involves emergent listening (Davies, 2014).

Emergent listening enables the listener to enter into composition *with* the pond, with a knowledge of the pond that comes from "sensory attentiveness to nonhuman forces." Emergent listening is open to what it doesn't know, and in some sense works against the self of the listener and the desire for fixed, striated, already-given concepts and methods. Through emergent listening, we open ourselves to the entangled vital materialities, our own and others', and to an awareness of their capacity to affect each other: "Our capacity to affect each other, to enter into composition with others both enhances our specificity and expands our capacity for thought and action" (Davies, 2014, p. 20). Such agency is distributed and multiple, and within that entangled multiplicity, each being is both emergent and vividly alive—open to being affected, not just by words, or within the terms of existing relations, but by percepts and affects, by things in the world (both human and more-than-human), whose force may be both uncanny and vital.

Imagination

Curiously, near to the pond of this story, there is another larger pond where a very different scenario plays itself out repeatedly. Fathers and their children can be seen peering into the pond and pointing. The bigger pond is full of eels that occasionally snatch small birds landing on the surface. The larger birds may also be seen snatching small eels. No one throws sticks into this pond—rather they stare with rapt attention at the lifeworld of the pond, wondering about it. The pond of my story, by contrast, does not have such attention-grabbing, gory features. Apart from the obelisk, its delights are subtle, and it takes more work to imagine what might be going on.

What if the mother had stood by the pond with the boy and drawn his attention to the wonder of the family of moorhens with their bright red legs and faces, and ducks duck-diving, tails in the air, foraging for food at the bottom of the pond, or marveled with him at the reflection of the trees on the surface of the water, perhaps showing him how to make small movies on her iPhone of their rippling reflections. In entering into composition with the pond, her own vitality might have revived, and she might have carried her son with her into a quite different assemblage that was open to the unexpected and the uncanny.

She might have listened with him to the trickling sound of the small waterfall or looked with him at the ibis's feet as it stands on the railing, toes curled around the rail like fingers and thumb, then turning around and shifting all toes in the same direction. They might have marveled together at the fact that the ibis's feet, while made up of the same bones as his own feet, have got the dexterity of a hand as well as the strength of a foot. They might have looked up at the spreading canopy of the Giant Water Gum[4] and seen the intense blue of the sky through its leaves. Such observations do not need to be heavy and didactic, but playful open-ended wondering and listening with all their senses, to each other and the pond. Children love to put their imagination to work beside water, and they gain great pleasure from doing so, as Somerville's research with children by the river has shown (Somerville, 2017).

Curiosity

There are so many questions that might pique curiosity once the vitality of the pond is registered in its material relation to the human bodies by its side. Where does the water come from into the pond? It is possible to discover a series of

---

[4] A *Syzigium Francisii*—rainforest tree of northeastern NSW and south Qld.

waterfalls and bridges, and still further up, to find the pipes through which the water flows in, from under the city (Fig 11.4 and 11.5).

And where does it come from before that? Is it in fact part of the same Tank Stream that the First Fleeters found in 1788 that enabled them to live here and colonize this country? Did the building of the city and the sealing of the roads destroy the wetlands that supplied the water in the first place? Does Sydney have any wetlands left? Can we discover more about wetlands and the work they do in filtering the water? Can we explore the way sandstone acts as a water filter and was used as such by the early settlers? Were any of the sandstone walls, still there, built by the convicts who came out on the First Fleet? The possible questions are endless.

Such listening, imagining, and questioning can work to interrupt the striations of unquestioned human dominance and exploitation, and open the possibility of a sensuous enchantment with the pond. Such enchantment is dependent on the moods and sensibilities that emerge in intra-action with the shared, material vitality of the pond. Such openness enables the

Figure 11.4 The first small waterfall

Figure 11.5 Water flowing from under the city

letting go of the desire for "identity" (of one and self) and opens instead the possibility of experiencing oneself as a vital materiality, and as such, one of many things in intra-action with a world of things: "Human power is itself a kind of thing-power ... [Our bodily materiality can be understood as] lively and self-organizing, rather than as passive or mechanical means under the direction of something nonmaterial, that is, an active soul or mind" (Bennett, 2010, p. 10).

Ethical encounters depend on the development of such affective sensibilities: "If a set of moral principles is actually to be lived out, the right mood or landscape of affect has to be in place" (Bennett, 2010, p. xii):

> Moments of sensuous enchantment with the everyday world—with nature but also with commodities and other cultural products—might augment the motivational energy needed to move selves from endorsement of ethical principles to the actual practice of ethical behaviors. (Bennett, 2010, p. xi)

(In)Conclusion: Ecological encounters

Bennett makes a strong claim that

> the bodily disciplines through which ethical sensibilities and social relations
> are formed and reformed are *themselves* political and constitute a whole
> (underexplored) field of "micropolitics" without which any principle or policy
> risks being just a bunch of words. There will be no greening of the economy,
> no redistribution of wealth, no enforcement or extension of rights without
> human dispositions, moods and cultural ensembles hospitable to these effects.
> (Bennett, 2010, p. xii)

I began this chapter with a chance encounter by a pond, open to the pond, but at
first not open to the boy-stick-obelisk-mother assemblage on that particular day.
I was peculiarly affected by the boy and his participation in the *spacetimemattering*
of human domination over the waterway. As Schulte observes:

> We don't always have the power to decide which problems receive our attention,
> nor do we have the leverage to decide how long we linger with them. Rather,
> problems arise from and are contingent [on] the encounters we have with
> something or someone, encounters that force thought to rise up and that move us
> to think something we never thought we could ever think. (Schulte, 2016, p. 147)

The encounter with the boy and his assemblage took me in very surprising
directions, toward new ways of thinking about ethical encounters, not just
among humans but also with the more-than-human. The trail of thought and
affect brought me to a point similar to Guattari when he said that the problems of
ecology are "as much a matter of culture-and-psyche formation as ... of watershed
management and air quality protection" (Bennett, 2010, p. 114). I came to an
understanding that our capacity for ethical encounters with others, both human
and more-than-human, depends on some of those shifts in understanding
that come from a comingling and entering into a shared composition with the
pond. Bennett offers a challenge to old refrains that emerge from this newfound
appreciation of matter:

> Each human is a heterogeneous compound of wonderfully vibrant,
> dangerously vibrant, matter. If matter itself is lively, then not only is the
> difference between subjects and objects minimized, but the status of the
> shared materiality of all things is elevated ... Such newfound attentiveness
> to matter and its powers will not solve the problem of human exploitation or

oppression, but it can inspire a greater sense of the extent to which all bodies are kin in the sense of inextricably enmeshed in a dense network of relations. (Bennett, 2010, pp. 12–13)

And so … I have invited you here, to sit by my pond and to comingle with it, and with the ibis, the trees, and the boy. I have asked you to come with me in imagining a world not full of moral judgment and lack but a world full of wonder and response-ability. I have asked you to shed some old refrains and open yourself up to new ways of imagining your place in the world and new ways of listening to the world—and to wondering what is possible.

References

Bansel, P., and Davies, B. (2014). Assembling Oscar, Assembling South Africa, Assembling affects. *Emotion Space & Society*, *13*, 40–45. http://dx.doi.org/10.1016/j.emospa.2014.04.002.

Barad, K. (2003). Posthumanist performativity: Toward an understanding of how matter comes to matter. *Signs: Journal of Women in Culture and Society*, *28*(3), 801–831.

Barad, K. (2007). *Meeting the universe halfway: Quantum physics and the entanglement of matter and meaning*. Durham, NC: Duke University Press.

Barad, K. (2014). Diffracting diffraction: Cutting together-apart. *Parallax*, *20*(3), 168–187.

Bennett, J. (2010). *Vibrant matter. A political ecology of things*. Durham, NC: Duke University Press.

Cixous, H. (1976). Fiction and its phantoms: A reading of Freud's Das Unheimliche (The "Uncanny") (Trans. R. Denommé). *New Literary History*, *7*(3), 525–548.

Collins, D. (1798). *An account of the English colony in New South Wales*. Vol 1. Sydney: A.H. and A.W. Reed.

Davies, B. (2008). Re-thinking "behaviour" in terms of positioning and the ethics of responsibility. In A. M. Phelan and J. Sumsion (Eds.), *Critical readings in teacher education: Provoking absences* (pp. 173–186). Rotterdamn, Netherlands: Sense Publishers.

Davies, B. (2014). *Listening to children: Being and becoming*. London: Routledge.

Deleuze, G. (1980). "Cours Vincennes" 12/21/1980. Accessed February 10, 2010. http://www.webdeleuze.com/php/texte.php?cle=190andgroupe=Spinozaandlangue=2.

Deleuze, G., and Guattari, F. (1987). *A thousand plateaus: Capitalism and schizophrenia*. London: Athlone Press.

Deleuze, G., and Guattari, F. (1994). *What is philosophy?* New York: Columbia University Press.

Mitchell W. J. T. (2005). *What do pictures want? The lives and loves of images*. Chicago: Chicago University Press.

Schulte, C. M. (2016). Possible worlds: Deleuzian ontology and the project of listening in children's drawing. *Cultural Studies ↔ Critical Methodologies*, *16*(2), 141–150.

Somerville, M. (2017). (Becoming-with) water as data. In M. Koro-Ljungberg, T. Loyonten and M. Tesar (Eds.), *Disrupting data in qualitative inquiry: Entanglements with the post-critical and post-Anthropocentric* (pp. 35–48). New York: Peter Lang.

Wyatt, J., and Davies, B. (2011). Ethics. In J. Wyatt, K. Gale, S. Gannon and B. Davies (Eds.), *Deleuze and collaborative writing. An immanent plane of composition* (pp. 105–129). New York: Peter Lang.

12

Questions of New Materialist Ethics

Heather Kaplan

University of Texas at El Paso, USA

As a self-proclaimed early childhood art education researcher, questions of ethics are inherently always a consideration in my work as a researcher. Indeed, these considerations begin with the institutional review board's classification of children as a special population requiring additional protections and provisions. This is by no means where concern for children as research subjects and ethical consideration end. The fields of childhood studies, early childhood education, and early childhood art education are deeply invested in the question of how a researcher and research project are ethical when acting and being enacted with children (Corsaro, 1985; Davies, 2014b; Gallacher and Gallacher, 2008; Schulte, 2013; Thompson, 2009, 2017; Thorne, 2001). Thus, it is a tradition in our fields to consider the researcher's position in relation to the children we study.

More recently, we have as a field taken up questions and methods of new materialism that have further complicated this ethic and how research with children changes when its social and material realities are expanded to include objects, things, and other nonhuman actors. Where once early childhood may have asked what is ethical when working with children, we now ask, "How does this research provide for or emerge within a relation that embodies a greater ecoethic between researcher, child, and objects" (Davies, 2014a, 2014b; Kaplan, 2017; Kind, 2013; Lenz Taguchi, 2009; Murris, 2016; Mustola, 2017; Olsson, 2009; Pacini-Ketchabaw, Kind, and Kocher, 2017; Schulte, 2016; Trafí-Prats, 2017) or "How does research emerge from an action produced by actants, Bennett (2010) and Latour's (1988) term meaning elements—subject and object—that produce an action?" This shift away from being a researcher and being ethical toward doing research and possibly doing ethics is a hallmark of relational and new materialist approaches to research. It indicates what Davies

(2014b) refers to as an "emergent process, in which subjects and objects become different in the encounters through which they emerge and go on emerging differently" (p. 740).

As a researcher who claims the subject position of researcher and who studies with children and objects, I wonder about the location of ethics in a relation. Can the researcher release his or her ethical responsibility to the relation? Is there something inherently subject-centered about the researcher's position and role that cannot or possibly should not be relinquished to the forces of the relation? I also wonder if there is more involved than a mere shift from thinking to practice or in other words, a shift from being ethical to doing ethics? In order to explore these questions, this chapter describes differences in research practices, positions, and ultimately ethics assumed during two qualitative research endeavors. The first endeavor involved a relational, new materialist approach to research that was conducted in a childcare center that was affiliated with a large Midwestern university. The second involved (ultimately failed) forays into observational research attempted at a local high school in the Southwest. This chapter will compare approaches and research assumptions in both experiences and the comparison will assist in thinking about the nature of ethics in relational and new materialist research and will act as a way of troubling and questioning the location of ethics. Ultimately, this chapter asks if ethics in research are truly able to unsettle the subject-centered researcher regardless of claims to co-constitutiveness.

Completing my dissertation research in an early childhood center in a Midwestern university felt very different from another (failed) research foray in a local public high school. This had much to do with the difference between the circumstances of each study, including a more situated researcher position, differing site experience with research in general and especially with emergent research and curriculum, and different expectations of the research findings and outcome. The following paragraphs describe the studies in order to give a background understanding of each. Later, I will discuss the "location" of the ethical decision to not continue the second study.

The first study

The first study involved a relational approach to research in a university childcare center in the Midwest. My relationship with the site did not begin as a formalized research relationship. I first entered this site hoping to volunteer with a class that was interested in artmaking, and I did this in the hopes of gaining more knowledge about young children so that I could feel more authentic in an undergraduate class that I was teaching and to be of more help to my students. I spent an entire year volunteering one day a week (on Wednesdays) where I observed and made art with young children ages three to five. Throughout this time I built relationships with them and the co-teachers in the classroom. In that first year the teachers asked me to take a more active role of helping to plan and facilitate art experiences with and for the children.

It was not until after over a year of volunteering and helping to facilitate art experiences that I approached the teachers and administration with the intention of doing more formalized learning and research. This is significant because it meant that I had not only formed relationships with the children, co-teachers, and administration, but I was also already a participant in the classroom, making my research position that of a participant observer and part of a relation.

According to Bernard (2011), a participant observer does "all the everyday things that everyone else does" and "become(s) inconspicuous by sheer tenaciousness" (p. 259) while separating enough to observe (collect) and analyze data. For me this meant that for two and half years I was a weekly participant in the preschool classroom performing activities alongside both the children and the teachers. Among other things, I played with blocks, Magna-Tiles, Legos, and Matchbox cars, explored the sensory table, drew pictures and made art, read books, and sat side-by-side in circle time with young children. I also purchased and prepared art materials, planned art activities, tied shoes, monitored the restroom, mediated children's disagreements, helped with documentation, shared in student successes and concerns, and supported the children along with the teachers and other adults (university student workers). While these activities were performed and enacted with and among others, I also maintained my position as researcher—observing and analyzing.

The relationship that I had established in the classroom and the co-teacher's emergent approach to curriculum and knowledge were also significant in how my position was understood and the research process came to be. Because the co-teachers were familiar with emergent curriculums and approaches to knowledge and because they were familiar with a variety of approaches to educational research through their affiliation with the university as graduate school attendees and master's degree holders, they were open and supportive to my relational research and inquiry-based approach to artmaking. Ultimately, this allowed me the flexibility to ask different research questions and to approach the act of research as relation, meaning that I could consider Gallacher and Gallacher's (2008) understanding of subjectivity (including researcher subjectivity) as "ontogenetic" or as an "emergent, constitutionally unfinished 'almost-not-quite' ontology," which "rather than seeing actions as produced by the conscious intensions of preexisting subjects ... suggest(s) that subjectivity is performatively produced through the continuous unfolding of action" (p. 510). Here, this allowed me to not only consider how children and teachers, in the words of Barad (2007), "intra-act" or act in a relation, but it allowed me to look at the ways that objects and materials like paintbrushes, toy cars, and chalk pastels can act on others within a relation. This also meant that as an early childhood art education researcher, not only was I considering the ethics of how to be or how to act in a relation with children, but because paintbrushes, toy cars, and chalk pastels (and children for that matter) were considered active participants, the very constitution of the research ethic had shifted beyond the notion of possessing or being ethical and toward a notion of the ethical as performed, enacted, or shared.

The second study

The second research foray involved an invitation to learn more about a local high school's transition from a traditional art program to an integrated art program designed as a school within a school. The original art program was held in high regard and was what many might claim to be the heart of a high school that served many underprivileged students who might be making their transition into American life and culture. The new program promised similar opportunities for the underserved, but the role and function of art within it was yet to be clearly defined. Apparently struggling to make sense of art's pairing with one of the core subjects (science, in this case biology), the art teachers asked if I would be interested in coming to and observing a variety of the program's functions (student group exhibition night, team building with the (corporate) program facilitator, and observing the classroom) to learn more about the program with the implied understanding that this new program created many questions about the role of art in the high school curriculum. After observing the program both as an outsider and as a supervisor of student teachers that we placed in the school, I approached the teacher most involved with the new program about the possibility of doing research about art's role in the programmatic shift. He seemed excited at the idea and I proceeded to gather the correct permissions and access from both the university and the school district.

While readying the permissions, I got the sense that much of the reason that I was invited into this space to do research was that my expertise as a university researcher would help provide an expert understanding of programmatic change. However, I began to realize that that researcher position didn't feel right and was not aligned with how I wanted to conduct my research. Rather than my role feeling like that of an observer the need for me grew to feel at times interventionist or reactionary, and at other times it seemed like I was isolated and would not be given access to observe certain processes and relationships.

Ultimately, the project didn't proceed beyond the gathering of informed consent and student assent due to the extremely low rate of return of signed informed consent forms from the students enrolled in the classes. This and the lateness in the school year were the primary reasons that I did not force my way into the space and insist that we try to complete the project that semester or at the beginning of the next school year. A big factor in this decision was that access to and working within this particular population proved exceedingly difficult, but I would be remiss not to explore that very feeling that I would need to force my way in from outside, and how that positions me and my ethic as a certain kind of researcher and a certain kind of ethic.

> So what was it about this research that didn't feel right to me? And also, what does my unwillingness to pursue this research say about the location of research ethics?

The new materialist in me is tempted to say that the ethic rests or resides in the relation and might claim that the failure of the second research attempt is a shared failure between all the actants that would have co-constituted a relation or that never came to be in a relation. We could leave it at that, claiming that it was just a space where a relation never came to be. And yet, I know that as the researcher, this research endeavor was quite different from the first study, and much of that had to do with conditions and much had to do with my response as researcher to those conditions. Admittedly, my research position and subjectivity play a large part in this decision not to pursue the project. Some of the major differences included my heightened sense of expected expertise, that I was not a participant in the space, and that I did not have long-standing relationships with the school, students, teachers, and administration. In other words, I really wasn't embedded in the research site, and any entanglement that I was a part of seemed both larger than and inequitable to both myself and to the relation and the others in it. The work seemed to seek some objective truth larger than my research expertise but in this it also demanded an objectifying research approach I was uncomfortable performing. Furthermore, those who were involved in the study and most likely to regard the findings of my work of particular interest were not familiar with emergent approaches to curriculum or research and were for all intents and purpose alien to most forms of research.

That I had concerns about ethical research subjectivities and that I wasn't embedded in a ethnographic sense of research, combined with the sense that the school district "stakeholders" and teachers were hoping for definitive, applicable, replicable (positivist), and possibly interventionist answers to my observational study, were important factors in my decision not to retry the study the following year. I weighed these concerns against the knowledge that could have been generated by continuing the study and ultimately decided not to pursue this avenue of research.

A paradoxical asymmetry

This is where I think it gets complicated for thinking about ethics in a new materialist approach to research. Largely, this is because new materialism decenters the subject from its humanist position of privilege, and questions of ethics have been mostly centered around human thought and action. A big part of being a researcher, and also a big part of ethics, is this assumed humanist subject position. A large part of being a researcher, like being an artist, is calling yourself a researcher and what you do research. Like being an artist, being a researcher is about a way of seeing or approaching the world, but it is also a declaration, a naming, an act of representation from a subject position. It is a declaration that signals and claims that this is important, significant, and worthy. Moreover, a humanist ethic tells a researcher how to act or how not to act (upon their research subjects) in a research situation. New materialism complicates this understanding of ethical action as a location of humanist endeavor by proposing actors that are not human, such as paintbrushes, toy cars, and chalk pastels. Here, the shared action and agency of new materialism (among objects, things, and other nonhuman actors) presumably dislodges the researcher's assumed sole responsibility for ethical action. Released from the confines of humanistic research ethics that focus on the human as the subject of all ethical research action, we might ask, "What ethical actions do objects, things, and nonhuman actors perform?" Furthermore, considering research protections and historical precedent and previously established humanist protections, we might ask, "Can a paintbrush do harm?"

While objects and other nonhuman entities might act, we cannot presume that they can think through an ethical new materialist research relation, so this becomes the researcher's responsibility. Oddly this reveals a paradox in new materialism—one that creates a hyper-humanist sensibility, or an ethic in which the human actor becomes even more centralized when at the same time a hallmark of new materialism is how agency is dispersed from the human actor to the other actors in the entanglement. Bauman (1993) refers to this as the asymmetry of I-Thou and cites the following quote from Levinas (1985) to explain this relational asymmetry:

> Intersubjective relation is a non-symmetrical relation. In this sense, I am responsible for the Other without waiting for reciprocity, were I to die for it. Reciprocity is *his* affair ... I am responsible for a total responsibility, which answers for all the others and for all in the others, even for their responsibility. The I always has one responsibility *more* than the others. (p. 85)

Here Bauman (1993) explains that an ethical asymmetry is created that draws attention to the creativity or "condensation of creative power totally" (p. 86) (read agency) of the being that is human (read researcher) in comparison to others (human and non). Through its creative totality, this ethical asymmetry questions the dispersal of agency to the relation and to others (human and non).

Productive failure of thinking with research

Only now I can look past the sting of failure of the second site to see its inherent productivity. The complexities uncovered through thinking through the difficulty and unease of (not) doing research led to productive insights about the nature and experience of researching within the new materialist paradigm. While that does not reconcile the lost potential of the second research site, it has proved productive. Exploring these ideas has not only laid bare a contradiction within new materialist ethics but thinking through and theorizing them has strengthened my understanding of my own approach to research relations. In this way, the failure of the second site was what Bauman (1993) might consider an opportunity to repersonalize the problem of ethics and research, and it has given me reason to review the experiences at the first site, the childcare center, in order to acknowledge those practices.

At the first site, a Midwestern childcare center, much contributed to the sense of a productive new materialist research relation and to be entirely clear little of that had to do with my will to make it so. Rather, the relation seemed more to do with circumstances, people, practices, and ideas than anything that I alone could do—other than to respond and react to the relation. It was important to me that the teachers (at least) understood the varied nature of research. While it was convenient that they had participated in graduate study, this was not the only indicator that they understood the varied nature and value of research. Each worked to embody an emergent approach to curriculum and the entire childcare site, which consisted of multiple classrooms of infants, toddlers, preschoolers, and one kindergarten classroom, claimed to follow the Reggio approach. This meant that they were familiar with children's everyday explorations as forms of inquiry and investigation and it meant that they already understood the notion of research as emergent and unfolding around a set of questions. This more than anything else seemed to sustain the possibility of new materialist research at this site.

That is not to say that there weren't other cogent factors that this site provided. There were and they were important to establishing rapport and a research relation. They included such things as my sense of being embedded in the space as a participant observer, the co-teacher's underlying interest in art, children's artmaking, and an unsettled, explorative approach to materials and making, a dispersed and multiple sense of expertise and unknowing, and community support for the classroom program and my research by the site's administration, parents, and other teachers. While each of these was important to the productive research relation none of these were exclusive to a new materialist approach. To be sure each of these factors did contribute to an equitability in the ethical sense, but it was the parallel emergent approaches to curriculum and research that made this site equitable and ethical. Not only was the teacher's, parents', and children's exposure and understanding of research and its emergent character present but their understanding allowed for relations and intra-actions to unfold. Teachers and children curious to uncover material possibilities found themselves entangled with paint, clay, rain, Matchbox cars, with each other, and with me. Empathically this energy allowed me to be entangled with the research.

References

Barad, K. (2007). *Meeting the universe halfway: Quantum physics and the entanglement of matter and meaning.* Durham, NC: Duke University Press.

Bauman, Z. (1993). *Postmodern ethics.* Cambridge, NJ: Blackwell Publishers.

Bennett, J. (2010). *Vibrant matter: A political ecology of things.* Durham, NC: Duke University Press.

Bernard, H. R. (2011). *Research methods in anthropology: Qualitative and quantitative approaches* (5th edition). New York: AltaMira Press.

Corsaro, W. A. (1985). *Friendship and peer culture in the early years*. Norwood, NJ: Ablex Publishing Corp.

Davies, B. (2014a). *Listening to children: Being and becoming*. New York: Routledge.

Davies, B. (2014b). Reading anger in early childhood intra-actions: A diffractive analysis. *Qualitative Inquiry, 20*(6), 734–741.

Gallacher, L., and Gallacher, M. (2008). Methodological immaturity in childhood research? Thinking through "participatory methods." *Childhood, 15*(4), 499–516.

Kaplan, H. (2017). Circumspection in early childhood classrooms: Ontological forays into questioning, being, and making. In C. M. Schulte and C. M. Thompson (Eds.), *Communities of practice: Art, play, and aesthetics in early childhood* (165–183). New York: Springer.

Kind, S. (2013). Lively entanglements: The doings, movements, and enactments of photography. *Global Studies of Childhood 3*(4), 427–441.

Latour, B. (1988). Mixing humans and nonhumans together: The sociology of a doorcloser. *Social Problems, 35*(3), 298–310.

Lenz Taguchi, H. (2009). *Going beyond the theory/practice divide in early childhood education: Introducing an intra-active pedagogy*. New York: Routledge.

Levinas, E. (1985). *Ethics and infinity: Conversations with Philippe Nemo* (Trans. R. A. Cohen). Pittsburgh, PA: Duquesne University Press.

Murris, K. (2016). *The posthuman child: Educational transformation through philosophy with picturebooks*. New York: Routledge.

Mustola, M. (2017). Children's play and art practices with agentic objects. In C. M. Schulte and C. M. Thompson (Eds.), *Communities of practice: Art, play, and aesthetics in early childhood* (117–131). New York: Springer.

Olsson, L. M. (2009). *Movement and experimentation in young children's learning: Deleuze and Guattari in early childhood education*. New York: Routledge.

Pacini-Ketchabaw, V., Kind, S., and Kocher, L. (2017). *Encounters with materials in early childhood education*. New York: Routledge.

Schulte, C. M. (2013). Being there and becoming-unfaithful. *International Journal of Education & the Arts, 14*(1.5), 1–16.

Schulte, C. M. (2016). Possible worlds: Deleuzian ontology and the project of listening in children's drawing. *Cultural Studies ↔ Critical Methodologies, 16*(2), 141–150.

Thompson, C. M. (2009). Mira! looking, listening, and lingering in research with children. *Visual Arts Research, 35*(1), 24–34.

Thompson, C. M. (2017). Listening for stories: Childhood studies and art education. *Studies in Art Education, 58*(1), 7–16.

Thorne, B. (2001). Learning from kids. In R. M. Emerson (Ed.), *Contemporary field research: Perspectives and formulations*. Prospect Heights, IL: Waveland Press Inc.

Trafí-Prats, L. (2017). Learning with children, trees, and art: For a compositionist visual art-based research. *Studies in Art Education, 58*(4), 325–334.

13

Quantum Ethics: Intra-Actions in Researching with Children

Leslie Rech Penn

University of Georgia, USA

Lionel looks concerned. A lanky kindergartner in navy rugby and khakis, he stares at the camera, wide-eyed, knuckle in his mouth. Though I've been in his classroom six months and become a regular visitor during the class Writer's Workshop, it is only my second time video-recording Lionel's drawing. A fantasy enthusiast and Marvel Universe aficionado, Lionel often spends much of the writing period narrating action as he draws or explaining powers, gear, and relationships to his tablemates. Today he is quiet. He turns to stare at the empty page of his writing journal, a blank rectangle with lines underneath. His tablemates get organized with crayons and resources, Jonas already sounding out words for his story. As do many in the class, Lionel often spends more time drawing than writing and struggles to finish in the time allowed. Today, I'm unsure if he is more concerned about his work or the recording device, a small pink iPad, I hold upright in my lap. He stares at the white space, his fingers cramped around the stub of a pencil. Finally, he puts the tip to paper and begins—drawing first—starting with the teeth.[1]

The vignette above details an event in which Lionel, a six-year-old participant in an eight-month case study on drawing in a kindergarten writer's workshop, struggles to begin his classwork in the context of a busy classroom and a video-recorded research project. For me, this moment evokes what Barthes (2010) calls the *punctum*, the detail that pricks. It not only strikes an emotional cord in the possibility that I might be causing Lionel some discomfort but also illustrates many of the ethical issues with which I tangle when researching with children: the affect of observation, the agency of children (or lack of) in a research dynamic, and the ways research interpretations and writing shape, position, or fix phenomena, including children (Fig 13.1).

---

[1] Earlier versions of vignettes have been published in prior publications (Penn, 2019; Rech, 2016).

Figure 13.1 Lionel looks concerned

In this chapter, I examine the experience of researching with Lionel and ask myself a difficult question: Is my research practice ethical? What meanings do I conjure or leave out when I interpret or write about Lionel's classwork? What positions are employed? What politics are in play? Using Barad's (2007) diffractive method of analysis, I examine a drawing event that I have analyzed, presented on, and published about in the past in order to disturb the *apparatuses,* material-discursive practices such as observation, interpretation, and representation, embedded in qualitative research. I look critically at the intra-actions in research encounters with Lionel and posit the idea that a diffractive perspective offers an ethical intervention into the reflective tradition of representing children's experiences.

Researching children

Research on young children has historically been predicated on perspectives in which children were studied as objects in developmental or sociological phases of growth (James and James, 2012). From these points of view, children were relevant primarily in their progression toward adulthood. In the late twentieth century, academics in the social sciences advanced a sociology of children and childhood that focused on childhood as a concept, children as a distinct social group, and the child as an agentic social actor (Christensen and Prout, 2005; James and James, 2012; James, Jenks, and Prout, 1998; McNamee, 2016). This perspective reflects an ethical shift from the marginalization of children as immature and underdeveloped adults to children as active co-constructors of meaning in their own lives and in the social spaces of childhood. Today, *child-centered* research practices focus on research *with* children rather than *on* children, focusing on children's distinct voices, meaning-making, participation, and resistance (McNamee, 2016). Brostrom (2012) points out that postmodern perspectives have facilitated a child-centric focus in which researchers acknowledge "children's existing and emerging competencies, rather than on adult-like qualities they still lack" (p. 258). James and James (2012), however, warn that current research must maintain an ethical rigor that respects children "in their own right" throughout the research process (p. 17). One of the troublesome areas in observing, analyzing, and writing about children is that adults have a tendency to infer children's experience and that children have a tendency to perform for adults (Brostrom, 2012; Christensen and Prout, 2005). Brostrom (2012) argues that child-centered research attempts to account for issues with adult interpretations and ways in which "children themselves experience and describe their lives" (p. 259). But others caution that there are inextricable power imbalances and colonizing aspects in interpreting children's talk and actions (Meloni, Vanthuyne, and Rousseau, 2015; Waller and Bitou, 2011). Christensen and Prout (2005) suggest that multiple accounts of experience from children and adults will allow a deeper and more nuanced understanding than a "single version of the 'truth'"(p. 7). Likewise Meloni, Vantuyne, and Rousseau (2015) suggest that we consider ethics as an ongoing reflexive and relational dialog with children. I agree with both these points of view. I would also like to posit that critically examining and acknowledging our affect as researchers is also a valid way to engage in an ethical research practice. Within the discourses of validity and reliability in qualitative research, pointing out that researchers affect phenomena, change conditions, or influence subject and context, is a notion loaded with personal and professional tensions. But Barad's (2007) discussion of quantum theories, in particular Bohr's measurement interaction, the notion that measurement disturbs the object, that one cannot account for this unless the measurement *apparatus* itself is included in the equation, offers a way to consider mechanisms of qualitative research such as observation, interpretation, and representation as apparatuses—material-discursive practices that shape matter and meaning. Barad uses a *diffractive methodology*, a way of looking at phenomena that respects entanglements and illuminates differences, to disrupt the taken-for-granted knowledge and assumptions of the physical and social sciences. In her rich appropriation of quantum theories, she advocates for researchers to approach the universe, not as observers but as active participants that meet the universe halfway in its becoming. In this sense, she collapses Newtonian notions of distance and objectivity; "We are of the universe—there is no inside, no outside. There is only intra-acting from within" (p. 396). This perspective opens a space for a relational, entangled ethics of researching with children, one in which we acknowledge and embrace the responsibility that our affect as observers, measurers, interpreters has in co-constructing the world.

Agential realism

Barad's conceptions of *apparatus* and *diffraction* are embedded in a larger theory of agential realism, through which she uses the material interventions of quantum physics as a rhetorical tool to question human perceptions of knowledge and materiality. In agential realism, Barad (2007) adapts the theories of Niels Bohr to get at what she sees as the core lesson of quantum physics: "*We are a part of that nature that we seek to understand*" (p. 26). Necessary to an understanding of the world is an acknowledgment of our entanglement with it. Barad expands on Bohr's notion of phenomena as *intra-actions*, inseparable, mutually constituted components:

In contrast to the usual "interaction," which assumes that there are separate individual agencies that precede their interaction, the notion of intra-action recognizes that distinct agencies do not precede, but rather emerge through, their intra-action. It is important to note that the "distinct" *agencies are only distinct in relation to their mutual entanglement; they don't exist as individual elements.* (2007, p. 33)

Barad's theories move beyond a Newtonian physics in which objects have static, preexisting properties to the idea that matter is intra-actively produced via instruments of visualization or measurement, what Bohr termed *apparatuses*. She elaborates on the notion of apparatuses as material-discursive practices that produce matter and meaning. She points out that in certain experimental conditions and with certain measurement apparatuses, light behaves like a wave and in others, like a particle. Barad uses this example and others to illustrate how conditions, instruments, practices, and discourses determine the ways in which phenomena become defined. For example, changing historical practices and discourses in the sciences, those of calculation from geometry to algebra, from non-standardized to standardized reporting criteria, from geometric models to theories of physical optics, as well as political tensions within the science community, all contributed to the shifting form and meaning with which the phenomena of light has been measured and defined. She suggests that apparatuses are both political and discursive:

The basic idea is to understand that it is not merely the case that human concepts are embodied in apparatuses, but rather that apparatuses *are* discursive practices where the latter are understood as specific material reconfigurings through which "objects" and "subjects" are produced. (p. 148)

As well, Barad troubles the notion of representation in scientific research as a mirror image of reality: "Is the table a solid mass made of wood or an aggregate of discrete entities?" (p. 48). She uses the example of a scanning tunneling microscope (STM) that employs currents to feel around the surface of a specimen in a way similar to a blind person building up a mental image of an object by touching it: "Images or representations are not snapshots or depictions of what awaits us but rather condensations or traces of multiple practices of engagement" (p. 53).

Barad proposes diffraction as both a methodology of analysis and an alternative to representing reality. She draws from Haraway to distinguish between the concept of reflection, a mirror image, and diffraction, a fractured differential image:

As Haraway suggests, diffraction can serve as a useful counterpoint to reflection: both are optical phenomena, but whereas reflection is about mirroring and sameness, diffraction attends to patterns of difference. One of her concerns is the way reflexivity has played itself out as a methodology, especially as it has been taken up and discussed by mainstream scholars in science studies. (p. 29)

Barad sees diffraction as an apt way of engaging with the world. She proposes a diffractive apparatus, one that disturbs or interferes in discursive practices, as an ethical counter to reflective methods in which boundaries between object and subject or researcher and researched are predetermined:

Diffraction does not fix what is the object and what is the subject in advance, and so, unlike methods of reading one text or set of ideas against one another where one set serves as a fixed frame of reference, diffraction involves reading insights through one another in ways that help illuminate differences as they emerge: how different differences get made, what gets excluded, and how those exclusions matter. (p. 30)

In this chapter, my aim is to read my own research practice diffractively and to untangle the intra-actions in researching with Lionel and others. It requires drawing out the threads of cultural and historical discourses at play in my own work and illuminating the material-discursive apparatuses of qualitative research.

Qualitative apparatuses

Thinking diffractively about research with children, in particular about my research with Lionel, calls for a *genealogy*[2] of the entangled discourses at play, those of positivist science, qualitative research, developmental psychology, childhood studies, early childhood education, language and literacy education, anthropology, ethnography, thick description, photography, film studies, among others, including the more personal discourses of mother, teacher, and artist. To put it more succinctly, I need to consider how what has been said about something, in this case a child and his drawing, shapes my understanding of it. The "multiplicity of apparatuses," discursive practices whose trajectories intra-act in my research with Lionel determine the ways in which my work with Lionel was measured, imaged, and represented (Barad, 2007, p. 389). There is not

[2] Barad (2007) uses a Foucauldian genealogy to call attention to the discourses at work in the apparatus of the STM.

enough space in this chapter to account for all the intra-actions in this event, but in the following sections, I address the discursive apparatuses of observation, interpretation, and representation in narrative vignettes and images from one of Lionel's video-recorded drawing events.

Observation

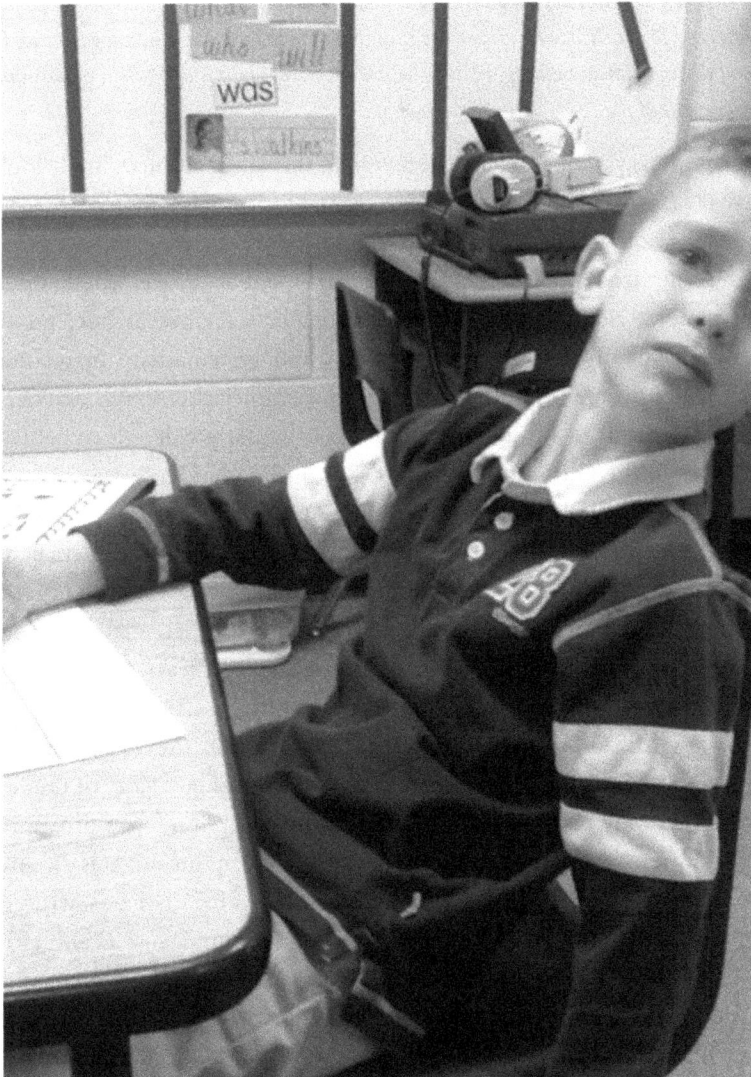

Figure 13.2 Lionel looks around the camera

Time is passing quickly in Writer's Workshop. Reluctantly, Lionel stops drawing and pulls out his folder of site words. He sounds out the first word in his story: "Ch … ba … ch … ch … ba … ka … chabaka … chabaka … cha … ba … ba … ba … aaaaa … ba … aaaa …" He looks at the video camera and then around the camera at me, "Can you please help me spell baa?" Though I'm still recording, I can't ignore a direct request for help. I mouth, "Ba … ahh …" He repeats, "Ba … aaaaaah," frowns, taps his pencil. He carefully writes one letter and looks up again, anxiety etched on his face. "Ch … ba … ka … U? U?" I have a difficult time remaining neutral and unengaged but tell him, "I can't help you when I'm filming. You can do it." He tries again, "Cha ba ka … Cha ba ka … Cha ba ka." His head begins to fall lower and lower. "I need a eraser," he mumbles. He throws out a hand, gesturing in silent dialog with something. Finally, he slumps in his chair and again looks around the camera at me, "Can you please help me?"

The terms *observation* and *documentation* in the social sciences imply looking objectively from a position outside the event. Documentation, particularly via field notes, photography, video recording, or audio recording, further removes the researcher from the event in that an instrument or device, whether pencil, paper, camera, video camera, etc., intercedes between researcher and event (Fig 13.2). Documentation, formalization, and systematicity in qualitative research have become signifiers of a rigorous empirical research practice (St. Pierre, 2016). In this way, documentation, particularly video documentation, contributes to the notion of objectivity. But in Barad's (2007) way of looking at things, all research is an intra-action. At the quantum level, observing phenomena disturbs it. In the event described above, the video camera behaves as both a disturbance and a measurement apparatus of the event. It intervenes with Lionel and I, becoming both a barrier and a surveillance mechanism, keeping us both in check. It also measures, visually at least, the intra-action between Lionel, site words, classroom spelling practices, discourses of success, failure, etc. As a recording device, it measures the height and width of a rectangle of reality. What it leaves out is the buzzing energy of the rest of the classroom, my body (a teacher-sized, authoritative body) in proximity to Lionel's, my tension in wanting to help, but not help. In this way it is discursive. It produces practice. It also prevents me from seeing that he's written an uppercase G and crossed it out and written another uppercase G and crossed it out. It's only when I go back and map the image of the actual drawing with the video that I see these two mistakes have occurred in an important term, that of the antagonist in his narrative: *solger*. This is a crucial intra-action to consider when trying to make sense of the struggle in Lionel's drawing event. The video data omits this reality. The video camera as a measurement apparatus has a perspective, one culturally embedded with a political agenda, video evidence as *truth*. Despite this, it is limited in its perspective. Researchers across disciplines (Barone and Eisner, 2012; Mitchell, 2011; Mohl, 2011; Pink, 2013; Rose, 2012) warn of the *iterative* nature of images. When we point the lens, focus it, frame it, we edit reality out of context. When we publish the image, we produce what we've edited. Barad (2007) explains the generative propensity of apparatuses: "Apparatuses produce differences that matter—they are boundary-making practices that are formative of matter and meaning, productive of, and part of, the phenomena produced" (p. 146). In this case, the video camera played and continues to play a part in several intra-actions: as a barrier between Lionel and I, one to which I was more susceptible to than he; as a frame for reality that edits material elements; and as a source of data that, on at least one occasion, limited the scope of my analysis. My point is not to frame video documentation as a suspect practice but to read it diffractively in multiple ways and to acknowledge it as a discursive practice. The video camera functions as both the apparatus of measurement and the meaning-producing medium. It blurs the line between object and subject. In Barad's (2007) view, understanding the inseparability of apparatus and object requires "multiple forms of literacy to make explicit the different apparatuses that are a part of the phenomenon being investigated" (p. 361).

Interpretation

Lionel is on word five of his story—Soldier. He wrestles with the sounds, "Sol-ger, sooool-ger, sol-ger, sol-ger." Lionel's tablemate, Jonas, has given up on his own work and leans on the table to watch Lionel cross out a mistaken letter. Lionel looks up, sees Jonas watching, and freezes. He gestures silently as if to say, what are you looking at? Jonas continues to stare. Lionel flushes and puts his head down, face in the crook of his arm. The tips of his ears are red (Fig 13.3). I can see him swallow. Jonas frowns, but makes no move to commiserate. It is a tense moment. Within a few seconds, Lionel pulls himself up, pulls his shoulders back, wipes his face on his sleeve, and sniffs. With only a few more minutes until lunch and recess, Ms. Walcott reminds the class to stay motivated, "C'mon, focus, focus". Lionel whispers the next big word in his sentence: "Strong, strong ... str ... ooooooooongggg ... str ... ooooooooongggg."

The video camera as apparatus is an easy analogy, one through which Barad's theories become clearly visible. More difficult to articulate is the idea of

Figure 13.3 Lionel puts his head down

interpretation in qualitative research as a discursive apparatus. The discourse of interpretation, grounded in traditions of anthropology and ethnography in which researchers infiltrate social groups and cultures to study, better understand, and explain meanings in everyday practices, implies that there is an underlying language to things that researchers can access in careful observation and analysis (Prasad, 2005). Interpretation as an instrument of research is fraught with tensions between observer, observed, spoken, unspoken, visible, and invisible and particularly problematic in research with children. For example, Meloni, Vantuyne, and Rousseau (2015) suggest that information can be interpreted from children's silences: "Silences, as withdrawals, need not be treated as non-data ... We may learn much more from interpreting these silences and hesitations than from analyzing what more vocal research participants have to say about a topic" (p. 118). But I would argue that in the silences, the tense moments in which we most want to help, researchers are more likely to reach for and infer meaning. In the vignette above, I inferred a particular frustration in Lionel's silence, framed it as a struggle: frustrated with his work, upset to the point that he has to stop, he hides it from his peers, the camera, me. I attributed the source of his frustration to anxiety about class expectations, peer evaluation, and the tensions of being video recorded. I also inferred that he experienced a resilient moment, one in which he experienced a renewed strength or focus that allowed him to continue. The manner in which I transcribed the video recording, the thick description of interpretation in the vignette, the choice I made to focus on that moment in particular in my analysis, all make up the larger picture of interpretation in which a meta-narrative of the child as hero emerges. The discourses I called on or put into play when I interpreted the event in this way include boys, boyhood, resilience, resistance, and every book I read as a child in which a child struggles, perseveres, and emerges stronger. Other interpretations are possible. It could be the case that the experience ruined the rest of Lionel's day or that what I interpreted as frustration was embarrassment triggered by an event between he and Jonas or Ms. Walcott's urging to *focus, focus*. I've often thought about what Lionel would have said if I'd shown him the video, asked him what he was experiencing in those moments.[3] Certainly, asking Lionel to comment on and collaborate in the interpretation of the event would have better met the ethics of *multiple accounts of experience* called for by Christensen and Prout (2005). But this also approaches something I've theorized on occasion when asking my sons about their drawings and listening to the stories change in the multiple retellings; the idea that meanings for children are both fluid and playful and that interviewing and asking questions are intra-actions that not only provoke but produce new meanings. Interpreting as an apparatus then becomes less like transcribing a hidden language and more like producing a collaborative hybrid of co-constructed meanings. Thinking diffractively about ways in which researchers make sense of phenomena engenders a shift from the perspective of researcher as interpreter to one of co-contributor to a shared account.

---

[3] In my apprehension about taking up school time, the complexity of accounting for children's performances, and the immediacy and fluidity of drawing events, I had made the decision to refrain from directly interviewing students during drawing events over the course of the project.

Representation

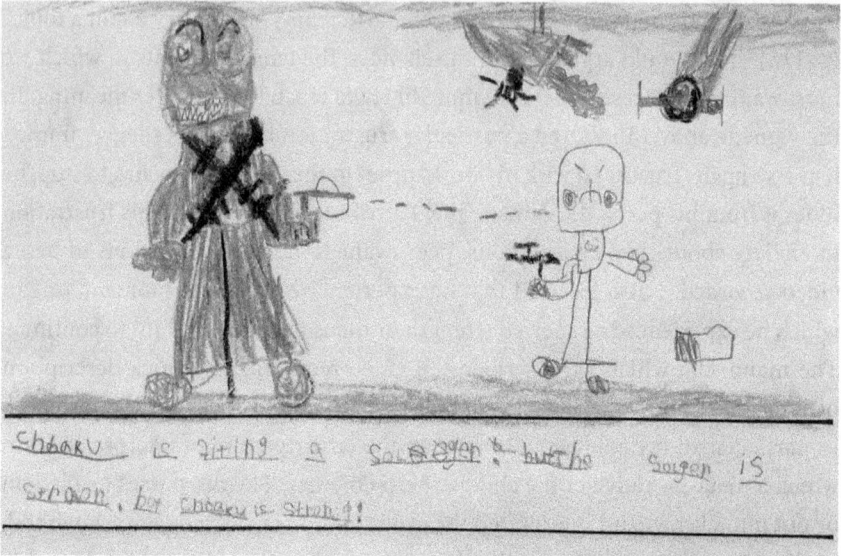

Figure 13.4 Lionel finished

It is the end of the writing hour. Ms. Walcott calls each table to line up for lunch. Only Lionel is left, still working. He looks up, looks at the camera, puts his head back down and continues to write. Ms. Walcott responds quickly, "Ms. Nanda, can you please bring Lionel with you? He is really focused over there and I don't want to mess that up." The rest of the class, lined up at the door with coats and lunchboxes, chatter quietly. Lionel is bent over his work, left hand framing the text as he writes, carefully laying down the final letters. He sits back and puts his pencil down, "Finished."

In the final vignette, I frame a happy ending. Lionel, despite the struggle, shows perseverance and finishes his work. But there are other ideas embedded in this moment that I don't draw attention to in the description: the academic pressure for both children and teachers to finish, to have a completed record for evaluation and evidence of learning, the fact I am still recording, the possibility that Lionel was still working when the class lined up because Ms. Walcott did not call him to line up or that she suggested he was *too focused* to leave. Like the video camera, I framed an image and focused its meaning. In reporting, both qualitatively and quantitatively, we leave out more than we represent and rarely question that dynamic.

Barad (2007) describes Eigler's first experiments moving atoms with an STM and the images produced not as snapshots but as "condensations of multiple material practices across space and time" (p. 360). She points out that discursive apparatuses such as the microscope and the history of microscopy produce the illusion of reality when, in fact, what we are looking at are images defined by the mechanisms of the apparatus. What images of children have emerged via the language, images, and artifacts we use to describe them in research? In Lionel's case, I've juxtaposed the drawing event, the drawing, Lionel's struggle, classroom expectations, and tensions in video recording in text and images. The image that emerges is one of resilience. If I acknowledge research as a matter of intra-action and representation as a discursive apparatus, then writing, like experimenting, is a material practice. There are consequences. In my representations of Lionel and others, what meanings do I impose and put into play? What do others?

Conclusion: Ethical questions

> Do I dare disturb the universe is not a meaningful question, let alone a starting point for ethical considerations … We are of the universe—there is no inside, no outside. There is only intra-acting from within and as part of the world in its becoming. (Barad, 2007, p. 396)

It has been three years since my intra-actions with Lionel and others in his classroom. I continue to recount events from my time with them in papers, presentations, and discussions. Though he assented and his parents consented to his participation in the project, what agency do assume when I appropriate his image, interpret his story, and retell it over and over again? I struggle with the idea that I am not co-contributing but colonizing Lionel's classroom experience, laying meanings over events and in the telling and retelling, claiming them as mine. On the other hand, I argue with myself as Barad might that *because* of our intra-actions, *his* story becomes *our* story and that it is my responsibility to tell it in ways that do not close meanings, but open them and that telling it over and over is part of this process. Investigating my research practice with a diffractive perspective, one designed to disturb itself, using new materialist theories such as agential realism to disturb the historical discourses of qualitative research, is also part of this process. Each moment I, as a researcher, observe, interpret, present, and write about my research, I intra-act with those events and phenomena. My affect is inextricable. As Barad (2007) argues:

If we hold on to the belief that the world is made of individual entities, it is hard to see how even our best, most well intentioned calculations for right action can avoid tearing holes in the delicate tissue structure of entanglements that the lifeblood of the world runs through. Intra-acting responsibly as part of the world means taking account of the entangled phenomena that are intrinsic to the world's vitality and being responsive to the possibilities that might help us flourish. (p. 396)

An ethical practice of researching with children requires an accounting of the entangled material-discursive practices of researching children, including those continuing to unfold. Recently, I saw Lionel and his parents at a school function. His mother pulled him over and gestured in my direction, "Lionel, remember, this is the researcher who watched you draw in kindergarten?" Lionel, much taller now, scanned my face and looked back at his mother blankly. "Remember?" she prompted. He looked back at me without recognition, smiled politely, "Oh. Yeah." I might co-construct this exchange in several ways, but reading into the silence, I offer the thought that my intra-actions with Lionel, my presence in his classroom, my recording and note-taking, my attention to his drawing and writing, all blended into the history and layers of less memorable school experiences, a bittersweet thought, but one with which I am on easier terms than others.

References

Barad, K. M. (2007). *Meeting the universe halfway: Quantum physics and the entanglement of matter and meaning.* Durham, NC: Duke University Press.

Barone, T., and Eisner, E. W. (2012). *Arts based research.* Thousand Oaks, CA: Sage.

Barthes, R. (2010). *Camera lucida: Reflections on photography.* New York: Hill and Wang.

Brostrom, S. (2012). *Children's participation in research.* Great Britain: Taylor & Francis.

Christensen, P., and Prout, A. (2005). Anthropological and sociological perspectives on the study of children. In S. Greene and D. Hogan (Eds.), *Researching children's experience: Methods and approaches* (p. 42). Thousand Oaks, CA: Sage.

James, A., and James, A. L. (2012). *Key concepts in childhood studies.* Los Angeles: Sage.

James, A., Jenks, C., and Prout, A. (1998). *Theorizing childhood.* Williston, VT: Teachers College Press.

McNamee, S. (2016). *The social study of childhood: An introduction.* New York: Palgrave.

Meloni, F., Vanthuyne, K., and Rousseau, C. (2015). Towards a relational ethics: Rethinking ethics, agency and dependency in research with children and youth. *Anthropological Theory, 15*(1), 106–123.

Mitchell, C. (2011). *Doing visual research.* Los Angeles, CA: Sage.

Møhl, P. (2011). Mise en scène, knowledge and participation: Considerations of a filming anthropologist. *Visual Anthropology, 24*(3), 227–245.

Penn, L. R. (2019). Room for writers and monsters: Performativity in children's classroom drawing. *Contemporary Issues in Early Childhood, 21*(3). https://journals.sagepub.com/doi/abs/10.1177/1077800418810728.

Pink, S. (2013). *Doing visual ethnography.* Los Angeles, CA: Sage.

Prasad, P. (2005). *Crafting qualitative research: Working in the postpositivist traditions.* Armonk, NY: M.E. Sharpe.

Rech, L. (2016). *Children's drawing in a kindergarten language arts curriculum* (Doctoral dissertation). Retrieved from University of Georgia Electronic Theses and Dissertations database (Accession Order No. 9949081365302959).

Rose, G. (2012). *Visual methodologies: An introduction to researching with visual materials.* Thousand Oaks, CA: Sage.

St. Pierre, E. A. (2016). The long reach of logical positivism/logical empiricism. In N. Denzin and M. Giardina (Eds.), *Qualitative inquiry through a critical lens* (pp. 19–29). New York: Routledge.

Waller, T., and Bitou, A. (2011). Research with children: Three challenges for participatory research in early childhood. *European Early Childhood Education Research Journal, 19*(1), 5–20.

14

Thing-Power-Child Entanglements: A Resituated Ethics of Research with Young Children

Sonja Arndt

University of Waikato, New Zealand

Marek Tesar

University of Auckland, New Zealand

Thing-power is a force exercised by that which is not specifically human (or even organic) upon humans.

(Bennett, 2010, p. 351).

What happens, then, when we realize that thing-power and not-specifically-human matters matter in research with young children? What happens when we question the traditional divisions that remain dominant in contemporary conceptions of young children and the ethics of researching with them, where that which is not human, the matter, is considered as "passive stuff, ... raw, brute, or inert" and where we ourselves, humans, and children are considered as the sole experience of "vibrant life" (Bennett, 2010, p. vi), and as somehow more capable, developed, or feeling? In this chapter we disturb and question some of these conceptions, as we unsettle and disrupt our pedagogies of researching with young children. We argue for a stance that is at the same time uncomfortable and freeing. It is a stance that recognizes the equally affecting vitality of the things, energies, and forces that emerge in our rethinking of the powers of materiality, the matter with matter (Barad, 2003), in children's and our own lives and research (Tesar and Arndt, 2016; Tesar and Koro-Ljungberg, 2016).

Rupturing dominant thought is unsettling and raises tensions. What Bennett (2004) calls a materiality where "human being and thinghood overlap" (p. 349) intrudes into and complicates what otherwise appear to be overt, logical, understandable research processes and ethical standards. With this intrusion comes a loss of control, for us as the human researchers. It adds uncertainty to the pressures of reporting on, being accountable for, conducting and following the processes to which we commit in our grant applications, ethical review board approvals, and other structural demands of our research institutions. When we realize that, actually, "the us and the it slipslide into each other ... [where] we are also nonhuman and ... things too are vital players in the world" (Bennett, 2010, p. 349), our research with young children is revealed as *already* a thing-power materialism. It sets our own ethics and pedagogies in our research with young children into something of a freefall, as we attempt to find new ground in this thing-power-child thinking. It leads us to the juxtaposition in this chapter, involving Barad's (2003) questionings on material-discursive shifts, in an attempt to articulate in words, powers, and forces what we simultaneously argue eludes words. In this chapter we use Kristeva's philosophical work on the uncertainty, openness, and continual construction of subject formations, in an attempt to elucidate conceptual shifts that arise as we bridge human and more-than-human mattering in our conceptualizations of the ethical implications of our research encounters with very young children (Arndt & Tesar, 2019).

Blurring boundaries

Thinking with Kristeva's (1982) philosophy of the subject offers us a critical entry point through which to reorient not only our thinking but our being in our research encounters with young children. Barad's (2003) elevation of matter frames our re-thinking of our human exceptionalism. When we research with young children, "[w]hat compels the belief that we have a direct access to cultural representations and their content" for example, "that we lack toward the things represented?" And "[h]ow did language," which we are asked to utilize to articulate our research encounters, findings and reports, "come to be more trustworthy than matter"(p. 801)? In what ways do such reifications of the human, of us, as human researchers, dominate and already predetermine our research, while "matter is figured as passive and immutable, or at best inherits a potential for change derivatively from language and culture" (p. 801)? Wondering what this could mean that we do differently, if we alter our orientations toward materialities, in a "brute reversal" of established and deeply entrenched beliefs, "when materiality itself is always already figured within a linguistic domain as its condition of possibility" (p. 801)? Our performance of ethical pedagogical encounters in children's mundane childhoods is undisputedly affected by the forces exercised, as in the opening quote, upon children, ourselves, teachers, and others. Blurring human-thing-material-discursive boundaries Kristeva's thinking is a powerful guide into the nuances of what we acknowledge as an already complicated ethics of things, actants, children, their lives, and matter.

This blurring is situated in a context and time where children remain often treated as cute and innocent, and considered to be ethically in need of adult protection (Prout, 2008). We consider liminal subject-thing-matter ruptures in our orientations as in-between spaces where conceptional, physical, and ethical boundaries are neither fixed, stable, or normalized. In such spaces particular labels of childhood no longer fit, and notions of cuteness, innocence, or protection become at the very least blurred and most likely questioned to their very foundations. For example, theorized through Kristeva's (1991) notion of the subject, all of us are always in constant process, evolving, in-construction, in formation. As subjects-in-process, Kristeva insists, we are constantly affected in knowable and unknowable ways by a meaning-making inner drive, which she calls the semiotic. The semiotic drive affects the human subject in a variety of ways as the subject interacts with the world and life and is acted upon. The semiotic links us, and children, as subjects-in-process, to our surroundings, landscape, and wider milieu, of space, place, and our relationships within our surroundings, which Kristeva calls the symbolic. In addition, the semiotic counters the homogeneity of the symbolic structures by which we are governed, and it represents that which preexists us as human subjects. The semiotic is thus an energizing force that heterogenizes in nuanced ways, in the intricacies through which it acts, adding meaning to and moving beyond any overt sign systems or the symbolic structural environment (Prud'homme and Légaré, 2006).

Crucially for us, the meaning-making in the semiotic works both in ways that are nameable and knowable and in other ways that are not. It shifts our research framing in important ways, as an increased focus on matter and mattering with, by and in relation to children shifts us away from set expectations for outcomes, outputs, "new," or even any, knowledge. Immersed, then, in what Duhn (2014) has referred to as our "wild ideas" that shift us beyond "dead end structures," thinking through Kristeva's philosophy on subject formation pushes us to reorient ourselves more openly toward matter as not only "passive and immutable" but rather as inhering always already in those liminal spaces between what can be known and what cannot. In the following sections we share some of our struggles with the potential for sensing, in other ways, what matter might be, when it is not embedded and determined already through language and culture. Using the potential of the semiotic creates an opportunity for us to reconceptualize our research with young children and how we think of the children themselves. It helps us to de-elevate the human subject and to elevate that which is other than human. To begin this reconceptualization, we draw on the affecting influences of the semiotic as meaning-making in—and beyond—research "subjects," through its work in connecting the subject to its context.

Linking research subjects to their context

As researchers, the semiotic links us and the young children with whom we research to the early childhood context and the wider milieu of their and our lives. That is to say, none of us can be separated from the context, but instead, we are all always evolving in relation to our local and wider context (Kristeva, 1991). This means that the semiotic recognizes the signifying and communicative aspect of the social and cultural life of our context (Lechte, 1990), including the written and unwritten societal, cultural, legal, and political structures by which we are bound. However, semiotic meaning-making is un-representable, non-discursive, and outside of what can be represented in linguistically. That is, its sensing, affect, and work lies beyond what language can express or capture. The semiotic, then, might arise, for example, from young children's sensing, feeling of the rhythms, tones, energy, and pleasure, or desire, and also in their experiences of fear, disgust, or hatred. The semiotic thus connects us and the young children in our research to that which is around and in relation to us, by affirming the affective impacts of our surroundings on all of our constantly forming subjectivities. It thus does not eliminate our concern for the children themselves, as humans within the milieu, in a similar way to Braidotti's (2013) reminder, that the human is not banished in a posthuman way of thinking. Rather, the semiotic makes way for a shift beyond the human-centric context and connections, to recognize connections between us all also to the other vibrant forces and energies to which Bennett (2010) alerts us. It alerts us to the "matter with matter" (Barad, 2015) and to the inter-species and other-than-human relationships that inhere in young children's local and wider surroundings (Haraway, 2007).

Furthermore, the semiotic connects us to our context, not in a singular event, feeling, or identifiable "thing" that can be captured or recognized. It lies mostly in the unconscious, and it "speaks," that is it gives meaning, or signifies, in what has been described as an "uncanny strangeness" (Kristeva, 1991, p. 83) of meaning. The semiotic gives meaning to young children's and our own forming subjectivities through the unnameable sensed experiences, affects, and relationships in and with the collective known or unknown ways of being in our contexts (Kristeva, 1998). In other words we might say that it recognizes the complexity and unknowability of the effects and affects that are constantly relating to and shaping ours and the children's subjectivities. Once we become aware of the workings of the semiotic, it becomes impossible for our thinking to remain on a superficial, homogeneous level—about our research, about our practices, about our relationships with the children and with the rest of our context by which they and we are surrounded.

Myriad complex factors complicate early childhood contexts and any attempts to simplify them. As the semiotic always exists in counter-definition to the surrounding symbolic structures, it too is always complex. In Aotearoa New Zealand, the symbolic context includes biculturally determined and locally premised pedagogies and practices, espoused through the principles of *Te Whāriki* (Ministry of Education, 1996, 2017), the early childhood curriculum framework. Despite its relational aspirations, the curriculum framework and wider governing regulatory systems simultaneously implicate us in the short-term goals and commitments of the globalized, neoliberal, wider economic, political and societal paradigm (Kelsey, 2015; Springer, 2016). Envisioning society as unpredictable and unreliable, as a state of "liquid modernity," as Bauman (2009) has, for instance, places young children and their early childhood settings within this shifting symbolic milieu. Bauman's framing of the state epitomizes an un-simple polis, in constant competition with itself and with its often-changing variations and seductions. Barad's questions alert us to the even greater implications of the fluid, un-simple, and unknown connections within this milieu. The semiotic, we argue, not only implicates us in the unknown realms of our forming subjectivities, as Kristeva's theory states, but it throws us off the pedestal that reifies and upholds only human thought, culture, and being and that which humans construct and are.

Certainly, by connecting us and the young children in our research to our context the semiotic offers us a way to recognize the un-static nature of the wider context. In this sense, it recognizes the influences of concerns that affect our research that arise out of neoliberal educational reforms (Koro-Ljungberg et al., 2017; Springer, 2016), for example, of the rapid increase in the marketization and privatization of early childhood education (Mitchell, 2011, 2014; Mitchell and Brooking, 2007) and of the unsettling and multiple professionalisms to which these public and private tensions lead (Duhn, 2010). At the same time, it affirms these pressures within the expectation that, more than ever before, early childhood education is seen globally as a key determinant of children's and society's future success. In this sense the semiotic ruptures conceptions that might exclude relationships that emanate from matter, things, and forces, and that complicate our research perhaps without us noticing them. Conceptualizing the semiotic as countering homogeneity allows us to delve into the possibility of a wider reimagination of the material-discursive, human-non-human binary that inheres in our research spaces and activities in early childhood education.

Countering homogeneity—The semiotic attack

The semiotic can be seen as an inner space, where human responses evoked by their surroundings are formed and play out. These responses determine how they, and we as researchers, react and practice within the regulatory symbolic early childhood and wider context. Such responses reinforce that the symbolic context and semiotic meaning-making are inseparable, always interdependent, and the individual subject is always entangled in both the semiotic and the symbolic (Oliver, 2002). Kristeva's positing of the subject-in-process represents a conceptual shift from viewing the subject as logically structured, for example in a Lacanian way through language. It is exemplified in conceptualizing young children's semiotic responses to their symbolic environment, validating the disruptive, heterogeneous forces and energies that ruminate in that process. An example of this is in young children's performance of their everyday, mundane lives, that is, in the "tonality, rhythms, contradictions, meaninglessness, disruption, and silence" (Widawsky, 2014, p. 62), that arise in the spontaneity of their responses to their surroundings and relationships, and that perhaps often go unnoticed by our adult-researcher mind. The semiotic thus counters and helps young children and ourselves to exist beyond the homogeneity that is often promoted by narrow governing rules, laws, and research processes and structures. In countering homogeneity, it is as if it releases us from an enclosure. The semiotic thus creates a space to break out of this enclosure, conceptually, temporally, and emotionally (Prud'homme and Légaré, 2006).

Following this thinking, our symbolic structure represents not only the obvious, overt, but also the hidden rules by which we are governed. The symbolic structure of the human subject is related in psychoanalysis to the ego, to what is knowable, to a stasis, and to stability (Oliver, 2002). In countering homogeneity, we see Kristeva's semiotic as an "attack" on the stasis (Kristeva, 1998; Prud'homme and Légaré, 2006). We see it, then, as a disruptive force, which is distinct from the symbolic and from its language, signs, and symbolizations (Kristeva, 1984).

In this "attack," the semiotic represents and forms the affective, emotional, sensual elements in developing subjectivities in unspeakable, unrepresentable ways (Widawsky, 2014). It is through the semiotic, then, that the rhythms, tones, and drives are discharged (Oliver, 2002), and thus the semiotic counters the homogeneity of conventional distinctions of matter, thing, human, and nonhuman, within the early childhood conceptional, regulatory, and structural environment. Acting through the nuances, the poetic, and what Kristeva calls the musicality, that arise in our drives and energies, the semiotic offers potential for reconceptualizing knowable and unknowable reactions to young children's and our own contexts.

The semiotic's constant reconstruction of the subject is unconscious, and it is unpredictable. This point reaffirms our earlier point, that it falls outside of what we can capture in language and is a "translinguistic" (Kristeva, 1984, p. 90) disruption to the symbolic structures. In this sense, it breaks the mold of set expectations, by transgressing and blurring rules, not only *because* it conveys meaning and significance but *especially* to do so. It directly confronts the question of language being more trustworthy than matter, as raised by Barad (2003), and following that it could offer a "potential for change" that pushes us as human researchers, to think, feel, and act beyond the security of known and knowable "language and culture." Seen within our own pedagogies in our research with young children, the semiotic might be that which motivates our energies and drives to interrupt normalized, homogeneous definitions and expectations of our research data, outputs, or recordings. It might be that drive emanating from the discomfort, excitement, or frequent "gut" feelings, felt in the difficult to pin down sensations that cause us, and also young children, to avert, distort, pursue, and elevate, or abandon, particular actions, practices, or beliefs. It could thus also be the unconsciously arising sensation that leads to young children's rejection of what is intolerable, inexplicable, but essentially affecting them and their lives, as enmeshed with and surrounded by the matter and forces that are driven, through the semiotic, beyond the discursive.

In alerting us to these drives and responses, thinking about the semiotic creates a space to recognize and to trouble the complexity of our—human— inner senses and responses to research situations. Fitting with the ontological and epistemological in-betweenness of the nature-culture entanglements in our context in Aotearoa New Zealand, of indigenous Māori and non-indigenous Pākeha beliefs, the semiotic also recognizes the conceptualizations and senses to which we do not have access but which are nevertheless present. This refers to the diverse ways of knowing and being, for example, in a Māori world, which

Pākeha, or non-Māori, don't and will never be able to know. It elevates recognition
of our own energies and the forces within and around us and how our responses
to them implicate not only our own being but the very relationships in which we
and the young children in our research are enmeshed.

According to Kristeva (1986), the semiotic complicates what she calls
intertextual processes. Intertextuality means that our subjectivities are always
inscribed with our past realities, as well as with those that are current and
with those by which we are surrounded. Already, then, our relationships and
engagements are entangled with our contexts, in mutually affecting ways.
Through the blurring of the material and the discursive that evolves as we engage
with a thing-power materialist view, this intertextuality becomes the bridging
between us and the "passive stuff, … raw, brute, or inert." Indeed, it emphasizes
it as at least as significant to the "vibrant life" (Bennett, 2010, p. vi), as we, the
humans and our own "stuff" are.

Energizing the subject

Our rereading of Kristeva's theory on the subject offers further revelations
in terms of the ethics of our research responsibilities with young children, in
the energizing effect of the semiotic. Recognizing the semiotic elevates the
interrelationships of human encounters with the heterogeneous forces that
they represent and that create energy in their unknowability and uncertainty
(Kristeva, 1984). They energize the subject-in-process through the affective,
emotional, sensual drives and impulses (Widawsky, 2014) described above, and
which we argue, bridge the human–nonhuman binary, to implicate the vibrancy
of forces and matter, which Barad (2003) and Bennett (2010) alert us to. By
expressing "the unspeakable and the frightening … the things that language
leaves out" (Iannetta, as cited in Sadehi, 2012, p. 1492), the semiotic creates a
space for us to question, with Barad (2003), what that actually means when we
reconstruct materiality outside of language and outside of culture?

Elevating such interconnectednesses draws us toward a posthuman ethics
and relationality. As Ceder (2018) proposes, in his theorizing of an educational
relationality, relationships are always already imbued with "movement, process,
entanglement, becoming, and transformation" as an "intra-relationality" (p. 8).
When the relationships, for example, with unknown influences of thing-powers
and forces become elevated in our work with young children, they move us beyond
an individualistic logic or separation. The inability to capture or necessarily
name all of these influences simultaneously places us in an increasingly complex

ethical and moral relationship of care and responsibility: to things, to relational forces, to the children's affect, and to ourselves. Expelled from what we know, we are then pushed to ask, are we even equipped to "think" outside of ourselves and the young children, to become energized by "sensing" a situation, group, person, or belief? Regardless, recognizing the semiotic validates un-categorizable, indescribable bodily and mind reactions to our symbolic context, energizing our complex intra-relationships in inarticulable, unimaginable ways, to respond and react.

Destroying logic

Finally, the semiotic not only helps to recognize but shapes our relationship with and within each one of us. In its challenge of stagnating or fixed conceptual structures, the semiotic is a constantly shifting dynamic realm that "destroys logic" (Prud'homme and Légaré, 2006, p. 4) and reflects Kristeva's deliberate intention to negate unitary conceptions of life, language, and our human and wider interrelationships. Kristeva's tendency to "open pathways," where others see a pessimistic impasse (Lechte, 1990; Oliver, 2002), connects life, meaning, and language, and seems to indicate a willingness to recognize the potential of the wider more-than-human influences on the signification of the subject in process through this semiotic energizing potentiality. Further, we argue here, it shifts our conceptions beyond them. The semiotic thus exposes meaning as "not the unified product of a unified subject," but rather it ruptures certainty by revealing that "meaning is Other and as such makes the subject other to itself" (Oliver, 2002, p. xviii). As subjects who are continually in-process, ours and the young children in our research's constant knowing and unknowing is energized further through the expulsions and rejections that drive our constant renewal (Prud'homme and Légaré, 2006). The semiotic attack that verifies this complexity within and beyond the known, conscious, symbolic, and conceptual structures thus leads to a further renewal, as an *undoing*, of our unitary beliefs and of our elevation of human knowledge, being, and the human subject in our research encounters.

Whichever way we orient ourselves toward human-centric and other-than-human matter, forces, and energies, attitudes play out in our research encounters. Our stance is therefore influential on the young children, on ourselves, and on our hope for the *ways in which* we entangle all of us in the ethical and moral complexities of these contemporary conditions and of young children's education (Arndt and Tesar, 2016). Kristeva's (1998) theory of subject formation is process-driven, always working alongside the wider context in which the human subject exists. In our research with young children, the early childhood and wider context and impact of inner processes form and transform subjectivities in both conscious and unconscious ways. In other words, our own and the young children's subjectivities are always shaped in ways that we may or may not be aware of, affected in ways that we might notice, or not notice, and implicated by and working always within the complications of our material, cultural, political, and historical milieu of beliefs, systems, histories, and desires.

Concluding comments—Discomfort and freedom

Barad's (2003) elevation of matter continues to frame and expose our human exceptionalism. In this chapter, the ways in which "direct access to cultural representations and their content" (p. 801) traditionally occur have been de-elevated using Kristeva's notion of the semiotic to open conceptual spaces for the complexities of thing-power influences and affects. We have attempted to insert and make more trustworthy those affective matters and forces, to which Barad and Bennett alert us, as always already present and affecting us and our humanly relationships. "Matter," then, might indeed become recognized as a "brute reversal" (p. 801) of established and deeply entrenched beliefs that shift how we ourselves matter with children and with our wider research environment.

As we grapple with these concepts and their thing-power in relation to our research and pedagogies with young children, we realize that at the same time as we attempt to engage with them, our very engagement is an intrusion. Similarly, it is perhaps futile that we attempt to articulate and commit to language, or to knowable concepts, that which may never be capturable. Perhaps, however, what we have done in this chapter will work against a frequent exclusion, which negates the power, energies, and forces that we have attempted to elevate in our researcher pedagogies as too complex, too difficult, and messy. As we continue to disrupt our affective and intra-active research encounters, our human and other-than-human ethics become ever-more called into question. In the end, our ethical relationships with thing-power forces, although exerted upon us as Bennett notes in the opening quote, may forever remain out of our reach and understanding.

References

Arndt, S., and Tesar, M. (2016). A more-than-social movement: The post-human condition of quality in the early years. *Contemporary Issues in Early Childhood*, *17*(1), 16–25. doi:10.1177/1463949115627896.

Arndt, S., and Tesar, M. (2019). Re-configuring an ethics of care in culturally diverse early childhood settings: Towards an ethics of unknowing. In R. Langford (Ed.), *Theorizing feminist ethics of care in early childhood practice*. London, England: Bloomsbury.

Barad, K. (2003). Posthumanist performativity: Toward an understanding of how matter comes to matter. *Signs: Journal of Women in Culture and Society*, *28*(3), 801–831. doi:10.1086/345321.

Barad, K. (2015). Transmaterialities: Trans*/matter/realities and queer political imaginings. *GLQ: A Journal of Lesbian and Gay Studies*, *21*(2–3), 387–422. doi:10.1215/10642684-2843239.

Bauman, Z. (2009). Education in the liquid-modern setting. *Power and Education*, *1*(2), 157–166. doi:10.2304/power.2009.1.2.157.

Bennett, J. (2004). The force of things: Steps toward an ecology of matter. *Political Theory*, *32*(3), 347–372.

Bennett, J. (2010). *Vibrant matter: A political ecology of things*. Durham, NC: Duke University Press.

Braidotti, R. (2013). *The posthuman*. Cambridge, UK: Polity Press.

Ceder, S. (2018). *Towards a posthuman theory of educational relationality*. London, England: Routledge.

Duhn, I. (2010). 'The centre is my business': Neo-liberal politics, privatisation and discourses of professionalism in New Zealand. *Contemporary Issues in Early Childhood*, *11*(1), 49–60.

Duhn, I. (2014). Making agency matter: Rethinking infant and toddler agency in educational discourse. *Discourse: Studies in the Cultural Politics of Education*. doi:10 1080/01596306.2014.918535.

Haraway, D. (2007). *When species meet*. Minneapolis, MN: University of Minnesota Press.

Kelsey, J. (2015). *The fire economy: New Zealand's reckoning*. Wellington, New Zealand: Bridget Williams Books.

Koro-Ljungberg, M., Löytönen, T., and Tesar, M. (2017). Introduction. In M. Koro-Ljungberg, T. Löytönen and M. Tesar (Eds.), *Disrupting data in qualitative inquiry: Entanglements with the post-critical and post-anthropocentric* (pp. 1–10). New York: Peter Lang.

Kristeva, J. (1969/1986). Word, dialogue and novel. In T. Moi (Ed.), *The Kristeva reader* (pp. 34–61). Oxford, UK: Blackwell Publishers Ltd.

Kristeva, J. (1982). *Powers of horror: An essay on abjection* (Trans. L. S. Roudiez). New York: Columbia University Press.

Kristeva, J. (1984). *Revolution in poetic language* (Trans. M. Waller). New York: Columbia University Press.

Kristeva, J. (1991). *Strangers to ourselves.* New York: Columbia University Press.

Kristeva, J. (1998). The subject in process. In P. French (Ed.), *The Tel Quel reader* (pp. 133–178). London, UK: Routledge.

Lechte, J. (1990). *Julia Kristeva.* London, UK: Routledge.

Ministry of Education (1996). *Te Whāriki—he whāriki mātauranga mō ngā mokopuna o Aotearoa: Early childhood curriculum.* Wellington, New Zealand: Learning Media.

Ministry of Education (2017). *Te Whāriki he whāriki mātauranga mō ngā mokopuna o Aotearoa early childhood curriculum.* Wellington, New Zealand: New Zealand Government.

Mitchell, L. (2011). Enquiring teachers and democratic politics: Transformations in New Zealand's early childhood education landscape. *Early Years: An International Research Journal, 31*(3), 217–228. doi:10.1080/09575146.2011.588787.

Mitchell, L. (2014). Parent decision-making about early childhood education: Reducing barriers to participation. *Early Childhood Folio, 18*(2), 22–27.

Mitchell, L., and Brooking, K. (2007). *First NZCER national survey of early childhood education services.* Retrieved from Wellington, New Zealand, from: http://www. nzcer.org.nz/pdfs/15318.pdf.

Oliver, K. (2002). Kristeva's revolutions. In K. Oliver (Ed.), *The portable Kristeva* (pp. xi–xxix). New York: Columbia University Press.

Prout, A. (2008). *The future of childhood.* London, England: Routledge.

Prud'homme, J., and Légaré, L. (2006). The subject in process. *Signo [online], Rimouski (Quebec).*

Sadehi, C. T. (2012). Beloved and Julia Kristeva's the semiotic and the symbolic. *Theory and Practice in Language Studies, 2*(7), 1491–1497. doi:10.4304/tpls.2.7.1491-1497.

Springer, S. (2016). *The discourse of neoliberalism: An anatomy of a powerful idea.* London, UK: Rowman & Littlefield International.

Tesar, M., and Arndt, A. (2016). Vibrancy of childhood things: Power, philosophy and political ecology of matter. *Cultural Studies ↔ Critical Methodologies, 16*(2), 193–200. doi:10.1177/1532708616636144.

Tesar, M., and Koro-Ljungberg, M. (2016). Cute, creepy & sublime unnamed childhood monstrosities. *Discourse: Studies in the Cultural Politics of Education, 37*(5), 694–704. doi:10.1080/01596306.2015.1075708.

Widawsky, R. (2014). Julia Kristeva's psychoanalytic work. *Journal of American Psychoanalytical Association, 62*(1), 61–67. doi:10.1177/0003065113520041.

15

Finding Revolution in the Murmurations of Deep and Simple

Jaye Johnson Thiel
University of Georgia, USA

*Their bodies seem to float across the sky as they swing—higher and higher—
while deep-bellied giggles permeate the airwaves. Their happiness, joy, and
fearlessness spill out everywhere. It is contagious and as I sit here on the bench
I notice the moment I catch whatever it is they are sending out into the world.
It sneaks up, unexpectedly, and all-at-once I feel calmer, happier, more joyful.
It is a slowness that my body rarely finds in the spaces I traverse these days.
But in this moment, my research site is an exception. I take a deep breath in
and rock back and forth a bit in rhythm with the swings. I embrace the gifts
of this simple event: the space, the outdoors, the chill in the air, the swings, the
laughter, the slowness. I find myself wanting to lay on the ground and look up
at them as they swing—like one would a cloud floating by. But I don't because
the ground is muddy and I remember I am meeting someone for dinner later
with no opportunity to change the clothes I am wearing and to be honest, a
part of me reminded myself that I am an adult and maybe laying down would
be super weird to onlookers. Instead, I take it all in and much like the young
folks gliding across the sky on those blue plastic swing seats, I try to hang on.*

(Thiel, Fieldnotes, 2013)

Bodies. Everywhere I look. Bodies. One swings. The other sways. One zigs.
The other zags. One loops. The other knots. Bodies breathing. Bodies buzzing.
Bodies rusting. Bodies dying. The world is full of bodies, human, nonhuman, and
more-than-human alike. As educational researchers, we tend to look at human
bodies. Even when looking toward nonhuman or more-than-human bodies we
ultimately do so to better understand the human ones. In our research practices,
we often speak of Black bodies, brown bodies, men's bodies, women's bodies,
trans bodies, queer bodies, working-class bodies, children's bodies. Researchers

have become well versed in the customary practices of naming the bodies before us with revolutionary intent. Yet, revolution never quite comes.

Being revolutionary has become so expected in research practice, simple events like the one I shared at the beginning of this chapter are often disregarded, seen as uneventful and unmeaningful. Not containing enough "umpft"! And while as qualitative researchers we are taught to find the extraordinary in the ordinary and mundane, small moments are often forgotten for the bigger, more complex moments—the moments that scream out, demanding our attention with awe and disbelief, the moments that beg for justice and equity. Or collections of moments that seem to amount to something grander and greater than a simple moment swinging on a playset one January day with no particulars—the moments that seem to happen in spite of those bigger moments. I do not mean to imply these big moments aren't important. They deserve our attention and our outrage and our wonder. But in a world that is always searching for the answers to big social problems, could it be that the small moments, the moments of calmness, are equally important and have a great deal to teach us about the ways children actively and perhaps unknowingly work against the unspoken rules of a hyper-capitalist society and the ways their bodies get produced within it? Could it be that the murmurations of swinging and giggling and gliding on a thin plastic seat across a small portion of the sky is revolutionary in its own right?

In this chapter, I will dig into what it means to consider what Mr. Roger's called the deep and simple and the potentialities they might offer for research with children. I will begin by offering a glimpse into the way neoliberalism (Harvey, 2007) usurps concepts and emotions, tricking us into believing that we can only have revolution through complexity and giving up certain pleasures (i.e., love). I then offer up the concept of murmurations (King, 2017) as a way to focus on the deep and simple and as a way to rethink what counts as revolutionary. I conclude the chapter by illustrating the ways our research practices can work against neoliberalism through embodying a deep and simple approach.

Let's start by thinking about love in capitalist ruins.

Love in capitalist ruins (or the political project of neoliberalism)

Like kudzu (a climbing perennial vine), capitalism has a way of engulfing everything in its path. Native to Japan, kudzu's lush green leaves, sweet purple blooms, and its heartiness seemed appealing to folks in the United States as both a shade plant and a way to stop soil erosion. But soon, gardeners and farmers found that kudzu strangles everything in its path as it twists and grows. It has no natural enemies and thus extremely difficult to contain (Collins, 2003). Capitalism has worked a bit like kudzu, arriving with promises of potential that at first glance can seem appealing to onlookers. But given time, capitalism smothers, accumulating power and wealth.

Capitalism's story is one of colonization adhering to social practices that are philosophically connected to theories of neoliberalism. Neoliberalism is

> a political project carried out by the corporate capitalist class as they felt intensely threatened both politically and economically towards the end of the 1960s into the1970s. They desperately wanted to launch a political project that would curb the power of labor. In many respects the project was a counterrevolutionary project. It would nip in the bud what, at that time, were revolutionary movements in much of the developing world. (Harvey, 2016., N.P)

As a political project, neoliberalism uses the mechanics of capitalism and fuses those with conceptions of morality and virtuosity to convince humans that privatization, deregulation, and competitive outsourcing are for their own good. It is no wonder that revolution has been a slow go, when the political, social, and economic capacity for revolution has been squelched.

So, what happens when a concept, like the concept of love, becomes entangled with neoliberal (Harvey, 2007) practices? What becomes of love in education? It becomes a simulacrum of sorts that is contingent on the return in our investments rather than a deep and simple appreciation of another body's existence. It becomes conditional-love, a love that is often stitched together with a desire to "save" children from themselves and the worlds they live in. Words like "gap," "quality," and "rigor" would have people believe that education has to be about pulling children out of the mire and muck. But at the same time educators are pulling, larger social forces are pushing, and economic forces are gaining.

Love in capitalist ruins reaps both unintended and intended consequences. For example, lots of people claim to love children-bodies. Yet much violence is done to those bodies in the name of love. Take the ways education constructs children's bodies, as future-bodies—bodies that are never quite enough (Tait, 2017); commodified-bodies—bodies that make testing companies extraordinary amounts of money (Stauffer, 2017); and economic-bodies—bodies that will bring economic growth over time to cities and towns (GA Bright from the Start, 2016). An example of all three can be found in this excerpt taken from a document—*The Economics of Early Childhood*—put out by the executive branch of the US Government (2015) under the Obama administration:

An analysis by the President's Council of Economic Advisers describes the economic returns to investments in childhood development and early education. Some of these benefits, such as increases in parental earnings and employment, are realized immediately, while other benefits, such as greater educational attainment and earnings, are realized later when children reach adulthood. In total, the existing research suggests expanding early learning initiatives would provide benefits to society of roughly $8.60 for every $1 spent, about half of which comes from increased earnings for children when they grow up. (p. 3)

Love in capitalist ruins takes a universal understanding of love (fondness for another) and insidiously infuses it with the development of economic venture so that bodies are commodified seemingly under the guise of love itself. But in actuality, that commodification is for monetary gain. The aftermath of this love can be seen in a myriad of laws and policies that standardize bodies in neoliberal ways. It is clear that to claim to love children-bodies can also mean to love dollar-bodies—or more simply put to love the materialization of wealth that can be accumulated from bodies. It's easy to say I love someone-something therefore I will subject them-it to this pain for their-its own good and walk away feeling as if the right thing has been done when all the while, this is love with expectations, love with conditions. There is nothing radical or revolutionary about this love. This is love in capitalist ruins.

In his online interview in *Roar*, Horvat explains: "Love is work, it is something that is built. It is not something just given on the table. I think that this is the true radicality of love. The beauty of it actually lies in the hard and difficult work." Horvat goes on to discuss the dichotomies that have been built between love and revolution and believes dichotomies are rooted in the economic subject—the ridiculous notion that we can either love or revolt, have a career or a family, experience beauty or pain. What better way to control individuals than to suppress and control love itself? He urges something different, for us to see we can have both love and revolution because love, like revolution, is always political even though "the question of love is surprisingly missing" from "the upheavals all around the world" (Horvat, 2016, p. 2) and is missing because neoliberalism reduce bodies to classifications rather than reaching for the connectedness, the collectiveness, and the co-construction of it all.

There is something both complex and shallow in the act of naming bodies, classifying bodies, monetizing bodies, and revolutionizing bodies. For one, it is often done to bodies rather than bodies deciding what bodies they want to become. Furthermore, who and what benefits from these categorical acts, particularly in educational research? Stenger (2015) explains, "Practitioners ... could be capable of many other things than subjecting everything that moves to categories that are indifferent to their consequences ... worse, the knowledge that it produces has no other effect than to attribute even more power to capitalism" (p. 74). Because with capitalism comes a sense of conquering, narrowing, and isolating but also a pervasiveness that finds a way to commodify anything and everything.

Even the murmurs of love.

What we can learn from the murmurations of starlings (or things that fly)

If capitalism can manipulate love, it seems highly probable that the steady beat of neoliberalism pulsates in everything and everywhere, even in our research endeavors. But that is the thing about probability, it is a game of chance with outliers and multiple possibilities contingent on variability. But to find them takes an awful lot of listening for murmurs.

Like Harvey (2007), Stenger (2015), and Tsing (2015) both write of hyper-capitalism and its far-and-wide reaching grasp. Neither of these scholars romanticize a world untouched by capitalism but rather offer new ways of listening and producing the world so that we might find survival beyond the precarity neoliberalism produces. Stengers (2015) offers us the promise of narratives that drip with "the difficulties, the hesitations, the choices and errors" as much as "the successes and the conclusions arrived at" (p. 134), and Tsing (2015) teaches us to notice that which is thriving in spite of capitalism, to listen for the polyphonic rhythms. Both women call for an attentiveness to worldmaking amid capitalist-ravishing, paying particular attention to the subtle ways our everyday lives have been monetized and where murmurs of life can still be overheard among the seemingly forgotten and discarded. Perhaps we can find our way to these murmurs through a kinship with starlings.

At some point in your life, you have probably encountered the murmuration of starlings, although you may not have paid it much mind. Starlings are birds that when flocking together move in a darting and swirling coordinated pattern across the sky as they fly. These movements, called murmurations, look similar to ink blots when captured in a still shot and have a mesmerizing effect as they pull in and away from each other during these flights. Research has shown that "flocks of starlings exhibit a remarkable ability to maintain cohesion as a group in highly uncertain environments and with limited, noisy information" (Young et al., 2013, p. 1). According to the study, starlings manage these uncertainties almost effortlessly because each bird attends to seven of its neighbors and thus "part of a dynamic system in which the parts combine to make a whole with emergent properties" (King, 2017, N.P.). The results? A murmuration. Here, I am struck by the idea of managing uncertainty. Researching with children requires a certain comfortableness with managing uncertainty and I dare say that research as a practice is one of uncertainty writ large (or should be at least).

Furthermore, starlings are considered an invasive species, introduced to North America in the 1890s by those who adored Shakespeare and wanted every bird he ever mentioned to live among us on this continent (King, 2017). Viewed as menacing and aggressive, starlings are often considered troublemakers. But being labeled a troublemaker often means one did not conform to someone else's idea of normalcy (Shalaby, 2017). In a world where capitalism is ravishing us all, perhaps a little troublemaking is warranted?

I do not claim to be an expert on murmurations or on starlings for that matter, but in part, these murmurations remind me of the act of swinging on a swing, particularly a tire swing, moving back and forth, creating unexpected patterns in the sky. Yet, also the motion of a traditional swing set, as bodies move back and forth in patterns that change; as bodies move with various speeds through time and space, a polyphonic rhythm as it may be. But as far as rhythms go, murmurations can be fairly quiet, almost like white noise as a collective of wings flap in patterns across the sky—easy to push out of the mind for more noisy things, especially if you bear witness to murmurations frequently.

The small acts of young people, like the act of swinging, can often go unnoticed, too, especially if you bear witness to young people swinging frequently. Swinging can become white noise, particularly when looking for more noisy things.

Perhaps it is time to embody the uncertainty of less noisy things.

Embodying the deep and simple (or listening for things that murmur)

When we embody something, we do so subtly. Most of the time, it kind of just creeps in with little warning and unknowingly until—BAM!—it shows up when we least expect it. It can manifest in a particular way we do something and in what we say with automation. Or it can be more inconspicuous, embedded in a smell, a sound, a taste that we though was buried deep and forgotten but rushes back carrying the ghosts of yesterday, last month, last year with it.

As researchers, most of us have been taught to embody complexity. Complex reading. Complex writing. Complex thinking. Complex methods. Complexity doesn't always do the things we think it will. Often, the complex is merely shallow, a bramble of lots and lots of observations and artifacts and interviews that seem revolutionary but amalgamate to much of nothing overall. Complexity is noisy, and it tends to drown out murmurs. Murmurs, on the other hand, are deep and simple.

The idea of deep and simple originated from Mr. Rogers, a television personality who dedicated his life to the study of childhood. Deep and simple as a concept comes out of the fleeting moments, the mundane acts of our everyday lives, such as a diaper change. As Li (2018) explains, deep and simple acts are the ones that we often take for granted. For example, we may feel the important stuff comes from the big adventures we plan *for* young people such as visiting the Grand Canyon or taking a field trip to the zoo. But the simple act of eating a bowl of cereal every morning *with* a young person has a much deeper and more powerful impact because it happens every day.

Deep and simple isn't in the elaborate, one-time projects we plan, set up, and document. It is located in the unremarkable, such as swinging. Swinging is so commonplace; it is a murmur. Taken for granted. But there is much promise to be found in such a deep and simple act because deep and simple acts hold the potential for revolution. Swinging looks a lot like nonconformity, an act that finds itself outside of the purview of capitalism, if only for a moment. A complex and shallow approach might see swinging as meaningless unless some grand narrative of oppression embeds itself right into that swing. A deep and simple approach might see swinging as one of the most grandiose acts of resistance a young person can engage in—a big old "fuck you" to the neoliberal world that often marks their young bodies as too much or not enough—never just right.

My call is a humble one. Pay attention to the murmurations that young people create Every. Single. Day. But to find the murmurations, we must look for the deep and simple. Li (2018) offers us four lenses in which to locate the deep and simple: (1) sense of connectedness, (2) reciprocity, (3) opportunity resides in the smallest moments, and (4) sense of belonging. As researchers, we can embrace these four concepts and put them to work in our practices with children. To be honest, they are things we probably already all know but tuned out for more noisy things. To hear the mumurs, we must follow the murmurations. As Kontturi (2018) writes:

This way of following is not about shadowing a few steps behind, but about opening oneself up to a movement that exceeds the position one holds, the experiences one has had, or the knowledge one possesses. (p. 9)

In this vein, perhaps we can follow the murmuration of something other than capitalism by embodying the following practices in our research with children:

Sense of connectedness: One of the greatest things we can do as researchers is build a sense of connectedness (Li, 2018). It doesn't take long to feel if there is a connection or if we are being present with one another. Connectedness can't be one-sided. We can't be the only one who feels it. It has to be mutual. Otherwise, we risk commodifying bodies for our own research or scholarly agenda. We can't be there for the next paper or the next chapter or the next book. We have to be there because we want to learn how to be better humans in our worlding practices. We have to be there because we want to better understand what it means to be a young person in a society in capitalist ruins. We have to be there because we want to create new worlds and know that young people can help us create them because they already are.

Reciprocity: Being reciprocal means that interactions go back and forth and are mutually constitutive; no one person (or thing) is in complete control (Li, 2018). Control is a very complex and shallow way to create docile bodies, neoliberal bodies. Collectively producing the research space with children crafts a different story, one that is shared and intellectually robust with multiple imaginaries and opens possibilities other than neoliberal ones. Reciprocity also goes further than a grand gesture. It means that what the research is doing is mutually constructive. To practice deep and simple means to dig-in to the moment-to-moment interactions, day after day. To just be together and to listen for the murmurs.

Smallest moments as opportunity: Growth comes from trust—not from an ability to use or not use numbers or letters (Li, 2018). Trust comes from small moments of togetherness. Numbers and letters are merely a possible by-product of trust. If researchers are to craft something different than entrepreneurship, they must go deeper. Researchers must ask themselves what orients their acts of trusts and why? Who is benefiting from these acts of trust? What is that benefit? Is it worth it for everyone? Otherwise, the small murmurations are put at risk of being usurped and smothered by capitalism.

Sense of belonging: One must feel they have a place and are wanted in that place (Li, 2018). To feel wanted is much more than being wanted for a particular purpose. To be wanted in a place means someone wants you there just because you are you. Not because you can do something for them but just because you are. Just because you exist. As researchers, this means when someone comes to "the research place" (either the researcher or the young person) they should feel love—not love in capitalist ruins but love in its deepest form, an appreciation for the other without jumping through whatever research hoops planned for the day. An appreciation without strings.

Clearly the four practices outlined above are entangled in many ways. They do not live independently of one another. They are enmeshed and equally important to rethinking what it means to be revolutionary. Once researchers have done these things, they should ask, Where are these four things emerging in the lives of children and how? Where do young people seem connected to the world and when? How is reciprocity part of their practice and when? Where are the small moments? How do they unfold? When do they unfold? When, where, and whom do they trust? When, where, and how does belongingness flourish in their everyday lives?

If we attend to the deep and simple, perhaps, like the starlings, we too can manage uncertainty. Find these moments and we find the murmurations that leave capitalism and its neoliberal agenda behind, if only for a second or two.

And a second or two can change everything.

References

Collins, J. (2003). If you can't beat kudzu, join it. *Off the Wall. Duke Energy Employee Advocate*. Retrieved August 20, 2018, from http://www.dukeemployees.com/offthewall2.shtml.

GA Department of Early Learning (2016). Economic impact of the early care and education industry in Georgia executive summary. Retrieved September 25, 2018, from http://decal.ga.gov/documents/attachments/2016EconomicImpactSummary.pdf.

Harvey, D. (2007). *A brief history of neoliberalism*. Oxford, UK: Oxford University Press.

Harvey, D. (July 23, 2016). Neoliberalism is a political project. Jacobin. (Bjarke Skærlund Risager, Interviewer). https://www.jacobinmag.com/2016/07/david-harvey-neoliberalism-capitalism-labor-crisis-resistance/.

Horvat, S. (2016). *The radicality of love*. Cambridge, UK: Polity Press.

Horvat, S., and Davis, C. (2015). Love and revolution: An interview with Srećko Horvat. *Roar Magazine*. https://roarmag.org/essays/srecko-horvat-love-revolution/.

King, B. (January 4, 2017). Video: Swooping starlings in murmuration. *NPR Cosmos & Culture Commentary on Science and Society*, *13*(7). https://www.npr.org/sections/13.7/2017/01/04/506400719/video-swooping-starlings-in-murmuration.

Kontturi, K-K. (2018). *Ways of following: Art, materiality, collaboration*. London, UK: Open Humanities Press.

Li, J. (September 13, 2018). Putting Mr. Rogers deep and simple to practice. *HarvardEd Cast*. https://soundcloud.com/harvardedcast/putting-mister-rogers-deep-and-simple-to-practice.

Shalaby, C. (2017). *Troublemakers: Lessons in freedom from young children at school*. New York: The New Press.

Stauffer, R. (April 28, 2017). The business of standardized testing. *Huffpost*. https://www.huffingtonpost.com/rainesford-alexandra/the-business-of-standardi_b_9785988.html.

Stenger (2015). *In catastrophic times: Resisting the coming Barbarism*. London, UK: Open Humanities Press.

Tait, P. (May 12, 2017). It's time we educated children for the future, rather than limiting them to subjects of the past. *Telegraph*. https://www.telegraph.co.uk/education/2017/05/12/time-educated-children-future-rather-limiting-subjects-past/.

Tsing, A. L. (2015). *The mushroom at the end of the world: On the possibility of life in capitalist ruins*. Princetonm NJ: Princeton University Press.

US Executive Office (2015). The economics of early childhood investments. https://obamawhitehouse.archives.gov/sites/default/files/docs/early_childhood_report_update_final_non-embargo.pdf.

US Executive Office of the President's Council of Economic Advisors (2015). *The economics of early childhood investments*. Retrieved September 30, 2018, from https://obamawhitehouse.archives.gov/sites/default/files/docs/the_economics_of_early_childhood_investments.pdf.

Young, G. F., Scardovi, L., Cavagna, A., Giardina, I., and Leonard, N. E. (2013). Starling flock networks manage uncertainty in consensus at low cost. *PLoS Computational Biology*, *9*(1), e1002894. https://doi.org/10.1371/journal.pcbi.1002894.

16

(Non)Sensical Literacies, (Non)Sensical Relationships

Candace R. Kuby
University of Missouri, USA

Tara Gutshall Rucker
University of Missouri, USA

First the Egg[1]
A simple book with intricate cutouts,
outlining different life cycles.

Owen[2]: **Can I make a book like *First the Egg?***
Tara: Of course.

A simple question and a simple answer.
Yet, opportunity is at a stand-still.

Candace: **Does Owen have the supplies he needs to make the book?**

Pre-stapled books and lined paper
with a box for illustrations.
Pencils, crayons and markers available.
Stories, from the students' lives,
expected to fill the lines and boxes.

Questions, like thresholds, take us to unexpected places ...

*****

---

[1] See reference for Vaccaro Seeger (2007).
[2] All student names are pseudonyms.

> *Look for and construct the production of sense through nonsense. Do not look*
> *for solutions; look for and engage in the construction of problems and how*
> *this relates to the sense under production. Do not look for knowledge, look at*
> *learning processes, that is, look for and construct how the involved bodies join*
> *a problematic field. Do not look for methods, look for and construct how the*
> *entire culture surrounding the entering of a problematic field proceeds; take*
> *into account thoughts, speech, actions, but also material and environments.*
>
>   (Olsson, 2009, p. 119)

This quote by Olsson became a productive, provocative catalyst for our thinking
and writing of this chapter. As we composed poetry, read theory, and revisited
moments of teaching/learning from Tara's classroom, this quote was a refrain for
us that prompted newness. As the chapter proceeds, we thread this quote into
conversation with the poetry and thus the quote and our thinking/writing with
it becomes a refrain, a consistent rhythm for readers.

As we took up the invitation to write this chapter, we realized we had never,
since our partnership began in 2010, had an explicit conversation about *us*.
Separately, we often get asked how does your research partnership work? What
sustains it? Candace gets asked, how do you get a teacher to read theory with
you? To analyze and write with you? You really meet at night after your children
go to bed? Tara gets asked, you and Candace are *still* working together? What is
this article about? Thus, we took this opportunity to talk, think, contemplate *us* as
teacher/researcher partners. In doing so, we articulated experiences over the years
that are pivotal in our collaboration, several of which are included in the poetry
in this chapter. We discussed non-negotiables in writing together and our process
of "going public" with teaching/learning from Tara's room. For example, Candace
always discusses any possible writing project about Tara's classroom with Tara first
and they decide together how Tara will be involved. Sometimes as a coauthor,
sometimes as a co-analyst but not author, and sometimes to read drafts and offer
feedback. Over the years, we've created an easiness between us. For example, Tara
feels comfortable when Candace is in the classroom and often asks her to work
with small groups of students or become a part of a mini-lesson and co-teach.

Our collaboration together has focused on literacy desirings in Tara's first,
second, and fifth grade classrooms, specifically what Tara termed "Writers'
Studio"[3] or a space for children to produce literacies with a range of digital and
artistic tools. We write:

---

[3] For more on literacy desirings, see Kuby and Gutshall Rucker (2016); Kuby, Gutshall Rucker, and
   Darolia (2017); and Kuby and Gutshall Rucker (2015).

The concept of *literacy desiring* [is] to focus on literacy processes (the becoming of artifacts such as books, movies, dramas, 3-D models, wall murals, puppets, and so forth) and to emphasize the fluid, sometimes unintentional, unbounded, and rhizomatic ways multimodal artifacts come into being through intra-actions with humans and nonhumans (i.e., time, space, materials, environment). Literacy desiring is oriented toward the present (ever-changing) needs, wishes, and demands of students-with-nonhumans, but also with possible users of literacy artifacts in mind. (Kuby and Gutshall Rucker, 2016, p. 4, emphasis in original)

As we talked about this chapter, we realized that we have similar beliefs about children. We trust them, we respect them as fully human, invite them to learn/become/know/think in a lively world, and are (have become) comfortable not knowing where teaching/learning goes. We also realized these beliefs guide our relationship: we trust each other, we are respectful, and are comfortable without a firm plan. While this might seem trite or like a given in any research partnership, we aren't so sure it is. We began to see that what is critical in how we teach children is also critical in how we work together—our relationship is all of us (Tara, Candace, children, writing materials, theories, beliefs, and so forth). We all become together. As Jackson and Mazzei (2012) write, "The becoming is the something else, the newness that is created" (p. 87). For us, our becoming together (with children, policies, discourses on writing, theories, district curricular materials, digital and artistic tools, and so forth) is the newness that is created.

These becoming relationships have produced new ways to think about the teaching/learning of literacies. We don't have a set research plan, guiding questions before we begin (not even sure what the "beginning" would be), nor precise methods for producing data. Rather, we embrace a relational becoming as teachers/researchers/students/and … and … and … Therefore, this chapter is about our be(com)ing relational ethics, not as a fixed, solid thing but rather as a continual, constant unfolding. The phrase "relational ethics" emerges from our readings of poststructural and posthumanist scholarship (e.g., Barad, 2007; Biehl and Locke, 2017; Deleuze and Guattari, 1980/1987; Grosz, 2017) that sees the world coming into being through relationships. Inspired by these theoretical traditions, we find solace in Olsson (2009), "To do research [with poststructural and posthumanist philosophies] would in this sense mean to collectively invent rather than discover at a distance" (p. 97).

We invite you into the rest of the chapter by experiencing our poetry (i.e., verses) and refrains (i.e., excerpts of Olsson's quote alongside our thinking/writing). Inspired by researchers who think and write with poetry (e.g., Lahman,

2017; Lahman, Teman, and Richard, 2017; Lahman, Richard, and Teman, 2018), we found poetry as a way to explore and write about our relational ethics with children. Poetry invites readers to experience, imagine, and think in-between the lines of the poem. Instead of trying to "capture" our relational ethics of teaching/researching in a narrative or more traditional research writing form, we decided to take a risk and explore poetry together. Explore with us.

Threshold(ing)

Walking over the threshold of the classroom.

I[4] remember stepping into Tara's 1st grade classroom in 2009. In/through the threshold into peaceful, chaos of teaching/learning.

In a threshold, things enter and meet, flow (or pass) into one another, and break open (or exit) into something else.[5]

Thresholds take us to unexpected places.

If I get this job at Mizzou, I want to learn with/from Tara.

When you pass over them (thresholds), it takes you (to) a new direction.

Nine years later, we are (still) thresholding.

Threshold as a verb.

In a threshold, thinking flows, seeking connectives to interpret
(and to be interrupted).
Thinking is a productive force in its potential for difference.[6]

---

[4] Candace.
[5] Jackson and Mazzei (2018, p. 721).
[6] Jackson and Mazzei (2018, p. 722).

Moments, encounters that might seem inconsequential
produce new relationships with/in/between us.

Flying airplanes bumping bodies.
Did Owen have the supplies he needed to make the book?
Does Edward need a timeline?
Why does the book need to be finished?

Small but big moments.

Thresholds.
Thresholding.

Exiting Room 203

Thinking is a productive force in its potential for difference.

The summer after Owen's question, Tara asked Candace:
**What would it look like to "open up" writing workshop on the first day of
school?**

Materials:
Blank paper, lined paper, construction paper, cardstock.
Pencils, crayons, markers, Cray-pas.
Popsicle sticks, tissue paper, yarn.
Rulers, staplers, hole punchers, tape.

An invitation:
Be a writer!

Things enter and meet, flow (or pass) into one another, and break
open (or exit) into something else.

A group of students read *Bones*.[7]
Their curiosities flow, leading to new places–
a drawing of a giraffe reaching 19 feet tall.
When ready to display, it bends and breaks
out of the classroom and beyond the hallway.

Candace: **What is going to happen to the giraffe? Where might it fit?**

Tara wonders to herself:
The giraffe looks different than writing from other classrooms.
How will people respond?

Thresholding is a productive force in its potential for difference.[8]

The giraffe moved into an unexpected place:
the school commons
for everyone to see.

Fifth graders oohed and awed,
bending their necks to see it.
Kindergartners wondered:
How much tape was needed to hang it up?
How long did it take to make?

Moments, encounters that might seem inconsequential produce
new relationships with/in/between us.

Inviting children to be writers with a range of artistic and digital tools might seem like nonsense. One might say, that it isn't writing. You should spend your time on more important things in school. "Look for and construct the production of sense through nonsense" (Olsson, 2009, p. 119). Writing as books with intricate cutouts, as 19-foot tall giraffes, as airplanes. "Look for and engage in the construction of problems and how this relates to the sense under production" (p. 119).

As we threshold with students, discourses on writing, theories, and materials in Tara's classrooms, we are taken to unexpected places. Unexpected places of (re)thinking writing and literacies. Of the role of a teacher. Of materials for

---

[7]   See reference for Jenkins (2010).
[8]   Jackson and Mazzei (2018, p. 722).

literacy. Of what it means to research with/about young children in a more-than-human world. Of what to say or not to say when a paper airplane hits you in the head. Are these (unexpected literacies) problems to be solved? Solutions to be found? Or something altogether different?

For Owen to *not* create the book initially seemed like nonsense. He had "permission" from Tara to do so, yet he didn't create the book. As we tried to understand why, we realized the materials he needed were not made available to him. They were in the classroom, but in spaces that he didn't have access to. Additionally, Tara had not trusted or invited the students to move beyond the lined writing paper that provided a box for illustrations. This paper made Owen's *First the Egg* book unthinkable, perhaps impossible, given the desired format of cutouts. At the time, Tara hadn't considered what writing looked like beyond pre-stapled pages with lines and a box. Who would have thought that just putting out blank paper could make such a big difference in producing literacies?

Tara was uneasy about the 19-foot tall giraffe being displayed outside of Room 203. Candace sensed this on the day that children were measuring the walls inside and outside the classroom. It became clear that neither walls were tall enough for the giraffe. There were only so many places that a 19-foot tall giraffe replica could hang in the school. Tara knew this (and did want the children to share their learning from a project that lasted five months). However, the giraffe would have to "go public" and hang in a common area by the school's front door and office. Construction of problems: a physical problem of where do we hang the giraffe, a problem of what materials to use to create the giraffe (paper, markers, or real skin, as one student contemplated), and also the problem of going public. A problematic field. Once the giraffe is hung, people can ask questions about the giraffe but also our relationship and the pedagogies unfolding in Room 203.

In posing questions to each other, we weren't looking for a solution. Instead we questioned new possibilities. What if students had a range of materials readily available to them? What might writing become? Encounters such as these, perhaps seen as nonsense, and the back and forth of questions between us, have provoked us to (re)think literacies time and time again. Even the smallest cuts, a small question of where to hang the giraffe or if Owen has the supplies he needs, produce newness in the field. Newness in our relationship and pedagogies. This chapter is providing a space to map how questions that seem small are monumental. Relations and moments that seem inconsequential at the time aren't. Small moments are really big moments in our be(com)ing as teachers/researchers, as learners.

Mattering in Room 203

On the second day of school, a few boys make and launch an
airplane during Writers' Studio. The plane nearly hits Tara as she
conferences with another student.

Hesitation.

Will our work be shut down?

No response.

Blank paper folds again and another airplane flies across the room.

Does anyone even notice?

Tensions rise within Tara. The airplanes are noticed (and felt).
Should they be shut down?
They can't be.

The invitation stood:
Be a writer.
Explore the supplies.
Imagine how materials can be used
and support you as a learner.

The airplanes alter the course of Tara's plans.
Airplanes intervene.

Within days, the airplane group grows.

My airplane is Twister. I'll sell it to someone for 9,000 bucks!
The Lightning Striker is better. It will sell for 5 billion, kajillion dollars.

Play.
Imagination.
Endless possibilities.

Later that week, the group meets with Tara.
What do you want to do with the airplanes?

Host an airplane tournament.
... and keep score.

Create an obstacle course for the planes.
Make more airplanes.
Invite the class to watch trial runs.

Many desirings.
Logistics unclear.

Eleven days from the first airplane launch, Tara conferences with the group again. She conducts a mini-lesson, sharing different possibilities of how the students could host an airplane tournament. The group decides to teach the class how to make airplanes.

We will show the class how to make airplanes.
Then we can practice flying the airplanes.

The group models how to make airplanes.

Modeling, folding, practicing.

Everyone makes an airplane.
Even Tara.

Airplanes glide, soar, fly.
Planes crash, land, collide.

Next week we will have the tournament.

More excitement.

The day of the tournament, everyone carries their plane to the blacktop. The airplane group brings stopwatches and rulers to measure how long the airplanes stay in the air and the distance each one travels.

Airplanes alter the course of events
and undo what is known as writing.

Intervention with airplanes.
Matter.

In·ter·vene: Mundane Transformation(s)

/in(t)ər'vēn/

verb

- Come between so as to prevent or alter a result or course of events
- Intercede, involve oneself, get involved, interpose oneself, step in
- Occur in time between events[9]

Intervention, a word we hear often in school discourses.

In discourses about children.

In discourses about teaching/learning.

Intervention groups.

Intervention strategies.

Intervention programs.

We question intervention(s).

Can we (re)think and (re)claim intervention?

Intervention in what things could be.[10]

Intervene. A doing in between.

Altering a course of events.

Aren't we all already, always intervening?

That things could be different is the impulse of speculative thinking ... the speculative refers to a mode of thought committed to foster visions of other worlds possible.[11]

What are (our) ethics of intervening in pedagogies (and researching) with children
and more-than-human bodies?
What is our response-ability?

This involves political imagination of the possible, purposes of making difference with awareness and responsibility for consequences: speculative thinking as involved intervention—as speculative commitment.[12]

---

[9]   Definition retrieved from google dictionary on March 7, 2018.

[10] Puig de la Bellacasa (2017, p. 66).

[11] Puig de la Bellacasa (2017, p. 110).

[12] Puig de la Bellacasa (2017, p. 110).

Our thinking and commitments are to imagining the possibles of
literacies.
The otherwise (un)thinkable.
To intervene-with-children-discourses-iPads-paints-books-and-and-and-
Involved intervention.

Interventions ... [a] deep attention to materiality and embodiment in ways that rethink relationality, in ways that suggest
a desire for tangible engagements with mundane transformation.[13]

What do interventions-with-_____ produce?
Make possible?
Mundane(ly) transform?

- Come between so as to prevent or alter a result or course
  of events
- Intercede, involve oneself, get involved, interpose oneself,
  step in
- Occur in time between events[14]

verb
/in(t)ər'vēn/

"Do not look for knowledge, look at learning processes, that is, look for
and construct how the involved bodies join a problematic field" (Olsson,
2009, p. 119). Knowledge. Learning. These are the projects of education. A
focus on meeting benchmarks. Learning skills and strategies. A defined end
goal in mind. Linear trajectory. However, Olsson invites us to imagine and
be otherwise. To not stop the desirings of children-with-airplanes. Instead
to intervene through not stopping, not talking, not policing their becoming
literacies. Sense is produced from what seems nonsensical. Airplanes as
literacies. Nonsensical.

We often reminisce about how we were both in the room and a part of
airplane desirings coming into being. There was/is a culture between us that
was also in the classroom as the airplanes were flying. We can't separate us and

---

[13] Puig de la Bellacasa (2017, p. 112, emphasis added).
[14] Definition retrieved from google dictionary on March 7, 2018.

the classroom/children. Did Candace being in the room provide "permission" for Tara (maybe even unconsciously) to let the airplanes happen? We were both comfortable in the uncertainty, what perhaps felt like chaos to us. What if an administrator had walked in the room, would that have changed what unfolded (probably)? Nonsensical.

"Do not look for methods, look for and construct how the entire culture surrounding the entering of a problematic field proceeds; take into account thoughts, speech, actions, but also material and environments" (Olsson, 2009, p. 119). What is our pedagogical method in small, but big moments such as these? How are we already a part of intervening? What do we do with that responsibility as teachers/researchers? How are we all proceeding together, relationally?

We are nonsensical. We struggle to make sense of what we do as teachers/ researchers (although we've never verbally called ourselves "teachers/researchers," it seems the "right" language to use). We aren't sure how to articulate *us*, our relationship, when people ask. Our relationship makes sense to us, but we can't say what it is. Being co-researchers and co-teachers seems to have created an entanglement—a newness created between with/in/through us. We are always changing. We are a problematic field.

We also struggle with what is (or isn't) writing and/or literacies, as there are rich histories and traditions of what counts as writing and/or literacies, especially in schools. As you read this chapter, you too might struggle with the 19-foot giraffe and/or airplane examples as literacies. We invite you to enter into these problematic fields and the ethics of struggling with/in/through them.

The writing of the chapter is also a problematic field. It feels messy and impossible to try and pin down in language our relationship, our ethics together with children in a lively world. We can't write out recommendations or a how-to list of how we "develop" as teachers/researchers. Instead, we keep coming back to the notion that the smallest cuts matter. What seems inconsequential—a question, blank paper, a chance encounter—matters. Our ethics are woven with/in nonsensical relations of us with children, discourses, thoughts, speech, actions, and also materials and environments. (Non) sensical literacies, (non)sensical relationships. It is a lively ethics becoming each moment and in doing so producing us, realities, students, knowledges, teachers, and literacies.

Live(ly) Ethics

Live(ly) ethics: The tissue of ethicality that runs through the world.[15]

The difficulty here is that ethics in entanglement cannot be determined in advance[16] ...

... Something that cannot be organized, whose complexities cannot be settled or decided by "theories" or the application of more or less mechanical programs. Ethics, in this sense, is what happens when we cannot apply the rules. This means that ethics is an experience of responsibility, but that responsibility is not a moment of security or of cognitive certainty. Quite the contrary: the only responsibility worthy of the name comes with the removal of grounds, the withdrawal of the rules or the knowledge on which we might rely to make our decisions for us. No grounds means no alibis, no elsewhere to which we might refer the instance of our decision.

I would argue that ethics is what happens when we cannot apply the rules.

This ethics is surely too hard to think, and yet,[17]

We must think (about) ethics as we teach and research with young children
and the more-than-human bodies/world.
Live(ly) ethics.

Ethics is therefore not about right responses to a radically other, but about responsibility and accountability for the **lively** relationalities of becoming, of which we are a part. Ethics is about mattering, about taking account of the entangled materializations of which we are part, including new configurations, new subjectivities, new possibilities.[18]

New worldly (re)configurings.
New subjectivities.

---

[15] Barad (2012, p. 70).
[16] St. Pierre (2013, p. 150).
[17] St. Pierre (2013, pp. 150–151), original quote from Keenan (1997, p. 1). St. Pierre replaced the word "reading" from the Keenan quote with "ethics." We kept it as "ethics."
[18] Barad (2012, p. 69, emphasis added).

New possibilities.
New relationalities.
New pedagogies.
New inquiries (practices).
New literacies.
Live(ly) ethics.

Even the smallest cuts matter.[19]

Cuts. Our response-abilities to respond,
which can't be determined in advance but rather in-the-moment.
In-the-moment (agential) cuts.
Live(ly) ethics.
Candace-Tara relationship(s) matters in the pedagogies that come
to matter.
In-the-moment ways of knowing/be(com)ing/doing together.

Responsibility, then, is a matter of the ability to respond. Listening
for the response of the other and an obligation to be responsive to
the other, who is not entirely separate from what we call the self.
This way of thinking ontology, epistemology, and ethics together
makes for a world that is always already an ethical matter.[20]

Listening for/with children.
Listening for/with all bodies.
Listening for/with all discourses of what teaching/learning
should be.
An obligation.
Not (entirely) separate from ourselves.
Live(ly) ethics.
An obligation.

How are people in particular researchers, thinkers, and
theorists
[and teachers, and children, and more-than-human bodies],
involved in the making of the world[21]

---

[19] Barad (2012, p. 69).
[20] Barad (2012, p. 69).
[21] Puig de la Bellacasa (2017, p. 39), brackets and writing within added.

References

Barad, K. (2007). *Meeting the universe halfway: Quantum physics and the entanglement of matter and meaning*. Durham, NC: Duke University Press.

Barad, K. (2012). Interview with Karen Barad. In R. Dolphijn and I. van der Tuin (Eds.), *New materialism: Interviews & cartographies* (pp. 48–70). Ann Arbor, MI: Open Humanities Press.

Biehl, J., and Locke, P. (Eds.) (2017). *Unfinished: The anthropology of becoming*. Durham, NC: Duke University Press.

Deleuze, G., and Guattari, F. (1980/1987). *A thousand plateaus: Capitalism and schizophrenia* (Trans. B. Massumi). Minneapolis, MN: University of Minnesota Press.

Grosz, E. (2017). *The incorporeal: Ontology, ethics, and the limits of materialism*. New York: Columbia University Press.

Jackson, A. Y., and Mazzei, L. A. (2012). *Thinking with theory in qualitative research: Viewing data across multiple perspectives*. New York: Routledge.

Jackson, A. Y., and Mazzei, L. A. (2018). Thinking with theory: A new analytic for qualitative inquiry. In N. K. Denzin and Y. S. Lincoln (Eds.), *The Sage handbook of qualitative research* (5th edition) (pp. 717–737). Thousand Oaks, CA: Sage.

Jenkins, S. (2010). *Bones: Skeletons and how they work*. New York: Scholastic.

Keenan, T. (1997). *Fables of responsibility: Aberrations and predicaments in ethics and politics*. Stanford, CA: Stanford University Press.

Kuby, C. R., and Gutshall Rucker, T. (2015). Everyone has a Neil: Possibilities of literacy desiring in writers' studio. *Language Arts, 92*(5), 314–327.

Kuby, C. R., and Gutshall Rucker, T. (2016). *Go be a writer!: Expanding the curricular boundaries of literacy learning with children*. New York: Teachers College Press.

Kuby, C. R., Gutshall Rucker, T., and Darolia, L. H. (2017). Persistence(ing): Posthuman agency in a Writers' Studio. *Journal of Early Childhood Literacy, 17*(3), 353–373.

Lahman, M. K. E. (2017). Who cares? *Qualitative Inquiry* (online first) https://doi.org/10.1177/1077800417727.

Lahman, M. K. E., Teman, E. D., and Richard, V. M. (2017). IRB as poetry. *Qualitative Inquiry* (online first) https://doi.org/10.1177/107780041774458.

Lahman, M. K. E., Richard, V. M., and Teman, E. D. (2018). ish: How to write poemish (research) poetry. *Qualitative Inquiry* (online first) https://doi.org/10.1177/10778004177501.

Olsson, L. M. (2009). *Movement and experimentation in young children's learning: Deleuze and Guattari in early childhood education*. New York: Routledge.

Puig de la Bellacasa, M. (2017). *Matters of care: Speculative ethics in more than human worlds*. Minneapolis, MN: Minnesota Press.

St. Pierre, E. A. (2013). Ethics in entanglement. *Knowledge Cultures, 1*(5), 141–155.

Vaccaro Seeger, L. (2007). *First the egg*. New York: Roaring Brook Press.

Index

leadership role in classroom 81
Leafgren, S. 96–7
Levinas, E. 73, 169
Lewis, P. J. 83
Li, J. 207
"listening-as-usual" 92, 155
literacy 109, 178, 181, 213, 216–17, 221–2
literacy desirings 212–13, 212 n.3

MacLean, D. 10
Making Kin Not Population (Clarke and Haraway) 136, 143
Malaguzzi, L. 56, 89–91
Manning, E. 51, 54, 57–8
Marks, L. 139, 142
masculine modesty 116
masculine objectivity 116
masculinity 149–50, 152, 155
Massumi, B. 51, 58
mastery, learning 148
material acts, children and 49–51, 53
material-discursive practices 174, 176–9, 185–6
materiality 189–90
    of parenting 133, 136
    vital 152–5, 158
matter 192
    elevation of (Barad's) 190, 198
    of ethical encounters 147
Mazzei, L. A. 213
media culture, children's discussions of 41
    drawing event 42–5
Meloni, F. 176, 182
Merleau-Ponty, M. 24
method of equality, Rancière's 40, 45–6
Meyer-Drawe, K. 98
microethics 19
microscope, discursive apparatus 185
Midwestern childcare center 164, 169
minority group, children as 90
Mitchell, C. 105
Modest_Witness@Second_Millenium.
    *FemaleMan©_Meets_*
    OncoMouseTM (Haraway) 115–16
moments of uncertainty 84
Mondloch, K. 103
Montgomery, J. 14
moral judgment, ethics 148, 152
Morrow, V. 15
Moss, P. 72–3

motional-relational perception 56
Mukhopadhyay, T. R. 55–6, 60
multiculturalism in early childhood 119–20, 122–3
multivocality/multivoiced approach 83
murmurations 202
    learnings from 205–6
    listening for 206–9
Murris, K. 93, 95–6, 101
mutated modest witness 113, 115–19, 123–6

narratives 86, 101, 103, 110, 180, 205
    multivoiced 83
    writing 105
The National Statement on Ethical
    Conduct in Human Research
    (NHMRC) 11
neoliberalism 130, 193, 202
    political project of 202–5
new materialism 3, 147–8, 163–4, 167–70, 185
    analyses 147 n.1
    feminist 101, 103, 114–15
    new materialist ethics 147–8, 147 n.1
New South Wales (NSW) 150–1, 150 n.3, 156 n.4
No Más Hambre (Hunger Project) 104
normative masculinity 149–50

objectivity/objective scientific knowledge 116–18
observational research 5, 99, 113, 116, 124–6, 136, 156–7, 164, 168, 174, 176, 179–80, 182
Olsson, L. M. 91, 212, 221
onto-epistemology 97, 115, 136
orders of relations 130–1, 134
outsider science 116
Owens, A. 217

parental play 69, 72
    towards ethics of 72–4
Parent and Child Education (PACE) 104
parenting
    animalization of 131–2
    good 131–2, 136
    government intervention 131
    policy 131–3
    with posthumanist ethics of care 139

www.ingramcontent.com/pod-product-compliance
Lightning Source LLC
Chambersburg PA
CBHW050423280326
41932CB00013BA/1974